Monk: The Official Episode Guide

By Terry J. Erdmann and Paula M. Block

Star Trek: Deep Space Nine Companion

Star Trek: Action!

Also by Terry J. Erdmann

The Paramount Story

The Last Samurai Official Companion

Also by Paula M. Block

Star Trek: Strange New Worlds (coeditor)

St. Martin's Griffin ≈ New York

The Official Episode Guide

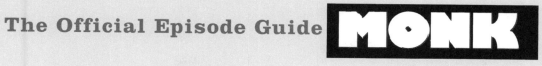

MONK

Terry J. Erdmann and Paula M. Block

www.stmartins.com

Design by Fritz Metsch

Library of Congress Cataloging-in-Publication Data
Erdmann, Terry J.
    Monk : the official episode guide / Terry J. Erdmann and Paula M. Block—1st ed.
        p. cm.
    ISBN-13: 978-0-312-35461-9
    ISBN-10: 0-312-35461-4
    1. Monk (Television program). I. Block, Paula M. II. Title.
PN1992.77.M595E73 2006
791.45'72—dc22   2006041764

First Edition: July 2006

10   9   8   7   6   5   4   3   2   1

Foreword

BY ANDY BRECKMAN

Monk is the first and only one-hour show I've ever worked on. People ask me how I did it. What's my secret? How did I create a hit series my very first time at bat?

The truth is: it's embarrassingly easy. Anyone can do it. You can do it. Your idiot brother-in-law can do it. All you have to do is follow these seven simple steps . . .

How to Produce a TV Show

1. **Have a miserable childhood.** Stay in your room and read comic books and Sherlock Holmes. Don't worry about making friends. Don't worry about sports. Just keep reading.
2. **Wait for David Hoberman to have a great idea for a show.** When he tells it to you, stay calm. Smile. Say this: "A cop with OCD? That's not a bad idea, David. Do you have a writer in mind?"
3. **Get the script to the USA Network.** They'll appreciate you. They'll support you. And—most important—they'll leave you alone.
4. **Hire the best writing staff on either coast.** Their names are Tom, David, Hy, Dan, and Joe. Put them all in a room. Close the door.

When they say something funny, or come up with a brilliant plot twist, write it down.

5. **Hire Randy Zisk and make him your partner.** Get him to direct as many episodes as he can. Work him hard. Don't let him sleep.

6. **Cast Bitty Schram, Traylor Howard, Ted Levine, Jason Gray-Stanford, and Stanley Kamel.** Turn the cameras on. Get out of their way. They'll make you look like a genius.

7. **Find Tony Shalhoub.** This final step may require some divine intervention, because Shalhoub is a Godsend. I've never used that word before, but that's what the man is—a Godsend.

Monk isn't perfect. Lord knows. Some episodes are stronger than others. Some storylines are—and I'm being kind here—nuts. Some scenes that were hysterical in the writers' room don't seem to play at all. But the show seems to work. People have embraced it. Families plan their Friday nights around it. I think I know why: they can tell *Monk* is a labor of love.

It's true. The cast, the crew, and the writers put their hearts into every episode. We want to thank Terry and Paula for writing this wonderful companion book. It's given us a chance to share our thoughts and memories, to take credit for the stuff that works and—more important—blame other people for the stuff that doesn't.

Have fun. See you around the campus.

obsessive-compulsive: relating to or characterized by recurring obsessions and compulsions, esp. as symptoms of a neurotic state.

Merriam-Webster's Collegiate Dictionary

Season One

"I am what I am"

"Someone once asked [former Beatle] Ringo Starr the secret of his success," relates Andy Breckman, creator and executive producer of the USA Network Original Series *Monk*. "And Ringo's answer was, 'When the boys asked me to join their little band, I said yes.' "

Breckman chuckles, tickled by the anecdote. "That's my secret, too," he confides. "The secret of my success in TV is that I said yes."

Monk, USA Network's critically acclaimed television series about the infamous defective detective, premiered on July 12, 2002. But its genesis dates back four years earlier to a completely different era for Breckman.

"I was writing features," explains the screenwriter of such comedies as *Moving, I.Q.*, *Sgt. Bilko*, and *Rat Race*. "It never occurred to me that I might want to be in the TV business. Ever. I had never written a television script. I had never even explored it. And then, in early nineteen ninety-eight, I had lunch with David Hoberman."

Hoberman, then president of the Motion Picture Group of Walt Disney Studios, wasn't exactly a stranger. "I had written some bad screenplays for David," Breckman relates. "Because writing bad screenplays was my specialty."

Be that as it may, Hoberman knew Breckman as an extremely funny man, a veteran from the writing staffs of *Late Night with David Letterman* and *Saturday Night Live*. He also knew of Breckman's fondness for mysteries. And that's what he was counting on.

Hoberman had heard that ABC Television was looking for a new detective show, something in the Inspector Clouseau (of *Pink Panther* fame) vein. The idea caught Hoberman's fancy and he began musing about variations on that theme. "And then, I don't know how the idea popped into my head, but I began thinking about the superstitions I had as a child, obsessive-compulsive stuff," he says. "And I thought, what if someone who was wracked with phobias and anxieties was also a brilliant detective. Someone who had trouble leaving his home, much less going out into the world and solving cases, but somehow he managed to every day."

Hoberman pitched—and sold—the concept to ABC. Not bad for a man who, like the character he would soon help to create, remains reluctant to ride in elevators.

It was then that Hoberman invited Breckman to that lunch. "David said, 'Do you think we could do a TV show about a cop with obsessive-compulsive disorder?' " the writer recalls, "and I immediately saw the possibilities. It was a vehicle where I could use my lifelong passion for mysteries. I grew up reading Sherlock Holmes and watching episodes of *Columbo*. I knew this idea was the perfect fusion of my passion for mysteries and my passion for comedy."

The next time Breckman spoke with Hoberman, he had a name for both the show and the character: "Monk." "I've always thought that 'Sherlock Holmes' was a great name and I

was determined to come up with something similar," Breckman says. "It had to be a simple, monosyllabic last name, with an unusual, colorful first name. 'Adrian Monk' sounded kind of quirky, and it was in keeping with the Sherlock Holmes mold."

The Baker Street detective provided more than just an inspiration for Monk's name. "People who know Sherlock Holmes recognize all the components of *Monk*," Breckman notes. "It's structured exactly as Conan Doyle structured his stories," which, he says, are quite different from the stories that other writers, such as Agatha Christie, crafted.

"Agatha Christie mysteries are about the intricacies of plot," Breckman explains. "Her plots are assembled like Swiss watches, and I always think reading them is hard work. Arthur Conan Doyle's Sherlock Holmes mysteries, on the other hand, are about the fun ride. Conan Doyle wasn't as concerned about the logic of filling every plot hole and making the story perfect. And *Columbo* was the same way. *Columbo* was about the fun ride. As soon as I saw that show, I knew I was in love. [*Columbo* creators] Richard Levinson and William Link did what Conan Doyle did, in that they were concerned with making the stories as much fun as their central character."

Breckman soon had sketched out a seventeen-page document, rough notes defining the show's structure and characters. "Monk is a remarkable man for two reasons," the notes began. "One: he's a great detective—a modern-day Sherlock Holmes. And two: he's nuts."

The rest of the document sketched out the primary beats for the pilot and suggested short storylines for ten possible follow-up episodes. Prior to taking on *Monk*, Breckman had never sat down to write a mystery. "However, I would often get ideas for them and make notes," he says. "I had a closet full of those ideas. One that I'd had for years was about what appeared to be a failed assassination attempt on a candidate, but was actually the successful murder of a Secret Service agent. I worked that into the *Monk* pilot story." Hoberman and Breckman developed the story into an hour-long dramedy (TV parlance for a hybrid comedy/drama series) and Breckman wrote a script that he called "Mr. Monk Meets the Candidate."

"From the very beginning I wanted to title the episodes as if they were children's fantasy books," explains Breckman. "Like 'Mr. Monk Goes to the Symphony,' 'Mr. Monk Takes a Vacation,' 'Mr. Monk and the Blankedy Blank.'" The titles hint at the detective's childlike nature and imply that every day is an adventure for Monk, who must try to carry out his grown-up job while dealing with a life that's completely dominated by childish fears.

"Everybody at ABC loved the script," says Jackie de Crinis, who at the time was Jackie Lyons, vice president of drama series at ABC. But there was a problem. ABC had bought the project with a "cast contingency" clause. The network had full control over who would play the title character and, notes de Crinis, "the right actor just didn't appear. ABC had a very physical type of comedian in mind, and that limited it."

"I can't express how depressing those casting sessions were," says David Hoberman (who is now president of Mandeville Films). "We had people coming in doing tics and Tourette's syndrome, and you name it. Everybody felt that they needed to embody an extreme physicality for Monk. But that would have gotten old and annoying very quickly."

Two development seasons—two full years—

passed as numerous actors were considered, most prominently, Michael Richards, after he had wrapped up his role as Kramer in *Seinfeld*. But eventually, says de Crinis, "Other projects started to trump *Monk* at ABC. Projects that sit on the shelf for too long become stale. People just get tired of hearing about them."

De Crinis, however, hadn't given up on the project and when, in November 2000, she moved to the USA Network as senior vice president of original series, she took a copy of "Mr. Monk and the Candidate" with her. "I thought that the quirky script probably made more sense for cable," she says. "When I showed it to the group here, everybody loved it, too."

"Jackie had been part of developing that amazing *Monk* script," says Jeff Wachtel, executive vice president of original programming at USA Network. "In the first thirty seconds of reading it, you knew you had something. It had a wonderful sense of familiarity yet was done in a new way. Which is exactly what we needed at USA. I said, 'We have a diamond here, and our job is to create the perfect setting for that diamond.'" The network executives made an offer to Touchstone Television, the Disney arm that was working with ABC, and soon acquired the show.

USA, being a basic cable network, didn't have the public awareness or the financial stability of premium cable channels like HBO, which made the chance to develop the project a groundbreaking opportunity. "At the time," Wachtel says, "USA was kind of uncharted territory. We wanted programs that would raise the bar for all of us and make viewers go to Channel 242. Now we'd been given the gift of this diamond, that's what our discussions on *Monk* were about."

That and, of course, casting.

"It was in casting hell, which is exactly what had brought it down at ABC," Wachtel says. The USA team considered a number of actors, including Dave Foley, John Ritter, and Henry Winkler. "The producers all wanted the network to say yes to one of them," Wachtel laughs. "It could have been the building's security guard who was reading for the part and they'd have yelled, 'Great! Let's just do this show!'" But Wachtel was unconvinced. "I thought we should find a brilliant actor who people outside of the professional community wouldn't know that well," he recalls, "someone who would get under the skin of the character and don him as his own. Then I suggested—insisted, actually—that we go after three actors, Stanley Tucci, Alfred Molina, and Tony Shalhoub."

Shalhoub was already aware of *Monk*. "My manager had read the pilot script because she was looking for roles for another one of her clients, a woman who she hoped could play the nurse character, Sharona," Shalhoub says. "And while she was reading for her, she thought of me as Monk."

As it turned out, Tucci and Molina were working and unavailable. Shalhoub had a different complication. He'd recently completed a pilot for a broadcast network, and was legally restricted from doing another until a decision was made as to whether that pilot would become a series. Nevertheless, USA decided to woo him.

"We brought Tony in and pitched the role to him," Wachtel says. "At the time, USA wasn't the most notable home to come to, so we really blew it out with the whole cheese plate, fruit salad, and designer coffee thing. We said, 'Tony, this is a career-making role. This is the one people are going to remember you for.' That was our pitch."

Wachtel laughs. "We never dreamed it would come true the way it has."

Shalhoub wanted to say yes, but his previous commitment prevented him from shooting a one-hour pilot. But USA had a contingency plan. The actor *was* allowed to do other formats, such as a two-hour movie, and, Wachtel points out, "One of the advantages we have at USA is flexibility. If we shot a movie and then Tony's other series was picked up, our movie wouldn't have to sit on the shelf. We could air it anyway. And maybe we could have done a whole bunch of made-for-TV *Monk* movies, a la *Columbo*."

To facilitate USA's contingency plan, "I was asked to do something that writers are almost never asked to do," Andy Breckman states, "and should never *be* asked to do. I was asked to take a one-hour pilot that, in my opinion, was perfectly written and working fine, and *expand* it." This is the antithesis of the usual writing process, he explains. "When you write, you tend to overwrite certain things, and then you cut out the stuff that isn't working. But I was asked to go back and put that stuff *back in*. It finally hobbled in at an hour and forty minutes, but that was enough for us to get Tony Shalhoub."

In fact, Shalhoub decided that he wanted to be even more involved with the show. "I wanted to have input," he says, "so I asked if I could become a producer." As a result, the actor signed on not only as the star, but also as one of the series' three executive producers (along with Breckman and Hoberman).

During the rewrite, Breckman tailored the script to Shalhoub's unique talents. "Keeping the comedic and the dramatic equal without having one undercut the other takes delicate balancing," Shalhoub explains. "'Candidate' had been around for almost three years, with different actors tiptoeing near it, so by the time I got to it, the comic elements had become a little too broad for me.

"I can't take responsibility for creating the character," the actor admits. "We collaborated in dialing back the comedic tone because we wanted to make a tragicomedy out of the show. But Monk was created by David Hoberman and Andy Breckman, who really fleshed it out. And they brought in all these other characters and created the universe of *Monk*."

All that work seemed to have paid off. The pilot episode aired successfully, and an additional eleven episodes filled out the series' first season. At the end of the season, the series won two Emmy Awards— Outstanding Main Title Theme Music for composer Jeff Beal, and Outstanding Lead Actor in a Comedy Series for Tony Shalhoub. In addition, Tony Shalhoub won a Golden Globe Award for Best Performance by an Actor in a Television Series—Musical or Comedy, and staff writer Hy Conrad was nominated for an Edgar Award for Best Televi-sion Episode Teleplay, for "Mr. Monk Takes a Vacation."

Dramatis Personae

In the creative process there is the father, the author of the play; the mother, the actor pregnant with the part; and the child, the role to be born.

–STANISLAVSKI, *An Actor Prepares*

Andy Breckman made no secret of the fact that his central characters were, if not reincarnations, then certainly direct descendents of the protagonists in Arthur Conan Doyle's Sherlock Holmes mysteries. As mentioned earlier,

Breckman had described Adrian Monk from the beginning as a modern-day Sherlock. His brother Ambrose (introduced in Season Two, in "Mr. Monk and the Three Pies") bears more than a passing resemblance to Holmes's older brother Mycroft. But while these, and others, were useful initial armatures for the inhabitants of Monk's world, they were only springboards to the unique personalities that viewers eventually saw on-screen.

Adrian Monk (Tony Shalhoub)

"Monk is a living legend," states Andy Breckman's initial story notes on the character. "Quick, brilliant, analytical . . . [with] an encyclopedic knowledge of a dozen unconventional and assorted subjects, from door locks to horticulture to architecture to human psychology."

The police call on him, the notes continue, whenever they are stuck on a case. Somehow, Monk has the amazing ability to see the things that they can't.

It's a gift . . . and a curse.

"Is Monk the smartest guy in the world or is he the luckiest?" reflects Tony Shalhoub. "Does he just happen to be in the right place at the right time to see or hear someone say the thing that triggers his insight? We talk about that all the time—the writers, producers, and me. I think perhaps Monk's antennae are just a little more finely tuned than most people. He's just superintuitive."

And yet, this twenty-first-century incarnation of Holmes is also, as the show's tagline loves to remind us, "defective." Breckman was pretty clear about that from the beginning: "Monk can barely function in the world. He's a walking bundle of fears and neuroses and obsessive rituals. A poster boy for obsessive-compulsive behavior."

"I don't know if there's any patient that has *all* of the things that bother Monk," acknowledges Breckman. "Generally speaking, he likes things to be orderly, he avoids germs, he likes things to be even, and so on. I'm not sure if that cluster of symptoms is found in the real world. I think that OCD patients might suffer from variations of some of that."

Playing Monk is probably almost (but not quite) as difficult as *being* Monk. "He's such a massive mess of complications," sighs Shalhoub. "He's proud and has a certain amount of arrogance, but he's *so* frustrated with himself that he can't do certain things. The will to do them is strong, but the phobias and compulsions overtake him. He loses so many of those battles. But I keep reminding myself not to get into self-pity. It's okay for the *audience* to feel sorry for Monk, but I don't want *Monk* to feel sorry for Monk very often."

It would be easy to fall into that trap, particularly since the strongest emotion in Monk's life is shrouded with tragedy—his love for his dead wife. "I think Monk always carries the memory of Trudy," says Shalhoub. "In some ways, it's not even memory. It stays in the present and he still holds Trudy as a kind of living entity. She's ever present." So ever present, in fact, that the two women who've portrayed Trudy over the course of the series, Stellina Rusich and Melora Hardin, are as familiar to viewers as regulars like Stanley Kamel, who plays Dr. Kroger.

Shalhoub tends to draw on childhood experiences in his portrayal of the detective. "There are a lot of childlike qualities to him,"

the actor observes. "He sees things in that kind of wide-eyed wonder, and that helps to give him a clear, objective view of things." Of course, the same quality also contributes to Monk's social ineptness and his ignorance about pop culture. "He's just a terminally unhip guy," Shalhoub grins ruefully. "He's decades behind in terms of music, television, and movies. He probably missed the sixties, missed disco, all of that stuff. He was *not* at Woodstock."

It's unlikely that Monk has ever seen anything on Tony Shalhoub's eclectic resume, either. (We know for a fact—see "Mr. Monk and the Airplane"—that he's never seen the TV show *Wings,* in which Shalhoub appeared for six years.) And the possibility that Monk has risked the sticky floor of a cinema to see such big-screen hits as *Men in Black* and *Galaxy Quest,* or even art-house favorites like *Big Night* or *Barton Fink,* is unthinkable. But rest assured, the people that count are familiar with his work. "Tony is one of the great character actors of our time," raves Jeff Wachtel. "Every week Andy Breckman builds this diving board and Tony jumps off of it."

Sharona Fleming (Bitty Schram)

As admirable as Sherlock Holmes and Adrian Monk are, they aren't exactly people that an audience can identify with. They're too different, too smart, too eccentric. Hence the need for a more audience-friendly everyman, a Dr. Watson type. In *Monk,* that everyman is an everywoman called Sharona, whose name brings to mind a very familiar ditty by rock band The Knack.

"I guess I was trying to think of a colorful name," muses Breckman. "Something that

would fit a blue-collar, working-class nurse who'd come from a tough neighborhood. The name just seemed to fit."

Like Watson, Sharona Fleming comes from the medical profession, a prerequisite that felt appropriate once Breckman understood just how screwed-up his main protagonist was going to be. "I realized that Monk was very low-functioning," he says. "He'd have a lot of trouble functioning in the real world. So he'd need a nurse, or a former nurse."

Sharona, he explains, was intended as the show's control character. "She was the one the audience would relate to, so it was important that she respond to Monk as they would. I think that any one of us, if he had to spend all day with Monk, would be thrilled—and also frustrated." Breckman notes that Sharona says it herself in the pilot: "It's the best job I've ever had, and it's the worst job I've ever had."

As indicated in the early story notes, Queen Latifah was the original prototype for Sharona: "Sassy. Outspoken. No BS." The producers toyed with the idea of offering the role to the rapper/singer/actress with the larger-than-life personality, but by the time the casting process began, "she'd gotten too busy," recalls David Hoberman. "So we opened it up to anybody. It was an unbelievably difficult role to cast. You needed someone cute with personality who could play a counterpoint to Monk. And she couldn't be annoying."

"I think that the people coming in to read had heard that the part was written for Queen Latifah," notes Jackie de Crinis, "so a lot of them tried to *be* her, and she's really one of a kind. They all went over the top. And then Bitty Schram came in and she just played it so real, as someone who had such compassion and was very grounded and oddly accessible. It was clear there was nobody else that made more sense."

"It was just one of those great auditions," says Breckman. "Bitty made it all work and then some. She added a dimension that we'd never even dreamed about."

Perhaps best known for her stage work and her film debut in *A League of Their Own* as the sobbing right fielder who's taken to task by Tom Hanks because "there's no crying in baseball," Bitty Schram was nothing like Queen Latifah. She had a personality all her own, one that was more reminiscent of a different Sharona prototype that Breckman had had in the back of his mind. "Someone like Marisa Tomei's character in *My Cousin Vinny*," he says. "Very smart and sexy. Bitty was in that mold."

So Sharona became a New Jersey girl, a so-called "bridge and tunnel" type, per Ileane Meltzer, costume designer for *Monk*. "Sharona was kind of stuck in the 1980s," she says. "Her hair was from that era, her makeup. Sharona would never wear skirts that came down to the knee. It was always going to be miniskirts for her. And tight pants."

And yet, somehow it didn't matter whether her wardrobe fit into the San Francisco scene or not. It certainly didn't matter to Sharona, who definitely marched to her own drummer, right to the end. And although she was very fond of Monk, who she thought of as a friend as well as an employer, there was never any doubt that her family always came first. Which helps to explain why she was able to cut the cord in Season Three and unceremoniously relocate to New Jersey with teenage son Benjy (played in various seasons by Kane Ritchotte and Max Morrow) to remarry her ex-husband.

Natalie Teeger (Traylor Howard)

Like Sharona, Natalie is a single working mom, albeit with a young daughter, Julie (played by Emmy Clarke). Beyond that, there's not much resemblance, a point that Natalie herself has to hammer into Monk's head when she first goes to work for him. She has less patience with Monk's worst habits and she won't put up with some of the things that Sharona had come to take for granted.

"As sweet as Monk is, he is *so* selfish," chuckles Traylor Howard, getting into character. "He sees everything through his eyes. So, in her initial relationship with him, Natalie tried to set up some boundaries. She was, and is, very assertive. She has a lot of respect for him but she won't hand-hold him."

Natalie is definitely not a blue-collar girl. She's the black sheep of a wealthy family—the founders of a toothpaste dynasty.

"Natalie's family has money, but she won't take it," says Breckman. "She was a very wild, untethered kid who has traveled around a lot. Her husband, Mitch, kind of tamed her and settled her down. There's a bit of mystery attached to her early life."

Natalie initially enters Monk's life as a client in mid third season, not long after Sharona had left the scene. "She had a million different jobs," says Howard, "and she's been trying to figure out what's going on in her life when she meets Monk, who's having his own crisis (over Sharona's departure)." Impressed with her capable attitude and take-charge personality, Monk asks her to work for him, and, despite some misgivings, she accepts.

The new dynamic took a while to work out (and for the Sharona-familiar audience to adjust to), but soon it was clicking along. A veteran of several television sitcoms, including *Boston Common* and *Two Guys and a Girl,* Howard brings a certain physicality to the role that Breckman appreciates. "As Natalie, she's very tough. She handles herself and, in some ways, she's fearless," he says. "If it weren't for her daughter, she'd be Wonder Woman out there fighting crime on her own."

Captain Leland Stottlemeyer (Ted Levine)

If Monk is Sherlock Holmes and Sharona/Natalie is his Doctor Watson, then that means the good captain must be Inspector Lestrade, the Scotland Yard inspector that always needs Holmes's help.

"Stottlemeyer's job is to serve and protect, and to catch the bad guy," says actor Ted Levine.

"And, if he's got someone around who can help him do that, he's going to use him. Monk is a tool to him."

"We wanted a legitimate police captain, a friend and a partner, a supporter and sometimes an adversary," says Jeff Wachtel. "Somebody real. That's why we went to Ted Levine."

Levine certainly has a solid track record playing smart cops and military commanders, notably in such films as *The Fast and the Furious, Evolution,* and the recent remake of *The Manchurian Candidate* (although he may have gained more notoriety for his creepy turn as psychokiller "Buffalo Bill" in 1991's *The Silence of the Lambs*).

"Stottlemeyer is a tough role," notes Andy Breckman. "He's a smart cop, but he's not *the* smartest cop. He has to feel a little embarrassed that he always has to call in Monk. He still has to have his pride. And Ted seems to be able to do all of that. I consider Ted our secret weapon. He's very funny and very smart and he anchors the crime stories for us in a way that nobody else could."

Referred to as "Chief Rockwell" in the original character notes for *Monk* that Breckman put together to pitch the show in 1998, Rockwell became Stottlemeyer somewhere between the pitch document and the shooting script for the pilot. Why? It's not quite clear other than the fact that Andy Breckman writes with the television on and often pulls names out of the electronic ether. "A sports game was on, it must have been either football or basketball, and the name Stottlemeyer was on the back of a player's jersey," he recalls. "I just picked it up. It's a great name."

As described in the character notes, Rockwell is a "crusty, veteran Deputy Chief of Detectives . . . ex-military, totally by-the-book."

In other words, a classic sonovabitch. Rockwell "resents Monk and ridicules him mercilessly," referring to the detective as "The Freak" and "Mr. Clean."

If that description doesn't quite jibe with your impression of the man who ultimately became Monk's boss, Ted Levine is probably to blame. "It was one of those things that evolved," says writer Hy Conrad. "Ted would play scenes nicer than they were written. And then we started writing nicer. Actors contribute."

In Levine's hands, Stottlemeyer also became more real. "I think in the beginning he was more exasperated by Monk," says Breckman. "I like their relationship now—there's a real warmth to it, although he's still driven crazy by the guy. He's as close to a friend as Monk has. I'd like to have a friend like Stottlemeyer."

Lt. Randall Disher (Jason Gray-Stanford)

Alas poor Randy. The things people say about him . . .

"He's the dumb cop to Stottlemeyer's smart cop," explains Jeff Wachtel.

"He was developed as a character that would idolize Stottlemeyer and was sort of groveling all the time," says David Hoberman.

"Disher *is* kind of obsequious and more ambitious than bright," Canadian actor Jason Gray-Stanford admits cheerfully. "Obviously, as the seasons go by, our characters grow and change. He's always viciously loyal to the captain and to the police force, which usually makes him the first to rebuff Monk's outlandish deductions. But at the same time, he's bright enough to know that Monk has the ability to make them all look very, very good. So he's

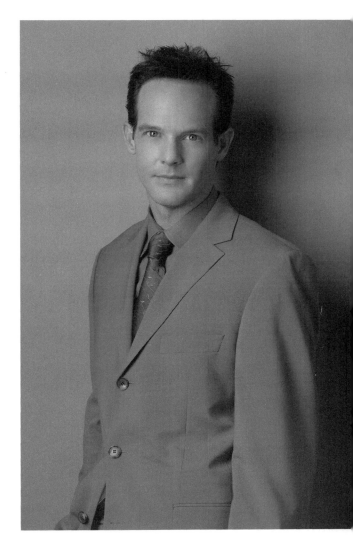

come to tolerate Monk and even have an affection for him."

The character was a minor one in the series pilot, a guest star rather than a costar. "The show was developed as a three-hander, with Monk, Sharona, and the captain," says Gray-Stanford. "But after the shoot, Andy Breckman took me aside and said, 'You know what? We got picked up—and it's a four-hander now.' And that's how I came to the show."

Gray-Stanford's new status required a small adjustment. "He was Lt. Deakins in the pilot," Breckman says. "But Disher sounded better. It says a lot about Jason that he made the character memorable. When we went to series, I couldn't have imagined doing it without him."

He may be the right-hand man to Monk's Lestrade, but Gray-Stanford has also had the opportunity to play the big man himself; he provided the voice of Holmes in the Scottish animated series *Sherlock Holmes in the 22nd Century*. He's probably better known to Monk viewers from his turns in the film *A Beautiful Mind* and the science fiction miniseries *Taken*.

Dr. Charles Kroger (Stanley Kamel)

"In any given scene," says Tony Shalhoub, "Monk has multiple agendas, needs, and objectives. And with Dr. Kroger, he's relying on him as a confident and as a friend, but he's also trying to impress him. Whenever he's there, I always feel like Monk is hanging on for dear life, trying not to completely unravel. He's guarded and needy at the same time, looking for help but not 100 percent convinced that Kroger is really able to help him. He has to be there because it's sort of required of him, but sometimes it feels like the process is moving too slowly."

"The scenes between them provide a quiet moment where Monk gets to express things about himself that he doesn't get to express at any other time," observes actor Stanley Kamel. "When Dr. Kroger is in the chair his job is to simply listen and talk to Monk. He's very comfortable in that chair."

If Kamel's face is familiar to television audiences it's because he's been in just about

everything, from guest spots on *The West Wing* and *Dark Angel* to recurring roles on *Murder One* (as an unscrupulous psychiatrist), *Beverly Hills 90210,* and *Melrose Place.*

Kroger was described only as an unnamed shrink in Breckman's initial character notes and defined as "an intermittent character; Monk probably has to see him once a month, like a parole officer."

As it turns out, Dr. Kroger sees Monk a lot more often than that—once a week on average (although viewers don't always see them together), and twice a week when he's really upset. And there are times when it's hard to tell which of them dreads the visit more.

"Well, they're both long-suffering people," chuckles Shalhoub. "And when you have two long-suffering people in the same room at the same time, it can only lead to laughs."

"Mr. Monk Meets the Candidate"

(Series Pilot)

Episode 1-01
Written by Andy Breckman
Directed by Dean Parisot
Original Airdate: July 12, 2002

GUEST CAST

Dr. Kroger . . . . Stanley Kamel
Benjy . . . . Kane Ritchotte
Warren St. Claire . . . . Michael Hogan
Gavin Lloyd . . . . Ben Bass
Sheldon Burger . . . . Rob LaBelle
Jesse Goodman . . . . Vincent Gale
Trudy . . . . Stellina Rusich
with
Miranda St. Claire . . . . Gail O'Grady

In a sunny apartment in Santa Clara, California, a small contingent of uniform cops, detectives, and forensic personnel has gathered to investigate the murder of Nicole Vasques, the young woman who lies dead on the floor. At the moment, however, Nicole is not the center of their rapt attention. That distinction belongs to the impeccably dressed man who is moving about the room, absorbing the details of the crime scene. This is Adrian Monk, once a highly respected member of the San Francisco Police Department, now the somewhat less respected private consultant who assists the local constabulary in some of their more perplexing investigations.

It's not that Monk's insight and investigatory skills are any less sharp than they once were; he's already discovered a number of useful clues in Vasques's apartment that the local cops missed. It's just that he has a few behavioral quirks that occasionally interfere with his ability to do his job. Quirks that have led some to refer to Monk as "the defective detective." Quirks that drove his former watch commander, Captain Leland Stottlemeyer, to take Monk's badge away and give him a psychological discharge.

Not that anyone actually blames Monk for his behavior. The detective's entire life fell apart after the murder of his beloved wife, Trudy, four years ago. Her death so traumatized him that Monk's lifelong compulsion for cleanliness, attention to detail, and orderliness in all things exploded into a severe anxiety disorder. Dealing with the world outside of his excruciatingly neat apartment became a terrible strain—one with which he's able to cope only with the assistance of his assistant Sharona Fleming, a former nurse. He's slowly improving and Monk harbors not so secret hopes that his psychologist, Dr. Charles Kroger, will recommend him for active duty on the force in the near future—but that's not likely to happen while he's still compelled to rearrange the pillows on Kroger's sofa whenever he visits.

In the meantime, however, there's his consulting work. Although Monk quickly ascertains that Vasques's murder was premeditated—not the work of a panicked burglar who'd been caught in the act, as the police had suspected—he doesn't have a clue as to who the murderer could be. As he grapples with the details, he's called in to work on a second case. Someone has just tried to assassinate upcoming mayoral candidate Warren St. Claire at a campaign rally. The shooter missed St. Claire but killed his bodyguard. The incumbent mayor wants the case solved quickly so he orders Stottlemeyer, who's overseeing the investigation, to call in supersleuth Monk. Stottlemeyer complies, although both he and his right-hand man, Lt.

Randy Deakins, have understandable reservations.

After meeting with St. Claire and his wife, Miranda, as well as St. Claire's business associate, Jesse Goodman, and campaign manager, Gavin Lloyd, Monk investigates the high-rise location where the would-be assassin was situated when he fired at St. Claire. To Stottlemeyer's surprise, Monk hypothesizes that the sniper may have been the same person who killed Nicole Vasques. Was Vasques involved with St. Claire's campaign? Monk asks Jake, a campaign staffer, to look into it—but not long after, Jake turns up dead. Although Jake's death initially looks like an accident, Monk proves that it was nothing of the kind—and Stottlemeyer discovers that right before he died, Jake had turned up evidence that Vasques was indeed a campaign worker; she worked with the campaign's bookkeeper.

After Monk is nearly run over by a mysterious black sedan, the defective detective is excited. He's sure it means he's getting close to the truth! He and Sharona begin to narrow the list of suspects. After discovering that Warren St. Claire is worth $150 million, Sharona expresses her belief that Mrs. St. Claire ordered a hit on her husband for the money. But Monk isn't so sure. Jesse Goodman may have motive; he's worked for St. Claire for a long time, yet never has been promoted to partner at the firm. *And* he's been having an affair with Miranda St. Claire. But while Miranda and Jesse each admit to the affair, they both deny any intent to kill Warren St. Claire.

In the meantime, Stottlemeyer tracks down the sniper who killed St. Claire's bodyguard, but the shooter gets away—thanks in large part to Monk's inability to climb a fire escape in order to stop him. But Monk did get close enough to

the man to realize one thing: the sniper wasn't the man who tried to run him down. There are *two* culprits at large, not one. And not long after, Monk realizes who the second one is. Reassembling everyone at the site of the campaign rally, Monk explains that the sniper wasn't trying to kill Warren St. Claire; he was actually hired to kill St. Claire's bodyguard. Why? Because Gavin Lloyd had tried to hire the bodyguard to kill Nicole Vasques, who'd inadvertently discovered that Lloyd was embezzling money from St. Claire's campaign. After the bodyguard refused to carry out Vasques's murder, Lloyd had to find a different assassin—someone who'd silence the bodyguard as well as the girl.

Monk produces his proof: a newspaper photo taken immediately after the shooting showing Lloyd pointing up at the location of the sniper. But, says Monk, because Lloyd's sight line to the building was obscured by a bunch of balloons, and because echoes of the gunfire off the surrounding buildings would have masked the direction of the shot, there was no way Lloyd could have known the location of the sniper. Unless, of course, he had hired him in the first place.

After the hired sniper takes a shot at Lloyd, Sharona takes off after him and chases him into the sewers—where he promptly captures her. Realizing her peril, Monk temporarily pushes aside several of his biggest phobias in order to capture the sniper *and* save Sharona, proving that with time, there may yet be hope of his returning to active duty.

"We open the show with this: fifteen seconds of total silence," states Andy Breckman's original notes for the *Monk* pilot.

Silence? Is this any way to launch a new TV show? With a trumpeting fanfare of silence? Isn't that counterintuitive? Ever since those seminal days of home entertainment when audiences were being drawn away from radio by a new technology that brought pictures into their living rooms, broadcasters intuitively have understood that, pretty pictures or not, television is an audio medium. Verbally elucidating upon what's on the screen allows viewers to raid the refrigerator for the very product being advertised without losing track of the dialogue, plotline, or message. So what's going on here?

"Monk is studying—'reading'—the crime scene," the notes continue. "It's almost Zen-like."

And somehow, just as the cops in the room are captivated by what they're seeing, so is the audience. We sense that we're in the presence of someone with a gift, someone magical, who's superior to us commoners—

And then Monk begins kvetching about his stove being left on. His assistant tries to reassure him, but he won't let the thought go, *can't* let the thought go. *The stove is on.* He can't focus, the heck with the victim, *check the stove.*

With that creative spark, Breckman had found an original way to introduce not only the title character, but also the show itself. This, his writing proclaimed, was going to be different. This was going to be something new.

The visuals shown under the opening credits contributed to that feeling. Credits are the place where, traditionally, a show about a detective will provide the viewing audience with shots of the protagonist looking at clues. And impressing a femme fatale with his brilliance. And punching out bad guys. Instead, the audience watching *Monk*'s pilot was treated to a sequence of scenes showing this new detective . . . attending to his personal hygiene. Doing housework. Dressing. Talking to himself. Preparing for a trip to his psychiatrist.

For an audience used to predictable "must see" type television, such an opening sounds like a death wish. But it was nothing of the sort. It was ingenious. And hilarious.

The audience got the message immediately. They weren't watching a traditional police procedural. They were watching *Monk,* a detective show that doesn't really operate in the real world.

"*Monk* is a fantasy," Breckman explains. "It just doesn't take place on the planet Earth. We have a police department that doesn't do forensics and doesn't deal with DNA. For the most part, they don't have computers and don't use informants. They live in an insane world that we've created. The show is a mystery/comedy/fantasy, with the fantasy as big a part of it as any."

Because the East Coast is familiar territory to Breckman, his original concept situated *Monk* in New York City, and he'd envisioned a chase through the city's subways for the pilot. But by the time the show was ready to go before the cameras, the series's setting had changed.

"We wanted to put Monk in an urban environment where people walk around, and where he would encounter life on the street," David Hoberman says. "In Los Angeles, you're in cars all the time." So L.A. was out. New York fit the bill but, as Hoberman notes, "shooting in New York is very expensive."

The producers settled on San Francisco, which had the right kind of urban feel. But while the beautiful city on the bay would receive some prerequisite location shooting to set the scene, the bulk of the pilot was shot in Vancouver, British Columbia. "You get more bang for the buck in Canada," comments Paulo de Oliveira, then senior vice president of creative affairs at NBC Universal Television Studios. "And Vancouver seemed the right place to double for San Francisco, because there aren't a lot of hilly streets in other cities, and hills are something that's recognizable for San Francisco."

But what about those subways? Shooting in Vancouver offered an opportunity to go in a different direction, although still underground. Monk, it was decreed, would walk through the sewers. "Vancouver has postal service tunnels that were built during the war," Tony Shalhoub observes. "We put water in them and for days people were standing in that water." The actor wrinkles his nose. "It was pretty scrungy."

As noted in the introduction to this book, the script for "The Candidate" was rewritten several times. However, the final draft wasn't completed until the fall of 2001, during a period when humor was difficult to generate. "Andy was working on it right after 9/11," recalls Tom Scharpling. "There was kind of a pall hanging over everything. The feeling for all of us was, 'I don't think I'll ever be able to be funny again.'"

But as anyone who's ever subscribed to *Reader's Digest* knows, laughter is the best medicine—and Breckman apparently tapped into a brand new strain of literary penicillin as he worked through the script for "The Candidate." He was matched, beat for beat, by the performance of lead actor Shalhoub, who brought every last one of Monk's eccentric quirks to life.

Finding the right director for what is, essentially, the prototype of a new series is always a challenge. Just as the actors have to

find that balance, the correct tone, so too does the director who must drive the filming forward. For "Candidate," the reins were handed to director Dean Parisot. "While we were trying to develop the show at ABC, the first person I went to was Dean," says Hoberman. Parisot's credentials included numerous television shows and films, including the uproarious sci-fi parody, *Galaxy Quest,* which, coincidentally, featured Tony Shalhoub in the cast.

Timing is everything. At the time Hoberman first contacted him, Parisot was unavailable. But after the show moved to USA, Jeff Wachtel explains, "Dean became available and he agreed to do it."

The director's tasks include finalizing the casting, and one of the actors he asked to see was Jason Gray-Stanford. "Dean had directed me in a pilot called *The Marshall,*" the actor recalls. "I auditioned to play the bad guy in *Monk*'s pilot, but after I finished, Dean said 'No, I want you to play a different part, the police captain's right-hand man," Randy Deakins (later Disher). Gray-Stanford has the honor of being the first person on-screen to refer to Monk as "the defective detective."

While working on the show, the filmmakers had used a temporary soundtrack of music by jazz guitarist Django Reinhardt to accompany the visual flow. When the time came to finalize the pilot, the producers sought out a composer who could match that sound, and also "deliver the comedy." Jeff Beal fit the bill. "They wanted music that was fun," Beal says. "We all liked the jazz guitar they'd been using, so I wrote a score in that style. We used a kind of bouncy beat because Monk can be like a little kid. But jazz also has the potential to be cerebral, with melodies that weave in and out like little puzzles, and I think Monk's whole take is to solve puzzles." Beal was surprised and pleased at the accolades his theme song received. "As soon as *Monk* premiered, I started getting tons of mail about the theme," he says.

The principle photography period went perfectly—and early edits of the pilot tested exceptionally well in front of trial audience screenings. In the end, USA Network executives, again taking advantage of the flexibility that cable broadcasting allows them, chose not to air the piece as a full-length movie. They shortened it to eighty-one minutes by cutting several nonessential scenes, including one in which Monk visits the home of two women known as the Street Sisters. But the extracted footage would not go to waste; the scene would show up intact in "Mr. Monk and the Billionaire Mugger."

The Quotable *Monk*:

"So that's the famous Adrian Monk."—First Cop
"Yeah, the living legend."—Second Cop.
"If you call that living."—Detective.

The Weirdest Clue: The drawstring to the blinds in the sniper's nest is kinked, as if it had steadied the gunman's shot—a Green Beret technique.

Idiosyncrasy of the Week: Fear of milk, fear of heights, fear of rat-infested sewers . . . you name it, he's got it.

The Clue that Breaks the Case: The newspaper photo of Lloyd pointing up at the location of the sniper.

"Mr. Monk and the Psychic"

Episode 1-02
Written by John Romano
Directed by Kevin Inch
Original Airdate: July 19, 2002

GUEST CAST

Dolly Flint	Linda Kash
Harry Ashcombe	John Bourgeois
Kate Ashcombe	Linda Trotter
Jennifer	Jenny Levine
Benjy	Max Morrow

Kate Ashcombe is driving much too fast for the twists and turns of a dark mountain road, but she doesn't care. Her beloved dog has been injured in an accident—or so her husband has just informed her via cell phone. As Harry Ashcombe fills her in on the grim details, he drags two large ramps into the middle of the winding road and urges his wife to hurry. A moment later, Kate's car hits the artificial incline at seventy-five miles per hour, and car and passenger sail over the side of the cliff road. Looking down from the top of the steep incline, Harry observes the mangled wreckage of his wife's car with satisfaction. It's the perfect murder—and he ought to know, seeing as he's the former San Francisco police commissioner.

Monk and Sharona offer Commissioner Ashcombe their assistance in locating his missing wife, but the body is discovered by so-called psychic Dolly Flint, a known charlatan who's been busted for fraud a number of times. Dolly claims to have been drawn to the scene of the crash by Mrs. Ashcombe's aura—but Monk, who doesn't believe in psychic powers, rejects that possibility.

After attending a memorial reception at the

commissioner's house, Monk begins to suspect that the death wasn't an accident. He and Sharona track down the woman they believe to be Ashcombe's mistress, Jennifer Zeppetelli. She readily admits to the relationship, but says she broke it off because she knew he'd never leave his wife's money. However, Ashcombe has continued to call her, and Jennie, like Monk, has some suspicions about Mrs. Ashcombe's death. Ashcombe, she warns Monk, is dangerous.

Monk is curious about how Dolly Flint could have found her way to the body, particularly after taking her usual dose of sleeping pills. The only access to the site is down a service road that people can't find under the best of circumstances. Monk thinks the commissioner killed his wife, but needed someone else to discover the body so he could claim the insurance money. But Monk doesn't think Dolly was working with the commissioner—at least, not so far as she knows.

Later, Monk and the police gather at Ashcombe's residence, where Dolly uses her "powers" to lead them to the body of Jennie Zeppetelli. After Dolly accuses the Commissioner of his mistress's murder, Ashcombe declares that Dolly is a fake. But, Monk protests, Dolly found Mrs. Ashcombe's body. The rattled Ashcombe blurts out that Dolly found nothing; *he* drove her to his wife's body!

The truth revealed, Jennie "miraculously" returns to life. The snare proved what Monk had suspected: Ashcombe's access to Dolly's police file led him to select her as the ideal candidate to find his wife's body. Already in a stupor from the sleeping pills, it was easy to drive her to the crash site in her own car. When Dolly awakened, she just assumed her bogus powers were real and that she'd come there on her own. Faced with the evidence, Ashcombe now declares that

he has nothing to say, but as Monk assures him, he's said enough.

By *Monk*'s second outing, it was clear to the USA Network that its defective detective was a winner. "*Monk* scores like crazy for USA," crowed the *Hollywood Reporter*, one of Tinseltown's preeminent showbiz trade magazines. The cable network was so pleased with the series's viewership—estimated at over three million homes—that it green-lit a second season.

But while the enthusiastic response warmed the writing team's collective hearts, "Mr. Monk and the Psychic," the first episode to air after the pilot, wasn't a creative favorite at their East Coast office. "Okay, we were just learning how to do this," Breckman laughs. "We didn't quite have a formula yet, so it was a little rough around the edges."

"Here's what happened," says Breckman, sounding uncannily like his titular character. "After the pilot tested well, the people at the network hired me to come up with three trial balloon episodes." Breckman chose three ideas out of the stash of mystery concepts he'd been keeping for years, and the newly assembled writing staff went to work, jointly fleshing out each story's key plot points and twists. Then the scripts were turned over to individual writers. Breckman himself would write "Mr. Monk Meets Dale the Whale," he and Tom Scharpling would cowrite "Mr. Monk and the Beatle" (which later became "Mr. Monk and the Red-Headed Stranger") and John Romano would write "Mr. Monk and the Psychic."

"John was the grown-up in the room," Scharpling says. "The rest of us were still just trying to figure out how many acts there were in

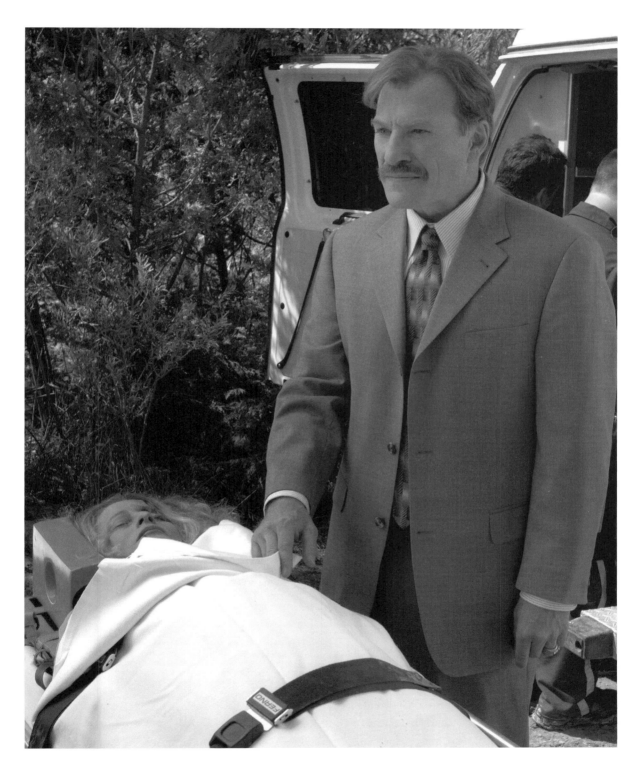

a TV show." Which explains why "Psychic" was the first of the three scripts to be completed— and to be filmed.

"We had asked the question, 'If a man killed his mistress and needed the body to be found in order to make his alibi work, what would he do if the body was then accidentally buried,'" Breckman recalls. "While kicking it around, we stumbled on the idea of a psychic that could be influenced [by the killer] without being aware of it." The gentle absurdity of the premise amused the writers and it stuck.

Unfortunately, things didn't play as well as they imagined when filming began. "I remember going to see the very first dailies," Scharpling says. "The footage was supposed to be the big summation scene where the body was buried. But it turned out that the owner of the location wouldn't let them dig a hole on his property and, as a result, they shot it so that the body was just lying there, with some leaves pushed over it. My gut feeling was, 'Well, maybe this could become a little cult show, but please don't let it be a punchline!'"

The filmmakers reshot the summation scene several weeks later, but somehow that first day had set the tone. "I guess the first episode of anything is going to feel less successful," sighs Scharpling. "But coming off the pilot, which was so elegant, 'Psychic' just felt rickety."

Having shot the pilot in Vancouver, the production started its regular episodes on sets on the other side of Canada, in Toronto. There were several reasons for the move. Permanent, as well as economic, production facilities were immediately available in the eastern city, and Andy Breckman's writing staff was located in New Jersey, so shooting the show in the same time zone would make the writers' trips to the set much easier.

One more change was made from the pilot. The actor playing Benjy, Kane Ritchotte, was recast. Sharona's son would be played by East Coast resident Max Morrow for the rest of the season. Ritchotte, however, would be back for Season Two.

The Quotable *Monk*

"Unless I'm wrong—which, you know, I'm not."

—Monk

The Weirdest Clue: The five empty Beaujolais bottles on Jennifer's mantle lead Monk to conclude that her affair with Ashcombe lasted five years.

Idiosyncrasy of the Week: Ataxophobia (fear of disorder). Monk "helpfully" tidies up Captain Stottlemeyer's desk.

The Clue that Breaks the Case: Monk realizes that Dolly, the psychic, couldn't possibly have found the service road that leads to the murder scene without some help.

"Mr. Monk Meets Dale the Whale"

Episode 1-03
Written by Andy Breckman
Directed by Rob Thompson
Original Airdate: July 26, 2002

GUEST CAST

Dale . . . . Adam Arkin
Dr. Kroger . . . . Stanley Kamel
Dr. Vezza . . . . Juan Chioran
Benjy . . . . Max Morrow
Louisa . . . . Lucia Fillipone

Sue Ellen	Jennifer Pisana
Police Dispatcher	James Downing

The late night call to 911 is unusual. Superior Court Judge Kate Lavinio sounds as if she's in a panic. A man named Dale Biederbeck has broken into her house and is going to kill her. Over the phone line, the police dispatcher can hear utter bedlam: furniture being smashed, animal-like growls . . . and finally the judge's scream of terror as the attacker breaks into her room. Then the line goes dead.

The next day, Monk and Sharona are summoned to the crime scene. Judge Lavinio has been murdered and Stottlemeyer wants Monk's input, although the captain already seems to know quite a bit. Inside, the home is a mess. There is a lingering smell of smoke in the air;

Stottlemeyer says the judge was cooking when the intruder came in, and the food burned. In the living room, a chair has been placed under a smoke alarm. The alarm is located in front of some windows; Stottlemeyer notes that a little girl walking past the house observed a fat man turning off the alarm. All of this seems rather odd—but not nearly as odd as Stottlemeyer's revelation that Lavinio identified her killer before she died. However, the man she mentioned couldn't possibly be the killer because Dale Biederbeck, a.k.a. "Dale the Whale," weighs over eight hundred pounds and hasn't left his pent-house apartment for years.

Monk is familiar with Biederbeck. Years ago, his wife, Trudy, wrote an unflattering magazine profile of Biederbeck and he sued her. Trudy spent a grueling year in litigation hell and the

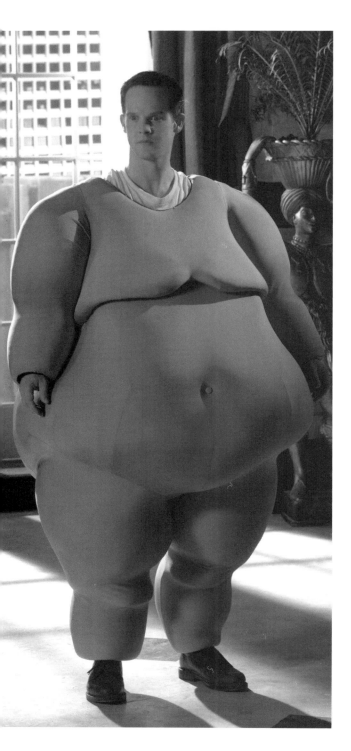

Monks lost all their worldly possessions in court costs. Monk is certain the fat financial despot is guilty; a ruling by Judge Lavinio caused him to lose hundreds of millions of dollars. That's all the motive he'd need.

Unfortunately, a visit to the Whale's luxurious abode confirms that he couldn't possibly get out of bed, let alone his bedroom, a fact his personal physician, obesity expert Christiaan Vezza confirms. Stottlemeyer can't convince a judge to issue a search warrant, so Sharona accepts a night nurse position with Biederbeck to gather evidence. But all she gets for her efforts is a peek at Biederbeck's videos of Lavinio's television appearances and a far more unnerving peak at his corpulent body, which confirms that all that blubber is nauseatingly real.

Monk's interview with the girl who saw Biederbeck inside the house plants a seed in the detective's fertile mind. A subsequent visit to Dr. Vezza's obesity clinic brings the thought to fruition. Monk has cracked the case. Biederbeck orchestrated the murder, although he didn't actually carry it out. Dr. Vezza—who imitated Lavinio's voice on the 911 call—killed the judge while wearing a fat suit from his own clinic, making sure that someone observed him in the house. Since Biederbeck couldn't possibly have committed the crime, the evidence would have represented a dead end for the police investigation if it hadn't been for Monk's sleuthing. After Vezza agrees to testify against his boss, Monk informs Trudy's old nemesis that he's going to jail—although they'll have to remove a window and lower him by crane to send him on his way.

*   *   *

"*Columbo* had completely 'open' mysteries," explains Andy Breckman. "You knew who did it, and why, and how. The question on the table in that show was 'How will Columbo break this man's alibi?' That's a great question to ask, but other kinds of mysteries ask different questions."

"Mr. Monk Meets Dale the Whale" is the series' first example of Breckman's favorite formula: the "semi-open mystery." "That's where Monk knows *who* did it, but he doesn't know *how* he did it," says Breckman.

The episode is also a great variation on a "locked room mystery," where someone is killed in a place that the murderer couldn't possibly get in or out of—a room that's locked from the inside, for example. In this case, however, the impediment to reaching the victim is killer Dale Biederbeck's own body! "I love that," Breckman says happily. "I love the idea that Monk suspects an eight hundred-pound man of murder, but the man can't even fit through the door."

"Mr. Monk Meets Dale the Whale" was the first episode Breckman wrote after the pilot. "I was trying to show the people at the network the kind of unique stories that I hoped to tell throughout the series," Breckman recalls. But while the setup was certainly unique, the resolution wasn't something that Breckman is quite as pleased about. Having a different character pose as the suspect while committing the crime wasn't clever enough, he admits. "It's not exactly an Edgar Award–winning mystery."

It didn't look as good as it could have, either, according to Tom Scharpling. "The production values fell a bit short," he points out. Dale the Whale should have looked awesome, and not in a good way, judging by Sharona's reaction when Dale plays "I'll show you mine" with her. "But

he didn't look great," says Scharpling. "It was as if they'd inflated a kid's wading pool over Adam Arkin's body and then just draped a blanket over the pool. When we saw that first shot, the air just went out of the office. We all said, 'Ooooh, noooo.'"

However, the fat suit that Dale's accomplice, Dr. Vezza, wore to kill the judge was a big hit with at least one of the cast members. "Wearing that suit was one of my favorite bits in the whole series," enthuses Jason Gray-Stanford. "It was like a scene within a scene. Monk was giving the summation, and there's Disher, demonstrating the fat suit and then trying to get off the chair and not knowing what to do." The humor surrounding Disher's predicament, he admits, was "a little broad, maybe too close to what I call the crazy zone, but it's also the kind of scene that keeps my character alive and three-dimensional."

If Disher had trouble with the fat suit, it's nothing compared to the problems the sound department has dealing with Monk's normal wardrobe. Actors are routinely fitted with tiny wireless microphones hidden under their clothing for scenes where an overhead boom mike would be seen in the shot. But Monk's constant fidgeting invariably causes the fabric of his snug-fitting clothes to rub against the mikes. The sound and wardrobe departments worked together on the problem, ultimately placing tiny sticky-backed "furniture feet" alongside microphones in order to make Monk's clothing lay smoothly while not rubbing on the sound equipment. Most of the time, they report, it works.

Although his appearance left something to be desired, Dale the Whale was certainly memorable, and the writers wouldn't hesitate to roll the pudgy villain back on-screen the following season, in "Mr. Monk goes to Jail," albeit with a different actor under the swimming pool.

"Mr. Monk Goes to the Carnival"

Episode 1-04
Written by Siobhan Byrne O'Connor
Directed by Randy Zisk
Original Airdate: August 2, 2002

GUEST CAST

Lt. Adam Kirk	Stephen McHattie
Leonard Stokes	Alan Van Sprang
Benjy	Max Morrow
John Gitomer	Rob Stefaniuk
Kitty	Elisa Moolecherry
Board Member #1	Bruce Hunter
Board Member #2	Carolyn Scott
Landlord	Phillip Williams

Lt. Adam Kirk arrives at a low-rent carnival amusement park to hook up with an informant named John Gitomer, but although Gitomer is the one who arranged the meeting, he's surprisingly uncooperative. He refuses to disclose his information out in the open; he wants Kirk to join him on the Ferris wheel. Minutes later, however, Gitomer starts screaming that Kirk is trying to kill him. The ruckus draws the attention of everyone on the ground and Kitty, the Ferris wheel operator, halts the ride.

Confused, Kirk leaps out of the basket. "What did you do?" Kitty asks accusingly, bending over Gitomer.

"Nothing!" Kirk responds. "I didn't touch him!"

But *somebody* obviously did; Gitomer has a knife sticking out of his chest. He's dead—and the only suspect is Kirk.

A short time later, Captain Stottlemeyer, Kirk's ex-partner on the force, grills his old friend about the incident. It looks like an open and shut case against him. Everyone saw him in the basket with the victim and Kirk has a history of using excessive force with suspects. Disher wonders if Monk can help clear Kirk. Stottlemeyer is reluctant to contact Monk—he's facing the police review board in an effort to win back his badge—but eventually the captain agrees.

Although impressed with Monk's improvement, the review board opts to reserve judgment until they hear from Monk's former commanding officer: Stottlemeyer. Monk is skeptical about Kirk's innocence, but he agrees to investigate because his cooperation may influence Stottlemeyer's testimony.

At the carnival, Monk finds a clue: a discarded claim ticket that fell from Gitomer's pocket. Monk and Sharona track the ticket to a dance club, where they claim Gitomer's knapsack, and the cell phone within. A check of

the call records establishes that Gitomer recently had been in touch with Leonard Stokes, an accused murderer who was jailed on the basis of Kirk's testimony. Stokes has long maintained that his confession to Kirk was beaten out of him; now that Kirk has been accused of murder, the judge has no recourse but to release Stokes. Clearly there's a connection between Stokes, Gitomer and Kirk—but what is it?

Monk is devastated when Stottlemeyer admits he didn't recommend him for reinstatement, but his keen mind refuses to stop analyzing the clues, and he solves the case. With the ostensible goal of discrediting Kirk, Stokes told Gitomer to claim that the detective roughed him up on the Ferris wheel. Then Stokes upped the ante on his revenge by having girlfriend Kitty, the ride operator, stab Gitomer after Kirk

exited the car, thereby framing Kirk for murder. A grateful Stottlemeyer tells Monk not to give up on his dream of reinstatement. When he's ready for it, it'll happen.

" 'Carnival' is the show where we hit our stride," observes Tom Scharpling. "The series took a step forward."

However, the original nugget for the episode seemed a little implausible to the folks at Universal. "Andy told us, 'I want to do an episode where a guy is alone on a ski lift and when he comes off the top he has a knife in him and he's dead,' " says Paulo de Oliveira, then senior vice president of creative affairs at NBC Universal Television Studios. "Now, that's impossible, so we were a little skeptical."

But that was the whole point, explains Andy

wheel and that's when the formula began to come together for us."

The episode contains two elements that would become a fixed part of the show, one that perfectly illustrates its style, and the other that sharply defines the relationship between two key characters.

Early in the episode Sharona and Monk argue about who's going to drive her car. "That scene goes on much longer than anyone at the network wanted it to go on," admits Breckman. "It was just a digression, a left turn from the mystery. But it showed that you *could* stop the mystery and just have fun. With that scene the show became *Monk*. It wasn't a straightforward procedural anymore. It was a fun ride. The fun ride trumped the mystery.

"The episode also has a great defining moment for Ted Levine," Breckman adds. "Stottlemeyer doesn't recommend Monk for reinstatement, and that sets up who Stottlemeyer is in Monk's world."

So despite the fact that the two men have a history together, and that the captain isn't unsympathetic to Monk's situation, the bottom line, according to Ted Levine, "is that Stottlemeyer's a cop. For him, that's what it's about."

Still another ingredient that contributed to the winning *Monk* formula was the addition of Randy Zisk to the production team. As the director of "Carnival" (he would later become an executive producer on the series), he admits to two snafus that occurred during his initial shoot.

"We had set up the carnival on an asphalt parking lot and the temperature was over one hundred degrees. I think it was the hottest week in Toronto in years. The people on the carnival rides were yelling, 'Stop the ride, stop the ride,' because they were passing out from the heat."

Breckman. "I had it worked out as an impossible murder," he says, so the initial skepticism didn't discourage him. There were, however, more insurmountable problems with setting the crime on a ski lift. "For one thing, we were shooting in the summer," Breckman notes. "For another, Monk lives in San Francisco. How could we explain him traveling? So we rethought the ski lift, and it became a Ferris

And there was a miscalculation with extras. "The first day we had fifty of them," Zisk recalls. "And that wasn't enough. It looked like *Monk* had rented out the carnival for a private party!" After an additional 350 extras were hired for the rest of the shoot, says Zisk, "the place looked really great. But to this day when I watch 'Carnival,' I can tell which shots are from that first day— although I think I'm the only one who can."

The Quotable *Monk*

"It's a gift—and a curse."—Monk

The Weirdest Clue: Ceiling fan + tube sock filled with batteries = the victim's bruises were self-inflicted.

Idiosyncrasy of the Week: Excruciating attention to meaningless detail. Monk knows how many jelly beans are in the jar at the carnival because he saw the discarded candy boxes in a pile of trash.

The Clue that Breaks the Case: The killer, Stokes, and Kitty, the ride operator, both wore orange "Straight & Sober" pins.

"Mr. Monk Goes to the Asylum"

Episode 1-05
Written by Tom Scharpling & David Breckman
Directed by Nick Marck
Original Airdate: August 9, 2002

GUEST CAST

Dr. Lancaster . . . . Dennis Boutsikaris
Jane . . . . Eve Gordon
Dr. Kroger . . . . Stanley Kamel
Benjy . . . . Max Morrow
and
Wurster . . . . Kevin Nealon

Monk arrives home with a bag of groceries and plans to make chicken cacciatore. But something isn't right. For one thing, he can't find the large casserole dish. For another . . . he's in someone else's house! As he turns to leave, Monk finds himself face to face with two uniformed police officers. Things go downhill from there, as Monk is escorted to the Medford Psychiatric Institute for two days of "observation and evaluation."

Dr. Kroger and Sharona try to be reassuring. At least no one opted to press charges. And the director of the facility, Morris Lancaster, is considered one of the top clinical psychologists in the country. After the pair departs, Monk has his first meeting with Dr. Lancaster, an avid sportsman with lots of fishing equipment in his office. Lancaster deduces that Monk went to the wrong house—a house that Trudy once lived in—because it was the anniversary of the couple's first meeting, something Monk had forgotten, at least at a conscious level. And Monk had wanted to make chicken cacciatore because that was Trudy's favorite dish. Impressed, Monk agrees to comply with Lancaster's prescription: take some time off from playing detective.

However, Monk finds it hard to keep his promise. Wurster, Monk's roommate at the facility, shares details of a murder that occurred there years earlier. Assistant Director Gould was shot to death, ostensibly by a patient who later overdosed on stolen drugs. But the murder weapon was never found, and Wurster says the alleged killer was a pacifist. The story piques Monk's interest, as does a different inmate's story that he saw Santa Claus hanging out near the building's chimney the night before. When Monk spots a swatch of torn red cloth on the chimney, he begins to wonder if there's a connection between Santa's appearance and Gould's murder.

When Dr. Lancaster hears about Monk's in-house sleuthing, he's extremely displeased. Not long after, evidence begins to surface that Monk is losing his mind. Even Sharona doubts his sanity until she discovers that Gould had been tapped as the institute's next director, a position Lancaster himself coveted. After Sharona manages to get that information to Monk, the detective is able to piece together the rest of the puzzle.

Four years earlier, Lancaster shot Gould, then framed and killed the innocent patient who was ultimately blamed for the murder. He stowed the gun in a long unused chimney. But now the institute's renovation work is about to reveal the crucial piece of evidence. That's why Lancaster has been up on the roof, "fishing" for the murder weapon in the old chimney. He wore a Santa suit because he knew the only person who might catch sight of him from his room was a delusional patient who believed in Santa Claus. Monk confronts "Santa" Lancaster on the roof just as the doctor retrieves the gun. He tries to shoot Monk, but the firing pin has oxidized over the years. As Sharona arrives on the scene with the police, Monk ruefully admits to Lancaster that, "Except for the murders and your trying to kill me, you really were the best doctor I ever had."

The concept for "Mr. Monk Goes to the Asylum" sprang from the mind of executive producer David Hoberman. "In every other episode, Monk

is the most screwed up member of any group," Hoberman chuckles. "I thought it would be interesting to put him in a psychiatric hospital where he'd be the sanest, healthiest person in the room."

The writing staff thought it was a funny idea, one that would work particularly well when conjoined with another idea they'd been toying with that involved a Santa Claus impersonator. "There's an old story about a kid who thinks he sees Santa Claus, but of course it's someone dressed up like Santa who's about to commit a crime," staff writer Hy Conrad explains. "That was our nugget. We changed the kid into a crazy man who's a super Santa Claus fan. He'd be in an asylum and Monk would be in the same asylum."

Besides the character of Manny, the Santa fanatic, the writers created Wurster (played by *Saturday Night Live* alum Kevin Nealon), Monk's amiable roommate who initially seems pretty normal. Wurster—who's named for a writer friend of Scharpling's—acts as Monk's guide through the asylum and intrigues him with details about Dr. Gould's mysterious murder. "We didn't want the guide to be somebody who's truly mentally ill, because then we weren't going to have any fun," Scharpling comments, "and it's a heavy episode to begin with. We made Wurster a kind of Zelig who assumes the identity of everyone he meets." Wurster's proximity to Monk not only gives the defective detective someone funny to play off of, but also serves as an investigative cohort at the asylum—a quasi-Sharona who comes in handy when Monk needs help in recreating Gould's murder.

The episode begins with a poignant mishap as Monk inadvertently breaks into Trudy's old house. "When Monk starts to focus on stuff related to Trudy, his emotions get in the way," Scharpling says. "That's his intellectual blind spot, and that's when he can be as wrong as he's usually right." At times like that, his brilliant mind seems to slip a gear. In this case, the subconscious memory of his first encounter with Trudy leads him to the place where she lived at the time. Memories of Trudy would again mislead

Monk in "Mr. Monk and the Billionaire Mugger," sending him to the home of Kelly Street, who doesn't know any more about Trudy's death than she did the first three times Monk visited.

Although the story takes place at a mental facility, the series' resident psychiatrist, Dr. Kroger, appears only briefly. Actor Stanley Kamel, who accepts the fact that his character is a seasoning, rather than a main dish, wouldn't mind seeing Kroger sprinkled a bit more liberally. "The pilot was bookended by Kroger scenes," Kamel observes. "Monk came to Kroger at the top of the show, went off and solved the case, and then came back to Kroger to wrap it up. That worked real well for me."

The Quotable *Monk*

"Be careful—there's a lot of gravity up there."—Monk

The Weirdest Clue: A piece of Santa's red suit, found attached to the chimney of the psychiatric hospital.

Idiosyncrasy of the Week: Acrophobia (fear of heights). Monk doesn't want to climb on the roof.

The Clue that Breaks the Case: Sharona learns that Dr. Lancaster was seriously unhappy when Dr. Gould was named director of the facility instead of him.

"Mr. Monk and the Billionaire Mugger"

Episode 1-06
Written by Tim Lea
Directed by Stephen Cragg
Original Airdate: August 16, 2002

GUEST CAST

Dr. Kroger	Stanley Kamel
Myra Teal	Jessica Steen
Sidney Teal	J. C. MacKenzie
Willis	Richard Chevolleau
Angie Deluca	Shannon Hile
Leo Otterman	Aron Tager
and	
Archie Modine	Peter Onorati

Billionaire software developer Sidney Teal leaves his mansion, ostensibly to deliver a lecture. But instead of heading for the college, Teal heads for the parking lot of a movie theater. There, he puts on a fake moustache and a hooded sweatshirt . . . and waits. Soon, Archie Modine and his girlfriend enter the parking lot. Teal confronts them. "Give me your wallet," he growls. "Don't be a hero!" Modine reaches into his pocket—but to Teal's surprise, his victim pulls out a gun and fires. The billionaire mugger collapses and dies.

Sharona is relieved when Captain Stottlemeyer asks Monk to investigate the botched mugging. Her most recent paycheck from Monk has bounced because Monk's last client hasn't paid the detective. Sharona urges him to bug Stottlemeyer for a raise, but Monk won't focus on anything but the investigation, which is complicated by the revelation that a uniformed cop ran from the parking lot in terror after Modine shot Teal. The press corps jumps on the "Fraidy Cop" story, much to Stottlemeyer's dismay.

Because Sidney Teal was a man who didn't need money, Stottlemeyer suggests the would-be mugger was having a mid-life crisis. Teal's widow supports that theory, adding that her husband had begun engaging in atypically risky activities. Sharona urges Monk to accept that rationale and wrap up the case so he can collect his fee. But there are too many unanswered questions for Monk. Why was Teal wearing kneepads? Why didn't Archie Modine mention that he and Teal belonged to the same fraternity in college?

Modine sheepishly provides the answer to the second question: he'd had a brief fling with Teal's wife. When he saw Teal coming at him in the parking lot, he figured he was facing a cuckolded husband and fired in self-defense.

The cops find the story credible. But Monk doesn't buy it and he refuses to turn in his invoice for the case. Frustrated, Sharona quits, but although she tries to walk away, she's drawn back to the case after learning that Teal was involved in a very similar mugging while he was in college. In that case, however, *he* was the victim. In fact, the mugger had used the very same words Teal had recently uttered: "Don't be a hero."

That information allows Monk to crack the case. Back in college, Teal and frat brother Modine had cooked up a plan to impress Teal's then-girlfriend. Modine pretended to be a mugger that Teal successfully fended off. Twenty years later, Modine called upon Teal to return the favor so he could impress *his* girlfriend. Teal had donned kneepads because he expected to engage in a staged tussle.

Unfortunately, Teal was unaware of Modine's real motives. That "fling" with Teal's wife was actually a long-term relationship, and the two had conspired to get him out of the way permanently. Modine hadn't counted on "Fraidy Cop," an actor Teal hired to add authenticity to the fake mugging. When Monk tracks him down, Fraidy Cop provides all the proof Stottlemeyer needs to put the murderers away. And as an added bonus, Monk uses Fraidy

Cop—in uniform—to convince his former client to settle his debts!

From a little acorn, a giant oak tree grows. In the case of "Billionaire Mugger," it was a rather inauspicious acorn: a comedy sketch that David Breckman had written while on staff at *Saturday Night Live.* The sketch, which never made it to prime time, revolved around an "Impress Your Date Service," where you hired somebody to mug you in front of your girl, then allowed you to beat him up instead.

"David and I were talking about that sketch," recalls brother Andy, "and over the course of things, it evolved into a nugget about [Microsoft founder] Bill Gates mugging a guy. We muse over these nuggets for months at a time—we kick them around, we go to lunch, we go to bed, always thinking, 'Is it possible that Bill Gates could be caught mugging a guy? How would that work? What are the ramifications? How do you get Monk into that story? How could that last for forty-one and a half minutes? Is there potential for comedy? Is there potential for an emotional moment?' "

At the same time, executives at the network and the studio ask similar questions. "During Season One, there were many conversations about comedy," says NBC Universal's Paulo de Oliveira. "We talked a lot about the Fraidy Cop character in this episode. We said, 'Andy, this Fraidy Cop just seems as if it's not going to be funny, it's going to be dumb and kind of silly.' And he kept saying, 'No, trust me, it's really gonna be great.' It turned out Andy was right."

Ironically, while the rather dark crime itself had evolved from a comedy skit, the played-for-laughs Fraidy Cop idea did not come from one of the comedy writers, but from the show's official crime consultant, Hy Conrad. "Fraidy Cop is the one thing I contributed to that episode," Conrad says. "The problem was that the setup mugging was a conspiracy, and the killer and victim were the only ones in on it. We needed some way for Monk to prove his theory, so we had the victim enhance the mugging by hiring a phony cop. That phony cop could later serve as a witness for the real cops."

Attentive viewers will notice that the marquee on the movie theatre that Modine and his date are leaving reads: "Hitchcock Festival—Now Showing—*Psycho* and *The Man Who Knew Too Much.*" And that the name of Teal's housekeeper is Mrs. Danvers, just like that of the sinister housekeeper in Daphne du Maurier's classic mystery *Rebecca*—also transformed into a film by Alfred Hitchcock. "That Hitchcock stuff hangs over the entire series," smiles Tom Scharpling. "Sherlock Holmes, *Columbo, Seinfeld,* and Hitchcock are the four lampposts shining down on us."

The sequence where Monk visits the "Street Sisters" may seem a bit disconnected from the rest of the story. That's because the scene actually had been shot for the pilot, "Mr. Monk Meets the Candidate," and later cut when the episode was shortened. The producers kept the footage and found a home for it here.

The Quotable *Monk*

"I think I just busted this case wide open."

—Sharona

The Weirdest Clue: The victim was inexplicably wearing kneepads and elbowpads.

Idiosyncrasy of the Week: Crooked things must be straightened. Monk pays a quarter just to straighten the display copy in a newspaper dispenser box.

The Clue that Breaks the Case: Sharona discovers that Teal and Modine were involved in a nearly identical mugging twenty years earlier.

"Mr. Monk and the Other Woman"

Episode 1-07
Written by David M. Stern
Directed by Adam Arkin
Original Airdate: August 23, 2002

GUEST CAST

Grayson	Nicholas Campbell
Monica Waters	Maria del Mar
Dr. Kroger	Stanley Kamel
Todd Katterskill	Patrick Garrow
Trudy	Stellina Rusich

As attorney Lou Pratt wraps up his day's work, a masked figure creeps into his office and murders him. The killer then breaks into the file room and burns the contents of a lone manila folder. By the time Monk arrives on the scene, the police have completed their initial investigation, and Stottlemeyer has a prime suspect: Lawrence Grayson, the man whose file was burned.

Monk thinks the evidence against Grayson is weak. Yes, Pratt represented the suspect in an unsuccessful lawsuit against Grayson's neighbor,

Monica Waters. Yes, Grayson threatened the attorney after he lost the suit. But if burning his own file was an attempt by Grayson to keep the police from connecting him to the murder, it was a clumsy attempt and it makes no sense to Monk.

Monk is immediately smitten when he meets Monica Waters, a strong, pretty woman who reminds everyone of Monk's late wife Trudy. Although Monica has little connection to the case beyond Grayson's futile lawsuit over the construction of her garage, Monk invites her to dinner, ostensibly to question her. It soon becomes obvious that Monk's interest is personal, but Monica doesn't seem to mind— although she does change the subject when Monk brings up her ex-husband.

At Pratt's funeral, one of the lawyer's elderly clients sits behind Monk, coughing continually. Unnerved, the detective berates him, and the old man keels over, dead. After an ambulance takes the dead man away, Todd Katterskill, the old fellow's nephew, chastises the embarrassed Monk for his thoughtless behavior.

Not long after, Grayson meets an untimely end in Monica Waters's garage, and suddenly *she* becomes Stottlemeyer's main suspect in both murders. Not surprisingly, Monk feels Monica is innocent, even when Stottlemeyer postulates that she killed her ex-husband and buried him under her garage! Startled by the accusation, Monica explains that her ex isn't dead—he's in an asylum in Switzerland. Now Stottlemeyer is stumped; they're back at square one and have no idea who killed Pratt.

Monk and Sharona return to Pratt's file room, where Monk finally finds the clue that breaks the case. At the reading of Old Man Katterskill's will, Monk reveals his discovery. The murderer of both Pratt and Grayson is Todd

Katterskill, who'd been cut out of the elderly man's will. Todd broke into the office of Pratt, his uncle's lawyer, to replace the will with a forgery that left everything to him. Because Pratt would have been able to identify the bogus will, Todd eliminated him, then burned a random file—Grayson's—to send the police in the wrong direction. He later murdered Grayson, thus insuring the police would continue to follow a false trail. Unfortunately, he didn't count on Monk's preternatural ability to spot out-of-place items, like the inappropriate tab on the bogus will's folder.

With the case solved, Monica tells a disappointed Monk that he's made her remember how wonderful her relationship was with her husband. She's going to Switzerland—and she's not coming back till he's better.

"Everyone knew that *Monk* was a very important series for USA, and the early scripts were often ripped apart and rebuilt," recalls Andy Breckman. " 'The Other Woman' was really reworked. In fact, it was rewritten more than any other script we've done."

The troublesome story had a simple beginning. Tom Scharpling suggested a robbery where someone breaks into a house and doesn't take anything. Instead, something is left behind. That intriguing concept begat a marathon series of talks, ultimately leading to a fleshed-out idea about a revised will that's left in a lawyer's file, and a different file that's grabbed at random. "The grabbed file is a red herring that leads to an innocent woman," says Breckman. "That, I think, is a really great story. The core mystery is strong. But the execution of the episode was not my favorite."

That was due, in part, to the script's early slot in production. Although "Other Woman" was the seventh episode of *Monk* to be aired, it was actually the third episode to be filmed. That explains why Disher and Stottlemeyer are so antagonistic toward Monk—despite the fact that they'd already begun to mellow toward him in some of the preceding episodes (which were written after "Other Woman").

The situation may have been complicated by the creators' lack of proximity to the set. In the aired episode, there is a scene in which Stottlemeyer grabs Monk and pushes him into the hands of a waiting policeman. But that rather physical bit of action was not written into the script; it was one of numerous choices made on the set during filming. "Those of us at this end of the country," Scharpling notes, "didn't think that was in Stottlemeyer's character." But back then, he acknowledges, "no one understood what the boundaries were. Everybody was just feeling his way. Now, three seasons later, *everybody* agrees that he wouldn't do that to Monk."

Even the romantic aspects of the script seem a touch out of step. The audience barely knew who Trudy was at this point—or the depth of Monk's devotion to her—yet here the writers were, creating a character whom Monk falls for, hard. "It ended up feeling like our 'Lifetime Movie of the Week *Monk* Episode,' " Scharpling admits.

The episode did, however, allow for some particularly eccentric—and funny—behavior from Monk: his "Princess and the Pea" type sensitivity to a very, very tiny pebble in his shoe, his pathetic attempt to fake eating, and his extremely prolonged efforts to freshen up at Monica's. "He goes into the bathroom, and comes out two hours later, without being aware of how long he'd been in there," chuckles Breckman. "Having Monk black out like that is something that we haven't done for a while and I miss it. I think it's really funny."

The episode is one of very few that lacks an epilogue. One was written—Sharona and Monk have one of their little walk-and-talks while Monk touches the poles they pass—but it was cut for time.

The Quotable *Monk*

"I don't mind change. I just don't like to be there when it happens."—Monk

The Weirdest Clue: Monk can tell that Monica's husband has been gone for two years by the amount of the pachysandra that's grown beneath the basketball net.

Idiosyncrasy of the Week: Monk doesn't want the different foods on his plate to touch—and believes other people don't either.

The Clue that Breaks the Case: The tab of the replaced folder is out of sequence with the other ones in the drawer.

"Mr. Monk and the Marathon Man"

Episode 1-08
Written by Mitch Markowitz
Directed by Adam Davidson
Original Airdate: September 13, 2002

GUEST CAST

Trevor McDowell . . . . Peter Outerbridge
Angie . . . . Paula Barrett
Tillie . . . . Arlene Mazerolle
Jenkins . . . . Martin Roach
Arthur Zaleski . . . . Richard Zeppieri
and
Tonday Mawwaka . . . . Zakes Mokae

Gwen Zaleski watches television coverage of the city's annual marathon race. She knows her lover is one of the runners, so she's surprised when she sees him in her apartment.

Moments later, Gwen's body hurtles twenty stories to the ground.

Not long after, Monk and Sharona spot Stottlemeyer in the center of a crime scene and stop to see what's going on. Stottlemeyer points out the body of Gwen Zaleski, noting that they haven't yet determined if the deceased jumped, slipped, or was pushed from her balcony. Monk feels she was murdered. Gwen has fresh nail polish on some—but not all—of her toenails. She was obviously interrupted by her killer.

In Gwen's apartment, Monk discerns the scent of chamomile and spots a blank space on her phone's speed dial directory. A tap of the corresponding button connects them to Trevor McDowell, Gwen's married lover. But the furniture magnate has an airtight alibi for the time of Gwen's death: he was participating in the marathon.

Monk believes McDowell is guilty. He and Sharona pay a visit to marathon headquarters, where the workers explain that every runner was tracked via a computer chip worn on the individual's shoe. McDowell's chip was scanned at every one of the marathon's twenty-six checkpoints.

Stottlemeyer theorizes McDowell removed his chip and gave it to another runner, someone who ran at McDowell's pace for the entire race. There was one runner who fits the bill: Tonday Mawwaka, a legendary marathoner whom Monk has worshipped since high school. Thirty years ago, Tonday's performance inspired Monk to take up running, and Monk did surprisingly well—until his burgeoning anxiety disorder caused him to blow a major relay race. Disgraced and humiliated, he never ran again.

Monk and Sharona visit Tonday, but Monk doesn't feel he's involved. Videotapes of the marathon show that Tonday and McDowell kept pace for a while, then McDowell dropped off-camera until the end of the race.

Monk traces a path from a blind spot in the marathon course to Gwen's apartment. There's a clump of chamomile at a spot where McDowell could have stopped to change his clothes, which may explain why the apartment smelled of the weeds.

Monk asks McDowell why he never returned his chip at the end of the race. He must have lost it, says McDowell, shrugging off Monk's theory that he murdered Gwen after she threatened to reveal their affair. The marathon computer says otherwise. He couldn't have detoured to Gwen's apartment unless someone else carried the chip—but if Tonday didn't carry the chip, who did? Watching the marathon tapes again, Monk realizes that it's not a *who* that carried the chip—it's a *what*: the television camera bike providing video coverage of Tonday during the race. McDowell must have attached the chip to the bike by putting it in a magnetic hide-a-key box.

Monk and Sharona arrive at the television station's parking lot just as McDowell retrieves the box and hightails it for the bay. Monk falls back upon his old running skills and overtakes McDowell before he gets to the water. But he's so excited by his recovered prowess that he fails to stop McDowell from tossing the box into the bay. Fortunately, the box floats—and the proof to McDowell's guilt is retrieved.

Of all the clues Monk has used to solve cases, Andy Breckman's *second* favorite is found in "Marathon Man." (For his first favorite clue, see "Mr. Monk and the Red-Headed Stranger.") "Monk knows the victim was interrupted while doing a manicure because several nails weren't finished," the writer says. "That's clever *and* it plays fair with the audience."

The idea for "Marathon Man" actually began with the killer's alibi. "I was working out with a trainer," Breckman recalls, "and he was telling me about a marathon that he'd run while wearing a computer chip that tracked him." It was, Breckman realized, a sensational alibi. But could a guy really commit a murder while running a marathon?

"Absolutely brilliant," concurs brother David Breckman. "How could the guy be in two places at once?"

" 'Marathon Man' is a good stand-alone episode," Tom Scharpling observes. "It's an example of a script that's not character-driven, just a good mystery. Ninety percent of the episode is the puzzle. It's very clean."

Nevertheless, the episode does rely on some of Monk's very personal idiosyncrasies for its humor, like the painfully awkward scene when Monk, as usual, uses a wipe after shaking hands with Jenkins, the African American security guard in the marathon office. Andy Breckman giggles at the memory. "The politically correct like to tell you what's appropriate, and what's offensive, but Monk in all innocence sometimes says and does things that are completely inappropriate," he says. "Sometimes a cigar is just a cigar. Sometimes he's just wiping his hands because he's Monk."

Viewers also get their first look at a very young Monk, circa 1974, the high-school-aged geek who used to run in school marathons (more flashbacks to Monk's school days would show up in Season Four's "Mr. Monk and Little Monk"). It's interesting to learn that Monk took up running after he saw Tonday Mawwaka in 1973, but it's a little disconcerting to hear that Tonday is Monk's absolute idol. "The episode is about Monk's favorite athlete . . . who we never heard of before . . . or after," Hy Conrad laughs. "He's totally devoted to a guy that he never mentions again!"

The Quotable *Monk*

"I'm the askew police."—Monk

The Weirdest Clue: Lack of nail polish on several of the victim's toes.

Idiosyncrasy of the Week: Phobia of uneven things, like the laces in his high school track shoes.

The Clue that Breaks the Case: Monk figures out that the tracking chip was attached to the motorcycle camera that followed Tonday through the race.

"Mr. Monk Takes a Vacation"

Episode 1-09
Written by Hy Conrad
Directed by Kevin Inch
Original Airdate: September 20, 2002

GUEST CAST

Rita Bronwyn	. . . .	Polly Draper
Benjy	. . . .	Max Morrow
John Fenimore	. . . .	Barry Flatman
Shawn	. . . .	Andrew Airlie
Stand-up comic	. . . .	Chuck Byrn
Tony Landis	. . . .	Graham Harley

Knowing that Monk can't handle being left alone, Sharona convinces the detective to accompany her and Benjy to the beach resort where she plans to take her first vacation in years. But they've barely settled in when Benjy, occupying himself with one of the resort's beachside telescopes, witnesses a murder in one of the hotel rooms.

Monk notifies the hotel and soon finds himself working with its chief of security, Rita Bronwyn. They investigate the room in question but find no trace of a crime. Indeed, the room is spotless. Its occupant, a wealthy businessman named Fenimore, claims he wasn't in the room when the alleged crime happened. Monk observes that Fenimore's wife, who's sharing the room, is conspicuously absent. Sharona suspects Benjy's imagination may have gotten the better of him, but Monk believes the boy, and continues nosing around with Bronwyn.

The theory that Fenimore killed his wife is quickly abandoned when Mrs. Fenimore shows up, unharmed. But there still may have been a crime. In the hotel's basement, Bronwyn finds evidence of blood, but she's attacked by an unseen assailant before she can investigate. By the time she gets back to the evidence, it's been cleaned up. In the hotel arcade, Benjy stumbles upon a dead body, stashed in back of an inactivate game. He races to find his mother and

Monk, but by the time they return to the game room, the body is gone.

Nevertheless, Monk is more convinced than ever that murder is afoot. He's found a sample of quicklime, a substance that can be used for gardening . . . or to kill smells. Later he discovers that someone has stolen three large bags of lime from the hotel gardener. Obviously the killer is using the lime to disguise the smell of the body, which means it's still in the hotel.

The extremely efficient clean-up of all those clues leads Monk to turn his attention to the hotel's cadre of four housekeepers. There used to be five, he learns. One quit a day ago—but, curiously, she left her street clothes behind. In the housekeepers' break room, Monk finds hidden digital cameras and, in those cameras, photos of confidential financial documents.

At last, Monk cracks the case. The house-keepers were stealing financial information from the resort's business guests and using the information to clean up in the stock market. But when one of the maids wanted out of the crime ring, the others killed her. That's the woman Benjy saw being murdered in Mr. Fenimore's room. Afterwards, the housekeepers cleaned up every trace of the crime. All Monk needs to prove his theory is the victim's body—but where have they hidden it?

A set of photos that Sharona took on the day they checked in provides the answer. In the hotel lobby, there's a display promoting a raffle for a cruise. Sharona's photo portrays the display with three big steamer trunks. But now . . . there are four! Bronwyn opens the new trunk, and they find the body of the missing maid. The housekeepers are arrested, and Monk happily declares that he is looking forward to Sharona's *next* vacation.

*　　*　　*

"It's an honor just to be nominated" may be an old saw, but to those who *never* are nominated, it couldn't be truer. The Oscars, the Emmys, the Tonys, and the Grammys are among the entertainment industry's most prestigious awards. But among mystery writers, no award is more coveted that the Edgar, the award presented by The Mystery Writers of America, and named after that organization's patron saint, Edgar Allan Poe. Hy Conrad was working as a consultant on *Monk* when he received the assignment to write his very first television script. No one could have been more surprised when the result, "Mr. Monk Takes a Vacation," received an Edgar Award nomination. "I'd never even thought of writing for TV before," Conrad says.

The script assignment gave him the opportunity to inject an important aspect into the show. " 'Takes a Vacation' marks the first time that Monk makes a deductive mistake," Conrad points out. "Early on he thinks that it was the husband who killed his wife in the hotel room. And then, of course, he barges into the surprise birthday party for the still-living wife. That's something I pushed for, that Monk is capable of making deductive errors. It makes him more human and gives us more plot possibilities."

The episode also was the first to incorporate Benjy Fleming into the mystery. "Andy doesn't like to put kids in peril," Conrad explains. "So this is about as close to that as we've gotten."

Benjy's mother, Sharona, was less involved in the crime but, then, she *was* supposed to be on vacation. Of course, that didn't work out very well for her and, as she had in both the pilot and "Billionaire Mugger," she threatens to quit. "That love/hate relationship between Monk and

Sharona has been part of the dynamic from the beginning," says Conrad, "just like it is in the Nero Wolfe mysteries, where Archie is always on the brink of quitting and Wolfe is always on the brink of firing him."

"Takes a Vacation" features a prominent guest appearance by Polly Draper (best known for her costarring role in TV's *thirtysomething*) as Rita Bronwyn, the tough but feminine hotel cop who assists Monk in his investigation. The presence of Rita gave the filmmakers a chance to have some fun with the classic Raymond Chandler-esque gumshoe stereotype. Rita's offer of a mint-flavored individually wrapped toothpick to Monk, accompanied by some jazzy music on Jeff Beal's soundtrack, invokes memories of people like Bogart and Bacall vamping over cigarettes long ago.

Unfortunately, Rita's presence nearly pushed Sharona's character into the background. "We learned something about the balance of incorporating a guest star into a show from the episode," says Tom Scharpling. "Guest characters have to complement our people, not replace them, and Rita almost smothered Sharona on that one."

Nevertheless, the writers found additional ways to incorporate Sharona into the action. "We'd heard that Bitty Shram was a semipro-level tennis player," Conrad says. "That's why we put in all of those tennis beats."

The Quotable *Monk*

"I tried doing that once, making every minute count. Gave me a headache."—Monk

The Weirdest Clue: Rita's infrared "Spectra-Light" reveals a lack of incriminating evidence in the initial suspect's room—but finds remnants of a disgustingly large quantity of bodily fluids in Monk's room!

Idiosyncrasy of the Week: Arachnophobia (fear of spiders)! Not to mention their webs!

The Clue that Breaks the Case: Sharona's photos of the hotel lobby disclose the final resting place of the murdered maid's body.

"Mr. Monk And the Earthquake"

Episode 1-10
Written by Tom Scharpling & David Breckman
Directed by Adam Shankman
Original Airdate: October 4, 2002

GUEST CAST

Gail	Amy Sedaris
Darryl	Cameron Daddo
Dr. Kroger	Stanley Kamel
Christine Rutherford	Janine Theriault
Benjy	Max Morrow
Father Hatcher	Damir Andrei

A 6.0 magnitude earthquake represents a lucky break for Christine Rutherford, who'd dearly love to inherit her millionaire husband Henry's wealth. Although Henry came through the quake just fine, Christine takes advantage of the circumstances by killing him and making it look like the temblor did the dirty work.

Sharona is stunned when she hears of Henry's death on the news. She's been working with the well-known philanthropist to raise money for a new church in the neighborhood.

Deciding to pay a condolence call on the grieving widow, Sharona opts to bring along the quake-addled Monk, who is temporarily speaking gibberish. Monk recovers quickly when he realizes that Christine's tale about Henry's tragic death is false. The heavy display case that the quake ostensibly tipped onto Henry looks as if it had some human help. But Stottlemeyer, overwhelmed with 1,001 quake-related minor emergencies, doesn't pay much attention to Monk's suspicions.

When Sharona heads home, she learns that her street has been blocked off due to earthquake damage; a gas line is ruptured and phone service is out. She and Benjy will have to stay with Sharona's sister Gail for a few days—not a pleasant prospect. On the other hand, Darryl, the handsome Australian journalist she meets at the police barricade surrounding her block, is *very* pleasant. Alas, their meeting isn't an accident. Darryl is Christine's lover; he's been dispatched by the widow to retrieve an incriminating tape from Sharona's answering machine. Although the police barricade has temporarily delayed that mandate, Darryl figures that feigning romantic interest in Sharona will allow him to keep an eye on her while he awaits his opportunity.

Monk is suspicious of Darryl, whom he catches in several lies. But he doesn't realize Sharona is in danger until he learns that a gas company employee was killed outside Sharona's building—perhaps when he came across someone breaking into her apartment. When Monk adds that to the fact that Christine's phone records indicate that she—or more likely Henry—called Sharona during the earthquake, he cracks the case. Since Monk knows Sharona wasn't home at the time, a message must have been recorded on Sharona's machine. And the message, he deduces, reveals both the fact that Henry was murdered—and who did it. That's clearly why someone wanted to get into Sharona's apartment.

But before Monk can warn Sharona, Darryl reveals his true nature and forces her at knifepoint to pass the barricade and return to her apartment. When Christine arrives as well, the two lovers take Sharona's answering machine and prepare to kill her. Fortunately, Sharona is able to hold her own against them, just long enough for Monk, Stottlemeyer, and Disher to arrive. With the killers in jail, things go back to semi-normal, with Monk evading the subject of Sharona's tardy paycheck by feigning the return of his earthquake-induced gibberish.

Should a writer feel guilty about inspiration? Catastrophic events devastate people's lives, whether they're the product of nature, like Hurricane Katrina—or the product of man, like the terrorist attacks on 9/11. So it's no wonder that David Breckman has some very mixed feelings about the genesis for "Mr. Monk and the Earthquake."

"Forgive me for admitting this," Breckman says, "but it occurred to me that with so many of the people who died in those towers unaccounted for, somebody could have committed a murder on 9/12, dropped the body in the Hudson River, and told people, 'She was on her way to the Twin Towers yesterday, and I haven't seen her since.' And they could get away with it."

Transferring that idea to a San Francisco setting made a lot of sense, given that the city by the bay has its own history of disasters—in the form of earthquakes. There was one problem, though: earthquakes cannot be predicted, which would obviously impinge upon the strategy of someone planning a murder. "The initial idea—a woman just waiting for the next earthquake to happen so she could act—was very far-fetched," Hy Conrad points out. "So we made it a crime of opportunity. She had been *thinking* about murder, the earthquake happened and she took advantage of the moment. That's feasible."

"But that only gave us the teaser," notes David Breckman. "Then Andy found a way to make an episode out of it. What if, unbeknownst to the killer, the victim had been on the telephone *after* the earthquake and left a message on someone's voice mail. So now the killer has to retrieve that incriminating voice mail. It's brilliant."

Earthquakes aren't, by nature, particularly funny. But imagining how Monk would react to one is. Thus Monk's dissociative episode came into existence. With the occipital lobe of his left hemisphere shorted out, per Dr. Kroger, the defective detective began speaking gibberish. It was up to Tony Shalhoub to voice that gibberish, although the writers did make some helpful suggestions in the script, such as, "Brogga hoook-a jogga, grora-ga!"

Ultimately, though, Shalhoub took over. "I just wrote it," the actor says. "It's not the first time I've done that, actually. I'd played a cab driver in one of my first movies, a Bill Murray comedy called *Quick Change*. The cabbie was of indeterminate ethnic origin and the script said he shouldn't sound identifiable by any one foreign accent. It just said, 'And the cabbie speaks gibberish.' But you can't just go, 'dah de dah.' So for my audition I invented a language by writing down phonetic sounds for myself. It was a lot of fun because when the script said, 'The cabbie speaks,' they had to let me just keep talking. I could just string it out as long as I wanted and pad my part! And for 'Earthquake,'" Shalhoub laughs, "I did the same thing!"

Monk's impaired linguistics skills made for some very funny sequences in the episode, including a summation scene that no one but Monk could comprehend. "We'd briefly considered having Monk speak gibberish throughout the entire episode," Andy Breckman says, "but we compromised by having him go in and out of the psychotic break."

"Mr. Monk and the Red-Headed Stranger"

Episode 1-11
Written by Andy Breckman & Tom Scharpling
Directed by Milan Cheylov
Original Airdate: October 11, 2002

GUEST CAST

Wendy Mass . . . . Jackie Richardson
Benjy . . . . Max Morrow
Sonny Cross . . . . David Anderson
Terry T. . . . . Neil Crone
Lil' Kenny Freedman . . . . Jay "Mad Dog" Michaels
Pete . . . . Bruce McFee
and
Willie Nelson . . . . Willie Nelson

An enthusiastic promoter informs living legend Willie Nelson that he's arranged for Willie to be interviewed on a San Francisco radio show. But Willie is distracted, and when road manager Sonny Cross approaches, everyone within earshot learns why. Willie icily accuses Cross of embezzlement and warns him that he expects the money to be accounted for immediately.

The next day, Cross arrives at the radio station and finds a note directing him to an entrance accessible through the alley. Then two shots ring out. A station engineer runs outside to find Willie hovering over Cross's dead body and a blind woman standing nearby, hollering for help.

The blind woman, Mrs. Mass, is the only "eyewitness" to the crime. Willie didn't see the shooting; he heard the shots from his car, and entered the alley to find Cross dead. Mrs. Mass says she was using the alley as a shortcut when she heard two men arguing, and then gunshots. Afterwards, one of the men threatened to kill her if she told anyone. She's certain that Willie's voice is the one she heard.

Mrs. Mass seems to be a credible witness. Stottlemeyer, his right arm in a sling following an accident, is reluctant to charge Nelson, but he may have no choice in light of the mounting evidence against him. But Monk, almost as big a fan of the singer as his wife Trudy had been, can't believe Nelson would commit murder. With Stottlemeyer occupied by the celebrity-obsessed press corps and an elusive streaker, Monk devotes himself to finding out the truth.

He begins by investigating Sonny Cross. A reckless womanizer and boozehound, Cross had briefly dropped out of the music industry while imprisoned on a vehicular manslaughter conviction. Monk also spends some time with Mrs. Mass, learning that she lost her vision at age sixteen in a car accident that also took her parents' lives. Although she still harbors some anger over the incident, she's not a bitter person. In fact, she received a concussion after falling in the local supermarket a year ago, but never thought of suing.

Upon parting, Mrs. Mass extends her hand to Monk, who suddenly recalls that when Mrs. Mass was introduced to Stottlemeyer, she extended her left hand for him to shake because of the Captain's incapacitated right arm. How could she know to do that if she couldn't see?

Monk sets a trap for her. The police have finally caught the evasive local streaker, so Monk bails the man out and hires him to run, au naturel of course, past Mrs. Mass as she sits in the park. Sure enough, Mrs. Mass turns her head to take in the unusual sight. Once in custody, she comes clean, admitting she regained her sight after the fall in the supermarket. She kept the miracle a secret so she'd be above suspicion when she took her revenge on Cross, the drunk driver who took away her family and her eyesight thirty-six years ago.

The charges against Nelson are dropped, and the grateful musician joins Monk for a very private performance—Willie on guitar, Monk on clarinet—at Trudy's gravesite.

"Red-Headed Stranger" is one of the three "trial balloon" scripts written immediately after the pilot to *Monk* aired, and it became one of the most popular episodes with cast and crew. "A lot of people talk about it," notes Tom Scharpling, who cowrote the episode with Andy Breckman. "It's a fun episode, one of the high-water marks of the series."

Although the script had been written early, it wasn't shot till late in the season. And in the time that transpired, it had gone through many changes. "Originally, the story was going to involve Ringo Starr being accused of murder, with Monk saying things like, "I don't think a *beetle* would kill anybody," Andy Breckman recalls with a chuckle. "But as we began to plot it out, we realized that having someone shot in an alley would remind too many people of John Lennon's death, and we felt we couldn't do it with Ringo."

"So I wrote a draft for Brian Wilson," says Scharpling. "Then I rewrote it for James Taylor, who actually showed an interest in doing it."

Scheduling problems soon took the very busy Taylor out of the running, and it seemed that the script had hit an impasse. "We knew that the more famous the character playing himself was, the more fun it would be," says Hy Conrad.

And that's when Andy Breckman suggested Willie Nelson.

"Andy wanted him," says David Hoberman. "So I just went after him."

This time, everything worked out. Nelson wanted to do it, he was available when they needed him, *and* he had quite a bit of acting experience, including roles in *The Electric Horseman, Barbarosa,* and *Wag the Dog.*

"Willie Nelson was a home run," Scharpling enthuses. "He just nailed the role. With all those twists and turns, we ended up where we should have been. Obviously, it was meant to be Willie Nelson."

"Just being around Willie and his band was one of the best experiences I've ever had," reminisces Tony Shalhoub. "In between setups they were just jamming. And Willie's such a gracious, warm human being. Even without saying anything, he's a spiritual guy. His whole essence is kind of inspired."

"That episode was a real shot in the arm from a production standpoint," Scharpling adds.

Meet the Writers

"I think we're unique in that no one on our writing staff, including myself, had ever worked on a one-hour episodic series before *Monk*," Andy Breckman comments. "None of us had any experience. We didn't even know what an act break was. And the series is better for it." Not surprisingly, one of Breckman's favorite TV shows is *Seinfeld*—another show, he says, "where you could tell that the writers were doing it for the first time. In the early *Seinfeld*s, it's wonderfully obvious that (writer/creator) Larry David had not spent a decade working on writing assignments. He just had this vision with Jerry Seinfeld, and he had the will to insist that it reach the screen intact."

The first writer Breckman hired to work with him on *Monk* was his friend Tom Scharpling, whom he knew from WFMU, a New Jersey radio station where both men host weekly talk shows. "At the time," Scharpling says, "I had written for *The Onion* and MTV, and I'd done some basketball writing. If somebody asked me to write something I'd say yes and then ask them what they wanted me to write."

The second person Breckman called was his younger brother, David. Like Andy, David had been a staff writer on *Saturday Night Live*. He also shared the Breckman delight in a good mystery. Bringing David on staff was akin to adding a second mystery/comedy database, making him a valuable resource. "I asked him if he wanted to be on staff in his first job in series TV, and he said, okay," the senior Breckman relates.

And so, with that inauspicious start, the *Monk* writers' headquarters opened. But it was a far step from the image most people have of a glitzy Hollywood enclave. "We were working out of an eight-by-eight 'rent-an-office' in New Jersey," Tom Scharpling relates. "We had a rented desk and a rented garbage can—and a receptionist answering about thirty different companies' names. It was like something out of *The Spanish Prisoner*. We didn't know what kind of fraudulent businesses were next door."

That office wasn't entirely staffed with novices, however. Understandably, USA Network executives believed that the inexperienced group would benefit by working with "veterans who had done it before," Andy Breckman notes. Among those who joined the group at the network's behest were John Romano, a writer/producer who had worked on dozens of shows, from *Knott's Landing* to *American Dreams*, and David Stern, former story editor of *The Wonder Years*, and writer of numerous episodes of *The Simpsons*. The veterans contributed fully to the show, but by the middle of Season Two it was clear that Breckman's vision was paying off, and the network stepped back, allowing him to fill out the staff with series-writing virgins.

> The pen is mightier than the sword.
> —Baron Lytton, *Richelieu*
>
> The only thing I was fit for was to be a writer, and this notion rested solely on my suspicion that I would never be fit for real work, and that writing didn't require any.
> —Pulitzer Prize winner Russell Baker, *Growing Up*

From the beginning, *Monk* had benefited from contributions by then Florida resident Hy Conrad—even before Conrad himself knew about it. "One day I got a call from a guy named Andy Breckman," Conrad says, "and he said, 'I'm stealing your plots so I guess I should hire you.'" Conrad had written eight books of "solve-it-yourself" mysteries that Breckman had found in a bookstore. "He'd been looking for plots and clues to pilfer," Conrad laughs. In addition to the books, Conrad had developed numerous games, mystery and otherwise, for Parker Brothers and Milton Bradley, and also some mystery-based interactive fare. He had not, however, written a script for television or film—making him a natural for Breckman's team. "I came on board at during the series's first season as a consultant," says the mystery writer. The following season he became a full-fledged member of the writing staff, commuting from his home, now Atlanta, a thousand miles to the south.

Above, left to right: Joe Toplyn (glasses), Dan Dratch, Andy Breckman, Peter Wolk, David Breckman, Tom Scharpling, Hy Conrad.

Also joining the staff for the second season was Daniel Dratch, whose previous writing credits included *The Man Show* on Comedy Central and *The Chris Rock Show* on HBO. "Andy wanted another comedy guy," Dratch reports. "I'd never done mysteries before, but I had written a spec script for 'Curb Your Enthusiasm' and I submitted that through my manager. That got me an interview with Andy. It must have gone well, because he called me . . . a year later!"

The Writers Guild of America requires that all registered shows offer work to a minimum number of freelancers, which accounts for the additional writers credited throughout the seasons. During Season Two, the work of one of those freelancers, Joe Toplyn, impressed the rest of the staff. Like Andy Breckman, Toplyn had been a staff writer for *Late Night with David Letterman,* although they'd met only in passing a decade earlier. Toplyn since had written for *In Living Color* and several sitcoms, including *Doctor, Doctor* and *Hangin' with Mr. Cooper*. He also teaches writing classes at The People's Improv Theatre in Manhattan. Heeding his own advice ("I tell my students, 'Write a spec script for a show that you watch because then you don't have to do any research'"), Toplyn pitched a *Monk* story to Breckman. The idea didn't fly, but Breckman liked it enough to assign him the script of "Missing Granny." "And then I came on board at the beginning of Season Three," Toplyn says.

"And that," laughs Andy Breckman, "is how we ended up with five guys who have never written for one-hour episodic television before."

By that time, of course, they'd moved into a larger office space.

"Everyone was tired at the end of the year, and Willie Nelson was such a nice guy that he just brought everybody up."

Per the script, Captain Stottlemeyer's right arm was in a cast due to a fall from a ladder. Because that seemed an odd tack for the writers, some fans speculated that perhaps Ted Levine had injured himself while away from the set. But only the character was injured.

"That was for the mystery," says Scharpling. "We had to facilitate the 'smoking gun' clue—the one that leads us to the killer. We pounded our heads against the wall trying to come up with it. It took a long time."

And then they had it—a blind woman reaching out to shake the left hand of a man whose right arm is injured. "That's my very favorite clue from the first four seasons!" beams Andy Breckman. "The blind woman shaking hands. I wish they all could be like that."

The Quotable *Monk*

"Oh, yeah, the Ramones. Yeah, they were great. I love that song they do about loving that woman all night long."—Monk

The Weirdest Clue: Monk knows that Stottlemeyer couldn't have injured himself on the dirt trails north of Highway 18 because they'd been closed for two weeks.

Idiosyncrasy of the Week: Monk can't play his clarinet because the mouthpiece has been in someone else's mouth.

The Clue that Breaks the Case: The blind woman knew that Stottlemeyer's right hand was in a cast.

"Mr. Monk and the Airplane"

Episode 1-12
Written by David M. Stern
Directed by Rob Thompson
Original Airdate: October 18, 2002

GUEST CAST

Leigh	Brooke Adams
Tim Daly	Tim Daly
Barbara Chabrol	Jennifer Dale
Stefan Chabrol	Carl Marotte
and	
Warren Beach	Garry Marshall

Sharona blindsides Monk by announcing that she's about to fly to New Jersey to visit her Aunt Minn. Monk has five minutes to make one of two choices. He can spend a week without her in San Francisco, or he can accompany her to New Jersey—she already has a bag packed for him. He's afraid to stay alone and equally afraid to fly. Obviously, he'll regret either choice, so Monk opts to go with her, and the nightmare of Monk's first trip on an airplane begins.

Unable to ignore the minutia around him even in his state of near panic, Monk observes an attractive married couple—the Chabrols—waiting to board the plane. They kiss, the woman standing on tiptoes to reach her husband's lips. Monk doesn't see what transpires when Mrs. Chabrol steps into the ladies' room, where she encounters a woman who could almost be her twin. But Mrs. Chabrol has no time to react; her doppelganger kills her and takes her place on the flight.

In the meantime, Monk boards the plane, in the process annoying every crewmember and passenger he encounters. As Sharona fawns over the TV celebrity in first class, Monk nervously studies the Chabrols. Mr. Chabrol boards late, explaining that he went to the wrong gate—although Monk saw him getting a shoeshine outside the correct gate moments earlier. And Mrs. Chabrol no longer has to stand on her tiptoes to kiss her husband; apparently, she's grown two inches since Monk first saw her. She's also forgotten that she's a frequent flyer and a vegetarian. Before long, Monk is convinced that the real Mrs. Chabrol has been killed and replaced with a look-alike.

Monk uses the in-plane phone to contact Randy Disher and convey his suspicions. Knowing Monk's hunches are nearly always correct, Disher begins checking facts for him. Mrs. Chabrol is an heiress, he relates. That presents a motive for the charade that's being conducted. Chabrol wants to be with another woman *and* continue to receive the yearly stipend from his wife's trust fund. So he has to pretend Mrs. Chabrol is still alive. Learning that Chabrol is a pilot—meaning he has free access to any area of any airport—Disher heads for the San Francisco airport to look for a body.

On the plane, "Mrs. Chabrol" fails to recognize an old family friend . . . who later dies an untimely death. Monk suspects this is another murder, but can't prove it. If Disher doesn't find the real Mrs. Chabrol's body soon, Chabrol and his mistress will make their connection to France, and it could take years to extradite them. After getting a close look at Mr. Chabrol's newly polished shoe—which has traces of cement on the sole—Monk advises Disher to look for a construction site at the airport. Disher discovers a likely site with freshly dried cement, but it will take an hour and a half to dig up. Monk makes a phone call to the airport manager and implies that the pilot of the Paris-bound flight is inebriated. The flight is delayed, the body recovered, and Chabrol and his mistress arrested.

*   *   *

Depending on your point of view, placing an entire episode on one small set has its good and bad points. On the positive side, it's economical—no set changes between takes means a quicker shooting schedule. On the negative side, after a commercial break or two, your viewers may begin to feel a little claustrophobic—the way they would during, say, a transcontinental flight. Which, coincidentally, was the proposed setting for "Mr. Monk and the Airplane."

"There was a lot of discussion about how much we would set on the plane," notes Hy Conrad. "The network wanted us to put less than half of the scenes on the plane and then have the characters get off the plane to do other things. But Andy Breckman and Tom Scharpling wanted it *all* on the plane."

Not that the writing staff couldn't see the other side's point. "There are only so many moves you can make on a plane," says Tom Scharpling. "Somebody getting up to go to the bathroom is considered an action scene."

And beyond the discussion about the set, there was that joke . . .

"That scene with the obnoxious little girl leaning over Monk's seat," recalls Jackie de Crinis, senior vice president of original programming. "Pete and Repeat were in a boat . . ."

"It went on for *two pages* of the script!" explains Jeff Wachtel, executive vice president of original programming. "They did the lines about *nine times*. We told Andy, 'It's funny the first two times, but at that point, someone should say, 'That was fun, but go talk to your mommy.' "

Ah, but that would be something a *normal* person would do in the real world. And Monk definitely doesn't reside in that world.

Andy Breckman has a mantra that he repeats

Out of the Closet: Monk's Wardrobe

Costume Designer Ileane Meltzer, whose credits include *Tuskegee Airmen* and *Tortilla Soup*, started working with *Monk* on the pilot, developing the characters' wardrobes, including the all important attire of Monk himself. "We felt that because of the character he is, Monk would be very restricted in his choice of clothing," Meltzer says. "So from the beginning we started with jackets that don't fit Tony properly, that are a little too tight for him. Then Tony and I came up with the idea of having his shirt buttoned to the top, but with no tie.

"We didn't want to do Inspector Clouseau, and we didn't want to do Columbo," Meltzer comments, "although we knew Monk was kind of like each of them. We had to create a look that would be all his own. That's when I came up with tweed, and pattern on pattern on pattern. Although it's very hard to see on television, all of his shirts have a checkered pattern, all of his jackets have a textured pattern, and all of his pants are textured.

"Brown was a good color for Monk because nobody else on television was using it at the time," the designer

> For the apparel oft proclaims the man.
>
> —Shakespeare, *Hamlet*,
> act 1, scene iii, line 65

points out. "I haven't deviated at all from the color or the texture, and Tony doesn't want to deviate. He likes it this way. It's very Monk.

"Originally, Monk was only going to have about four outfits. His closet would be full, but there would be four of the same jacket, and four of the same shirt," Meltzer explains. "I've expanded that a little as we've gone into the later seasons, but basically everything still looks alike," she says.

"A lot of people think he's always wearing the same thing, but he's not," Meltzer chuckles. "When we started, we were buying cheap clothing for Monk, and then we graduated from that. Everything still depends on whether the clothing has the pattern we're looking for, but we've actually gone from shopping at JC Penney and Sears, to the shop where I recently bought him an Armani jacket. We used it for the first time in 'Mr. Monk Goes to the Dentist.' It doesn't matter who made it, because it's the look that we want and the texture we want. And anyway," Meltzer concludes with a smile, "nobody can tell the difference on the screen."

whenever someone brings up a point like this. "He says, 'Please don't stop the fun train for plot,'" de Crinis chuckles. "We argued, 'But it doesn't even have a *punchline.*' And Andy answered, 'It'll be hilarious, trust me.'"

In the end, everyone realized that Breckman was right. "Monk couldn't *not* answer her," admits Wachtel. "It's in his core." And Tony Shalhoub's performance sold the joke 100 percent. "Each time the kid asked the question,

Monk went through a whole new set of tortures," he observes.

"When we finally saw the footage, we were crying from laughing so hard," de Crinis admits. "That was one of the last notes we ever gave on a joke, because Andy knows that the only one qualified to say 'I can't make this work' is Tony."

"Airplane," the final episode of *Monk*'s first season, has three notable guest actors in prominent roles. Brooke Adams, the real life spouse of Shalhoub, plays Leigh, the flight attendant who's wound just a little too tight. "We just love working together," comments Shalhoub with a big grin. "We met, actually, doing *The Heidi Chronicles* on Broadway together." Adams would return to *Monk*, albeit in a different role, during Season Three.

Actor Tim Daly, who starred in the television show *Wings* with Shalhoub, portrays—surprise—actor Tim Daly. The in-joke nature of his casting is enhanced by Monk's comment to Sharona about *Wings*: "Never saw it. Was it good?"

The third guest, Garry Marshall, perhaps better known as the director of such films as *The Princess Diaries* and *Pretty Woman* and creator of the television shows *Laverne and Shirley* and *Happy Days,* appeared as extension cord salesman Warren Beach.

Because of Marshall's extensive comic experience, the *Monk* staff let him improvise more than normally is allowed. "He was improvising all the way," admits Andy Breckman.

Beach's trademark line—"If it doesn't reach, call Warren Beach"—was one of his improvisations. "Garry came up with it," Scharpling laughs. "And we were ecstatic that *we* got credit for it."

The Quotable *Monk*:

"He always thinks people are killing each other."
—Sharona
"And I'll tell you why. Because they are."—Monk

The Weirdest Clue: Mrs. Chabrol seems to have lost several inches of height since Monk first saw her at the airport.

Idiosyncrasy of the Week: Kind of obvious, isn't it? Aviatophobia, a.k.a. fear of flying.

The Clue that Breaks the Case: The cement on the soles of Mr. Chabrol's shoes hints that he dumped his dead wife at a construction site.

Season Two

Go West, Young Defective Detective

Although USA Network was pleased with audience response to *Monk*'s first season and had, in fact, approved a second season of episodes, that didn't necessarily guarantee a timely start-up for Season Two. "We sweated it out for a long time," Tom Scharpling recalls. "We all felt that we'd earned a second season, but USA had to get their ducks in a row first." The first "duck" that the network put in the lineup for the 2003–2004 season was *The Dead Zone*. That was a simple decision because an outside company produced it. But *Monk* was USA's own baby; the network wrote the production checks. Important decisions, both financial and logistical, had to be made, not the least of which was where the series would be produced.

While shooting in Canada during the first season had certain economic benefits, shooting in Los Angeles offered others. "In the end, it's a trade-off," says Paulo de Oliviero. "The natural West Coast light matches San Francisco's more than the light in Toronto does. And L.A.'s architecture looks more like San Francisco's." Even so, there would still be times when the crew needed quick access to the city by the bay for San Francisco–specific location shots, and that would be a lot easier to manage with Los Angeles as the home base.

Finally the decision was made. The show would go on—and it would shoot in L.A. And to help run the show, Randy Zisk would become a full-time member of the team, serving as co-executive producer. "Tony is the star," Jackie de Crinis says. "And Andy's the creative genius behind the voices. But Randy is the awesome producer who makes everything else happen."

Zisk wasn't exactly an industry novice. Prior to directing "Mr. Monk and the Carnival" in Season One, he had directed over one hundred hours of episodic television, including such audience favorites as *Lois and Clark*, *NYPD Blue*, *Felicity*, and later helmed episodes of *American Dreams* and *House*. One of his first responsibilities as a producer was to oversee the construction of the new *Monk* sets in L.A., sets that would, for the most part, match the Canadian sets but be easier to shoot on. In other words, they were the same—but better. The audience may not have noticed, because there was a definite attempt to maintain continuity, but the people behind the scenes could. "We wanted to amp up the production values and make everything richer and fuller looking," Zisk says. "We gave the show a totally different feel and style."

One big change was Monk's apartment. "In Toronto, the apartment was kind of a cubicle, and it didn't have a lot of shooting possibilities," Zisk points out. "The rooms didn't line up with openings to other rooms, and I wanted to be able to put the camera in one room and shoot straight through." Zisk used the new layout in the very first episode of the season. "In 'Back to School,' we shot the opening scene through the door frame," he points out. "We couldn't do that on the Toronto sets. And we made all the walls wild [moveable] so we could always use longer lenses and get the camera way back."

After making similar changes to Sharona's apartment and the police station sets, they tackled the fourth permanent set, Dr. Kroger's office. "When we shot Kroger's office in Vancouver for the pilot," actor Stanley Kamel says, "we shot in a modern business complex that had a walled garden with a waterfall in it. Afterwards, people would come up to me in the grocery store and say, 'I love your waterfall.'" With the public so conscious of the set design, that original waterfall had to be reproduced in Toronto, and then again in Los Angeles. But a different detail didn't get reproduced—not exactly, anyway. "The Vancouver complex also had a balcony, so in the pilot the director opened up the scene with an overhead shot," Kamel relates. "On subsequent sets we haven't had the balcony, so now they just bring in a crane so they can shoot from that same angle."

The move affected three of the actors, although only two of the characters. In the pilot, Los Angeles resident Kane Ritchotte played Sharona's son, Benjy, but when the series moved to Toronto, Ritchotte was replaced by Toronto resident Max Morrow. With the move to Los Angeles Ritchotte got his old role back.

Toronto native Jason Gray-Stanford, too, was looking at some geographic displacement. But because Gray-Stanford was in almost every episode, commuting was out of the question. Relocation was the order of the day—but the actor behind Lt. Disher didn't mind. "It was cold as hell when we shot in Canada," Gray-Stanford says. "So there were no complaints out of me!"

Viewers may or may not have paid attention

to changes in the writers' room. Hy Conrad's consulting services evolved into a gig as full-time staff writer, and Daniel Dratch joined the team as story editor. But the home audience certainly took notice of the show's new theme song, "It's a Jungle Out There" by Randy Newman. Lots of people loved it—but there were quite a few die-hard fans of the old theme by Jeff Beal. Letters of protest about the change landed on the desks and filled the e-mail in-boxes of everyone involved with the show, from the network executives to the crewmembers on the set. In spite of the uproar, Newman's song won the year's Emmy Award for Outstanding Main Title Theme Music.

Also bringing home an Emmy statuette: actor John Turturro, who was named Outstanding Guest Actor in a Comedy Series for his role as Ambrose Monk in "Mr. Monk and the Three Pies." Tony Shalhoub was nominated for a second Emmy, but this time around, the award went to Kelsey Grammer, who was finishing his lengthy run on *Frasier*. Shalhoub did win a Screen Actors Guild Award for Outstanding Performance by a Male Actor in a Comedy Series, and he was nominated for a Golden Globe Award. Costar Bitty Shram also received a Golden Globe nomination. Even the *Monk* casting directors got into the act, with Anya Coloff, Amy Britt, and Lonnie Hammerman nominated for an Emmy, and Meg Liberman and Cami Patton nominated for the Casting Society of America's Aritos Award. In addition, writer Michael Angeli drew an Edgar Award nomination for Best Television Episode Teleplay for "Mr. Monk and the 12th Man," and Daniel Dratch earned a similar Edgar Award nod for "Mr. Monk and the Very, Very Old Man."

"Mr. Monk Goes Back to School"

Episode 2-01
Teleplay by David Breckman; story by David Breckman & Rick Kronberg
Directed by Randy Zisk
Original Airdate: June 20, 2003

GUEST CAST

Derek Philby	Andrew McCarthy
Nick Patterson	David Rasche
Arleen Cassidy	Rosalind Chao
Benjy Fleming	Kane Ritchotte
Iverson	Jamie McShane
Beth Landow	Erica Yoder

It's Saturday morning at Ashton Prep. But although it's a weekend, science instructor Derek Philby's classroom is full of Ashton High School students, who've just started their SAT exams. Five minutes into the test, at precisely 8:25 A.M., the class hears a loud crash, followed by the wail of a car alarm. Although Philby remains seated at his desk, most of the students rush to the window, where they see the body of pretty English teacher Beth Landow sprawled across the hood of a car parked at the base of Ashton's clock tower.

Landow's death appears to be a suicide, but vice-principal Arleen Cassidy isn't so sure. Knowing that her close friend from high school married a detective, she tracks down the friend's husband, Adrian Monk, and asks him to investigate. Monk is only too happy to comply. Trudy attended Ashton with Cassidy. Spending time at the school is like spending time with his late wife.

Monk is suspicious of the details surrounding Landow's death, particularly the

obvious grammatical errors in her printed suicide note. Landow landed on the car of fellow teacher Derek Philby, who parked right next to the clock tower even though there was a faculty parking lot close to the school. After a brief conversation with Philby, Monk is convinced that Landow's death was no suicide—and that Philby was her killer. Monk will need to spend some time at Ashton in order to gather the evidence he needs to crack the case, so Cassidy gives him a position as substitute teacher.

It's not hard for Monk to figure out that Philby was cheating on his wife with Landow, and with Sharona's help, Monk finds a motive for Philby's decision to kill his mistress. Landow was pregnant; she probably was putting pressure on him to leave his wife. But what Monk can't figure out is *how* the science instructor committed the crime. At the time of the murder, he was proctoring the SAT exam, surrounded by students.

Monk and Sharona investigate the clock tower one more time, and find a pair of glasses that belonged to Landow. But they're not at the top of the tower, where they'd be if Landow—

who was virtually blind without them—really had jumped. They're inside the "clock room," where the mechanism's gear works are located. Minutes later, Monk solves the case, and then lays a trap for Philby using the recovered glasses.

When the police move in to arrest the instructor, Monk reveals how Philby was able to appear to be in two places at once. He killed Landow on the tower at 8:00 A.M., and then carried her down to the clock room, losing her glasses in the process. At 8:15 A.M., he placed her body on the horizontal minute hand of the giant clock face, and then went to his classroom for the SAT test. At 8:25 A.M., gravity finished the job, dropping Landow to Philby's car below. If Philby hadn't gone to look for Landow's glasses, they'd never have been sure of his guilt; only her killer would have known they were in the clock room. Q.E.D., quips Monk. "*Quod erat demonstandum.* Thus it is proved."

"My brother David had this great idea," enthuses Andy Breckman, "that somebody could lay a body on the minute hand of a big clock in a tower and that hand would move—tick, tick, tick—until the body slides down. That, for me, is the gold standard for a clue. It fits all of my criteria: it's elegant, it's clean, and it's very low-tech, to the point that it could have occurred in nineteen-oh-five. Arthur Conan Doyle could have written that story. It doesn't rely on computers or any modern tricks. So I loved it."

David Breckman happily accepts credit for the nugget, but to this day, he has no clue as to how he came up with it. "Detective fiction has been around since Edgar Allen Poe," he says, "and I was convinced that somebody must have come up with the idea of putting a body of a

minute hand before I did." So the writer spent days researching the idea, looking at mysteries and scouring the Internet, only to come up empty-handed. "To my knowledge, it had never been done before," he shrugs, "so I'm tremendously proud of it. I think it's something that even Dame Agatha [Christie] would have been proud of. I'm just afraid that someday I'll find out that Paul McCartney or somebody actually invented it."

Resident crime and clue expert Hy Conrad doesn't think that's likely. "It's a pure David thing," Conrad states. "He loves those outrageous, quasi-possible things."

"Well, it's plausible in *Monk*world," David Breckman protests with a grin.

The killer's alibi—he couldn't have killed her because he was proctoring the SAT test—came from Rick Kronberg, a young production assistant on the show. Breckman jumped on it gleefully because it allowed him to use his favorite story formula. Like "Mr. Monk Meets Dale the Whale," in the first season, "It's a semi-open mystery," he explains. "Monk knows that Andrew McCarthy's character did it, but he just doesn't know how."

The series, which shoots on-location in various parts of Los Angeles nearly every week, found two different locales to serve as Ashton Prep. "One was in Pasadena and the other was in Brentwood," comments director Randy Zisk. "We played them as one school. There really was an eighty-foot clock tower at one of the schools, but we couldn't shoot in it because it was so small up there. So we had to *build* the interior of the clock tower," he notes.

The real tower can be seen as the body drops onto Philby's windshield—but it's not the windshield of an actual car. "We brought a windshield and clamped it to two metal stands

right in front of the tower," Zisk explains. "Then we dropped a dummy tied to a tiny wire so it would hit the glass."

At the time that "Mr. Monk Goes Back to School" was being written, Andy Breckman was courting a young woman named Beth Landau. What better way to win a girl's affections than to insert her name into an episode? "It's easy to give people you care about a name in a script," Breckman says. Given the nature of *Monk,* however, that generally means the name will be attached to either the killer of the week, or the killer's victim. Beth became the latter. The spelling of her last name, however, was changed to "Landow," not to protect the innocent, but to guarantee that the actors would pronounce it correctly—for the sake of romance.

The Quotable *Monk*

"You'll thank me later."—Monk

The Weirdest Clue: Being one of the few people in America who knows the difference between "it's" and "its," Monk is sure that an English teacher would use the correct one in a suicide note.

Idiosyncrasy of the Week: Monk tries to avoid treading on the cracks between the stepping-stones of a footpath.

The Clue that Breaks the Case: While looking up at the face of the giant clock, Monk realizes how Philby could appear to be in two places at the same time.

"Mr. Monk Goes to Mexico"

Episode 2-02
Written by Lee Goldberg & William Rabkin
Directed by Ron Underwood
Original Airdate: June 27, 2003

GUEST CAST

Captain Alameda . . . . Tony Plana
Doctor Madero . . . . Jorge Cervera Jr.
Lt. Plato . . . . David Noroña
Scott . . . . Corbin Allred
Michelle . . . . Emma Bates
Hector . . . . Marcelo Tubert
Captain Valez . . . . Rene Rivera

While on spring break vacation in Baja, lucky Chip Rosatti, son of an affluent friend of San Francisco's mayor, wins a free skydiving jump. Two friends cheer him on from the ground as he leaps from the plane, but their enthusiasm changes to horror as the boy plummets to his death before their eyes. Upon completing an autopsy on the body, the Mexican coroner, Dr. Madero, conveys some bewildering news to the local police. Chip Rosatti didn't die from the fall; he drowned in midair!

When Chip's father contacts the mayor with the bizarre news, the mayor knows exactly who to send to Mexico for the investigation: Adrian Monk. Because Monk hates to fly, Sharona drives them to San Macros—a good thing since Monk has packed eighteen suitcases for the trip, filled with pillowcases, backup pillowcases, prepackaged food and Monk's favorite brand of bottled water. Just moments after arriving at his hotel, however, Monk's suitcases are stolen, leaving the investigator dry-throated, distraught, and nearly deceased when a speeding truck tries to run him down.

Knowing that the sooner he solves the case,

the sooner he can leave, Monk interviews the youths who accompanied Chip to his skydiving appointment, and also the pilot of the plane. The free jump certificate, as it turns out, was a forgery, and Chip's chute was tampered with— meaning his death was premeditated. But why would anyone want to kill him? The local police suspect drugs; "it's always about the drugs," they observe. But then, they thought that a strange death the previous year was also due to drugs, even though Coroner Madero declared it was the result of mauling by a wild lion.

Another attempt is made on Monk's life, resulting in the death of the man who stole his suitcases and donned his clothes, and a bomb is found in Monk's hotel room. Suddenly it seems that the strange goings-on in San Macros may be more related to the detective than to Chip Rosatti. Or perhaps, joke the police, the killer may simply be someone who hates people from San Francisco. First the wealthy boy mauled by the lion, then Chip, and now . . . Monk.

In a flash, Monk solves the case. It was Coroner Madero who pronounced the bizarre circumstances under which both affluent victims died—each impossible, each from San Francisco, and each meant to inspire San Francisco's mayor to assign master detective Monk to the mysterious case. Why? Because the coroner—whom Monk had testified against two years earlier—wanted the opportunity for revenge. After Monk's incriminating testimony, Madero had fled from the United States, changed his identity, and hidden in San Macros, hoping that someday he'd be able to pay back the man who ruined his life. Unfortunately, he underestimated just how good Monk was at his job, even in a state of advanced dehydration!

*   *   *

Lee Goldberg and Bill Rabkin have been writing and producing partners for years, sharing credits on such shows as *Spencer for Hire, Baywatch, Diagnosis Murder,* and *Nero Wolfe,* among others. As fans of *Monk*'s first season, the pair knew it would be fun to freelance a script for the show. Having spent nearly twenty years in television, they thought they'd experienced all possible permutations of pitch sessions. Until they met Andy Breckman.

"The network scheduled a dinner meeting with Andy for us," Goldberg says, "and when we arrived, he wasn't there yet, although an old friend of his was." The friend told the writers that she and Breckman were going to a movie after dinner—which suggested that the pitch session was going to take place on the way to the movie! Goldberg and Rabkin jumped to the logical conclusion: "We just *knew* we were being blown off," says Goldberg. But when Breckman arrived, the pair gamely dived in and began discussing what they liked about mysteries. "And then we pitched something about a guy jumping out of an airplane. And Andy says, 'Okay. Do that one.' We left with the assignment."

"The pitch was about a parachutist being stabbed," Breckman recalls. "So I threw out a challenge and said, 'How about instead of being stabbed, he drowned.' I said it almost jokingly! But as we discussed it, the episode sort of revealed itself."

Goldberg and Rabkin soon found themselves breaking the story in the New Jersey–based writer's room. And although they'd been in hundreds of writers' sessions, this one, like the pitch meeting, was different. "Andy comes from a different world—features, sketch comedy, and joke writing for the Academy Awards," Goldberg notes. "He doesn't have all of the rules for hour-long episodic shows ingrained into the way he thinks. He thinks in a more free-form, creative way. He knows the rules, but he knows which ones to keep and which ones to not care about. And his writing staff just takes his free-form material and runs with it, because they're all still plugged into the whole comedy scene."

Goldberg points to an example of the comedic flow. "While we were in the room, someone came up with the idea of the Mexican cops being like Stottlemeyer and Disher," he says. As a result, the mustachioed Captain Alameda and young Lieutenant Plato not only looked and acted like Latino versions of Monk's friends, but also dressed like them. That idea would carry over into other episodes, most notably in "Mr. Monk and the Paperboy," where we see several international versions of Stottlemeyer and Disher who are helped by Monk.

The film crew didn't actually go to Mexico to shoot the show. "We shot it on the Universal Studios back lot," points out co-executive producer Randy Zisk. "They have a whole Mexican town square that looks perfect."

Ron Underwood, who helmed such movies as *City Slickers* and *Tremors,* directed "Goes to Mexico." "Ron and I had worked together years ago on a film neither of us lists on our resumes," Andy Breckman laughs. "He contacted us and wanted to do the show—not because of me or the script. I would say it was to get a chance to work with Tony Shalhoub."

The Quotable *Monk*

"One impossible murder, maybe. Two impossible murders? It's just not possible."—Monk.

The Weirdest Clue: Someone's been in Monk's hotel room. He can tell because the three-way lamp is on medium—and he left it on high.

Idiosyncrasy of the Week: Bacteriophobia. Monk takes a jumbo supply of bottled water, food, and bed linens to Mexico.

The Clue that Breaks the Case: Monk learns that the two victims were both members of wealthy San Francisco families with connections to the mayor.

"Mr. Monk Goes to the Ballgame"

Episode 2-03
Written by Hy Conrad
Directed by Michael Spiller
Original Airdate: July 11, 2003

GUEST CAST

Scott Gregorio . . . . Christopher Wiehl
Walker Browning . . . . Rainn Wilson
Lyle Turrow . . . . Michael B. Silver
Mrs. Jenkins . . . . Jane Carr
Benjy Fleming . . . . Kane Ritchotte
Lawrence Hammond . . . . John Sanderford
With
Dr. Kroger . . . . Stanley Kamel

Wealthy CEO Lawrence Hammond activates his car's electronic navigation system as he and his beautiful young wife Erin head for Skyline Hills Resort. While Erin listens to a baseball game on the car radio, Hammond concentrates on the instructions the GPS is providing, which don't seem quite accurate. The resort is supposed to be located on a lake, yet the car has been

directed to an industrial park. Annoyed, Hammond barely notices the man in a ski mask approaching the passenger side of the car, at least not until the man begins firing his weapon . . .

When Monk arrives at the scene of the crime, he quickly deduces that Erin was the primary target of the attack. She was killed first, shot multiple times, while her husband was shot only once, and lived long enough to utter a cryptic clue: "Girls Can't Eat Fifteen Pizzas." Not even Monk understands what it means.

Focusing on the wife, Monk learns she's been having an affair with Scott Gregorio, a baseball superstar on the verge of breaking previous champ Darryl Grant's single-season home-run record. Now, however, he may never reach that goal. Since Erin's murder, he's gone into a slump and Monk understands why. The handsome athlete really loved Mrs. Hammond. Monk observes that someone who knew about Gregorio's affair might have killed Erin to prevent the ballplayer from breaking the record. Gregorio reveals that someone tried to smash his arm with a bat a week ago—perhaps with the same motive.

The two men bond over their lost loves, and Monk offers Gregorio heartfelt advice about coping with his loss. In return, the athlete offers Sharona's son, Benjy, tips to bolster the boy's Little League performance. As Monk hears Gregorio relate a mnemonic device to improve Benjy's stance, he realizes that Hammond's last words were also a mnemonic device, pointing investigators to the license plate of the killer's car: "GCE15P." The tip leads the police to a stolen car, and in the backseat they discover the bogus computer disc that lured Hammond to his death. A security camera reveals a fuzzy image of the man who abandoned the car. Monk

is certain he's seen that face before—but where?

At Benjy's next Little League game, the boy hits a homer, winning the game. Stottlemeyer hands Benjy the ball as a souvenir—and Monk finally remembers where he saw the killer's face. It belongs to Walker Browning, the guy who caught the record-setting ball three years ago. The ball is worth millions at the moment—but if Gregorio comes out of his slump and breaks the home-run record, it will be worthless.

Monk and the police show up at Browning's home and learn that he's recently lost his job at an electronics company that makes global satellite equipment. He's also been contacting auction houses about selling his ball. All of which adds up to ample motive for murder. As

the police move to arrest him, Browning releases his vicious Doberman Toby. In the ensuing chaos, the baseball drops to the floor—and Toby disappears out the door with the world's most expensive chew toy.

The idea that led to "Mr. Monk Goes to the Ballgame" came to the *Monk* writers via Hy Conrad during the series' first season. Although Conrad, then a consultant, was considered a de facto part of the team, he recognized that his home in Florida was a long way from the writers' room in New Jersey. "I hadn't heard from Andy for a while, and I wanted to stay in touch," Conrad relates. "So I sent him an e-mail and mentioned that a baseball record was about to be broken, and that since there obviously was an old record holder, it could be a good motive for murder. Andy really picked up on that."

The record about to be broken was the 1998 tally of seventy home runs achieved by legendary slugger Mark McGwire. And sure enough, by the end of the 2001 season, San Francisco Giants' icon Barry Bonds had smashed an astounding seventy-three hits over the back fence. But it was what happened to the ball from that seventy-third hit that really clinched the nugget for Breckman. A fierce legal battle grew over ownership of Bond's ball, which was claimed by two different fans who'd been in the stands that glorious day. Ultimately, a San Francisco judge settled the dispute by ordering the two men to sell the ball and split the proceeds. At auction, the historic piece of horsehide drew a winning bid of $450,000 (by well-known comic book creator/producer Todd McFarlane—who also owns the previous record-holding home-run ball, McGwire's seventieth, in his collection).

"It was a fantastic motive," Breckman says, while acknowledging that the facts in the script differ greatly from those in the original news story.

While writing, the team did worry about one important detail. The fictional owner of the historic ball would have to be revealed early in the episode in order to set up Monk's trademark moment of realization about the killer's identity. But how could it be that in a way that wouldn't spoil the surprise for viewers?

Ultimately, they came up with the idea of showing some footage of the record-breaking game, complete with a rather grainy shot of the killer. "He's sitting in the bleachers waving the ball that he's just caught," Breckman observes.

"Who would ever dream that the kid in that stadium would grow up to be the killer? Who would ever see that coming?"

The theme of the episode offered a perfect place for the writers to use Tom Hanks's line to Bitty Schram in the film *A League of Their Own*: "There's no crying in baseball." Stottlemeyer would have delivered the line to Sharona. But when she saw it in the script, Schram asked that the line be dropped because she didn't want to capitalize on things she'd done in the past.

Obviously sports fans themselves, the writers formed a softball team during *Monk*'s second season. But, alas, Hall of Fame notoriety was not for them. They played a total of one game—against the writers of *Late Night with Conan O'Brien*. "We were pretty miserable," admits Hy Conrad. "It was only near the end of the game, when the opposing team had had quite a few beers, that we even got close."

The Quotable *Monk*

"Thank you, Adrian. I thought I'd thank you now, because in a half hour, you're probably gonna piss me off again."—Sharona

The Weirdest Clue: "Girls can't eat fifteen pizzas."

Idiosyncrasy of the Week: Let's just say you don't want Monk to be the umpire at your kid's Little League game.

The Clue that Breaks the Case: Monk sees a storm window commercial that features archival footage of the suspect—the fan who caught the baseball from Darryl Grant's record-breaking hit.

"Mr. Monk Goes to the Circus"

Episode 2-04
Written by James Krieg
Directed by Randy Zisk
Original Airdate: July 18, 2003

GUEST CAST

Natasia Lovara	Lolita Davidovich
Ariana	Lola Glaudini
Edgar Heinz	Mark Ivanir
Benjy Fleming	Kane Ritchotte
Nikolai Petroff	Ilia Volok
Sgt. Myers	Steve Monroe
Serge	Marek Probosz
with	
Dr. Kroger	Stanley Kamel

It's late but the San Francisco sidewalk café is jammed with customers, including Serge and his young date Ariana. Suddenly the culinary ambience is shattered as a mysterious black-garbed figure leaps into the café from the fire escape above and shoots Serge in the heart. Then, before anyone can bar the assassin's way, he jumps up to grab hold of the café's awning frame, flips around and over the bar like an Olympics gymnast, dives to the street, and makes a hasty exit.

When the police arrive at the scene with Monk in tow, it takes the detective only a few moments to put together the existing clues: an acrobatic ninja and remnants of sawdust on the ground . . . is there a circus in town? As it turns out, there is—Dratch & Denby Traveling Circus—and the dead man was the ringmaster.

Paying a visit to Dratch & Denby, Monk and Sharona question Serge's date, horse trainer Ariana, who is positive the masked killer was Serge's jealous ex-wife Natasia. Natasia, an exceptional acrobat and a skilled sharpshooter, made no secret of how much she despised her ex. But Natasia, they discover, has an excellent alibi: a broken leg in a cast, the result of a fall from the trapeze two weeks earlier. However, Natasia never saw a doctor after the fall—she set the bone herself—so Monk insists that she get an X-ray at a local hospital. To his dismay, the radiologist confirms that Natasia's leg is badly shattered. There's no way she could have performed the athletic feats at the restaurant.

Back at the circus Heinz, the elephant trainer, approaches Natasia and assures her that he will protect her secret. But while Natasia had been unaware that Heinz *knew* her secret, she does know what to do about it.

Still convinced that the cold-blooded Natasia killed Serge, Monk finds himself distracted by another icy female. Sharona is furious with the panicky detective for laughing at her own lifelong fear of elephants. Hoping to prove that he isn't insensitive, Monk tries to help Sharona get over her phobia by introducing her to Dede, the circus elephant. To demonstrate how gentle Dede is, Heinz allows Dede to put her massive foot on his head. But unbeknownst to anyone, Natasia has taped a walkie-talkie behind Dede's ear, and at the appropriate moment, she gives Dede the order to step down hard, killing Heinz instantly.

Monk considers the facts of the accident. There's no way the elephant could have made a mistake like that on its own. Suddenly, everything falls into place. He realizes that although Natasia's leg is broken, it didn't happen in a fall, nor did it happen two weeks ago. She was fine the night that she killed Serge. Then she returned to the circus and ordered Dede to step on her leg, shattering it. That's when unlucky Heinz spotted her—so Natasia had to get rid of him, too. After the police find the

hidden walkie-talkie, Natasia tries to escape, but an elephant blocks her path, saving Sharona in the process, and putting Monk's assistant on the road to recovery for her elephant-phobia.

Certain personalities have the ability to become the center of attention the minute they enter a room. In "Mr. Monk Goes to the Circus," Ti the Elephant easily commanded center stage.

"Ti had a better resume than *any* of us," laughs Director Randy Zisk. "She's been in many movies. And she was truly amazing—she'd stand on her hind legs, or get into a yoga pose. I'd never seen anything like it. And she was so gentle."

Which was probably a good thing, since the script called for her to step on the body parts of living, breathing people. "The elephant was supposed to break Lolita Davidovich's leg," Zisk says. "Lolita was a little spooked by it and I can't say I blame her." Although Ti's trainer had guaranteed it would not be a problem, Zisk always feels he can't ask an actor to do something he wouldn't be willing to do himself. "So I laid down and let the elephant lightly rest her foot on *my* knee," he says, smiling at the memory.

In the episode, the elephant also crushes a character's head, causing most of the squeamish onlookers to look away in horror. But strangely, Monk, the man who generally finds anything messy utterly repulsive, continues to stare. "Monk is repulsed and repelled by certain things," explains Tony Shalhoub, "particularly everyday things that other people can handle. But extreme things *fascinate* him. In this case he was probably thinking, 'Now, that's something you don't see every day.' "

Writer James Krieg has contributed to a number of animated television series, including *Spiderman, Extreme Ghostbusters,* and *What's New, Scooby-Doo?,* which may explain "Circus's" almost cartoonlike feel. "The earlier drafts of the script were even broader," notes Hy Conrad, with a lot more clown humor and physical hijinks. In those drafts, when Monk hears that the killer bounced off an overhanging bar above the café during his escape, he decides that he wants to recreate the getaway. So Disher is volunteered for the exercise. "Of course, when Disher duplicates the move, he gets hit in the crotch," Conrad adds. And although the painful result would have confirmed to Monk that the killer was a woman, and not a man, it was dropped from the episode.

One running bit of clown humor didn't get cut. While Monk is talking on the telephone, a clown starts mimicking everything he is saying, much to Monk's annoyance. Monk sends the clown away—but like most annoyances, he would return later on. "We established the Floppy the Clown early, knowing that we'd bring him back during the summation," Conrad explains. Why? "Just as a

way to make the summation different," he grins.

The man behind Floppy's makeup is Lance Krall, an actor who's worked with Tony Shalhoub on other projects. "Tony told me that I wouldn't get my real face on camera, but I could play Floppy the Clown if I could be as annoying as possible. I said, 'Oh, I excel at being annoying.' "

Krall's expertise in annoyance so pleased the producers that they brought him back to the series for roles as the bingo card checker in "The Three Pies" and the car salesman in "Takes His Medicine."

The Quotable *Monk*

"Just suck it up."—Monk

The Weirdest Clue: An empty sugar bowl at the café leads Monk to the circus's horse trainer, who stole the sugar cubes for her mare.

Idiosyncrasy of the Week: Monk obsesses about how much whipped cream is contained in a "dollop."

The Clue that Breaks the Case: . . . isn't quite there. In the script, during the scene where Sharona brings Monk his cocoa, Monk hears some static on the radio—and realizes he heard radio static just before Dede crushed Heinz's head. That leads to his discovery of the walkie-talkie behind the elephant's ear. In the aired episode, however, the static clue has been cut, and Monk goes from counting the marshmallows in his cocoa to realizing that the odds of an elephant making a mistake like that are a thousand to one. In both cases, the conclusion is the same—"It wasn't an accident"—but it's a lot easier to see how Monk reached that conclusion in the earlier version.

"Mr. Monk and the Very, Very Old Man"

Episode 2-05
Written by Daniel Dratch
Directed by Lawrence Trilling
Original Airdate: July 25, 2003

GUEST CAST

Karen Stottlemeyer	Glenne Headly
Dennis Gammill	Kurt Fuller
Mayor Rudner	Jim Jansen
Miles Holling	Patrick Cranshaw
Hiram Holling	Bill Erwin
Opal	Sonya Eddy
Kaitlyn	Audrey Wasilewski

As nursing homes go, the one that Miles Holling lives in is comfortable and extremely secure. At least, it *seems* that way until Holling, the world's oldest man, dies in his room the night before his 115th birthday.

The staff attributes his death to natural causes, but Captain Stottlemeyer's wife Karen—who made a documentary about Holling five years earlier—thinks it was murder. The captain humors her by assigning Monk to the investigation. But to his surprise, Monk agrees with Karen, forcing Stottlemeyer to push for an exhumation of Holling's recently buried body. After an autopsy proves that Karen was indeed correct, she kicks her husband out of the house, claiming that he doesn't respect her or her beliefs.

Hoping to repay Stottlemeyer for his support following Trudy's death, Monk offers him a place to stay, and the two men enter into a stressful period of cohabitation. As they attempt to unravel Holling's murder, Stottlemeyer drifts between irritation at Monk's annoying domestic quirks and moroseness over his inadequacies as a cop, a feeling that began five years ago, following the hit-and-run death of seventeen-year-old Darren Leveroni. Stottlemeyer never found Leveroni's killer, and the case continues to nag at him like a festering wound.

Eventually Stottlemeyer's simmering emotions boil over and he blows up at Monk. Packing his suitcase, the captain says he intends to go home and beg Karen to take him back. But Monk warns him that Karen won't take him back, not until he finally watches her documentary on Holling, something Stottlemeyer has successfully avoided for five years.

Stottlemeyer and Monk struggle to make it through the maudlin video, which concludes with a media event in which the mayor celebrates Holling's 110th birthday by burying a time capsule that contains "a letter to future generations," including a copy of Holling's life story and a personal reflection from each member of the mayor's staff. Afterwards, the mayor unexpectedly announces that if Holling lives another five years, he'll dig up the capsule and allow the old man to add another chapter to his book.

As Stottlemeyer takes in the implications of the event, he notices one more detail shown in the documentary: Deputy Mayor Dennis Gammill showed up at the ceremony in a rental car. Suddenly, Stottlemeyer has a Monk-like epiphany: he's solved the case!

After convincing the mayor to dig up the capsule, the captain finds the proof: Dennis Gammill's letter. In it, as Stottlemeyer suspected, the deputy mayor confessed that he was the one who hit Darren Leveroni with his car. That's why he was driving a rental car on the day of the ceremony. But although the confession had assuaged Gammill's guilty conscience, he'd never expected the mayor to dig up the capsule. Gammill figured that killing the old man before his 115th birthday would eliminate that possibility. If it hadn't been for Karen's documentary, and Stottlemeyer's willingness to look at it, he would have been correct. With a new appreciation for Karen's importance in his life, Monk's ex-roommate happily goes home.

"Stottlemeyer has a strange marriage," comments actor Ted Levine. "He and Karen were kids when they got together, fell in love, and got married. And they've stayed married for years."

The Stottlemeyers have had their share of problems. In the pilot, the captain has spent the night at a motel following a spat with the missus. He mentions having seen a marriage counselor in "Goes to the Circus," although in "And the Very, Very Old Man," we discover from Karen that the sessions didn't last very long because Stottlemeyer didn't "respect the process." But as different as they are, it's clear that there is genuine affection between them—and that's partly due to Levine's input.

"Early in the first season," he recalls, "a script included a scene where the two of them have had a fight and Stottlemeyer has smacked Karen around a little bit. But I said, hold on. Let's find out who Leland is first, and who his wife is. So instead of having what I think of as the clichéd 'divorced cop who's too rough for his family,' with an ex-wife who's weak, we looked for something else. And they cast Glenne Headly, making Mrs. Stottlemeyer a gorgeous, hardy woman."

Actress Glenne Headly, whose credits include *Dirty Rotten Scoundrels* and *Dick*

Tracy, already knew Tony Shalhoub and was also familiar with one of her costars. "Ted Levine and I had both acted in Chicago years ago, in different theatre companies," Headly recalls. "When I got to the *Monk* set, Ted told me that he was so glad that I was playing Karen because he'd had a minicrush on me back in the old days!"

The producers were very clear on just who Karen Stottlemeyer was. "They said they wanted me to play the polar opposite of Ted's character, and that she kind of wears the pants in the family," Headly recalls. "They didn't ask me to be a hippie, only that she was a documentary filmmaker, and they wanted her strong, despite her eccentricities."

Not so coincidentally, Andy Breckman's then girlfriend, Beth Landau, was (and still is) a documentary filmmaker. Consider it stage two— (following the use of her name as the victim in "Mr. Monk Goes Back to School")—in the courtship of Andy's future wife. "It just seemed to fit naturally," laughs Breckman.

The original idea for "Very, Very Old Man" had been on a card thumbtacked to the wall in the writers' room for quite some time before writer Daniel Dratch selected it as the basis for his first *Monk* script. "The question was, could there possibly be a motive for someone to murder the oldest man in the world?" Breckman says. As disparate as they seem, somehow that plot dovetailed with another idea that the writers had been kicking around, where Stottlemeyer moves in with Monk.

That unlikely pairing is exactly what drew Dratch to pick the story. "There were five choices up on the board, ready to go. I picked 'Old Man,' because of the *Odd Couple* element to it." And if ever there was a pair of unlikelier male roommates than Felix and Oscar, it's Adrian and

Leland. The episode is full of comedic collisions between the two that demonstrate Dratch's talents as a television sketch writer, like the confrontation over how to set the alarm clock that ends with Stottlemeyer threatening to shoot Monk if he enters the room one more time.

Yet one of those collisions ultimately provides some surprising insight to Monk and also brings the show to one of its sweetest tags ever. Monk, the supreme perfectionist, the man who insists on creating a grid pattern when he vacuums the rug, has an obsession for one imperfectly placed object: the coffee table in his living room. Why? Because Trudy used to position the table that way so she could put her feet up—and Monk could lay his head in her lap. "That tag at the end is as touching as anything we've ever done," says Tom Scharpling. "He's alone in the apartment reading, and Trudy fades in next to him, and we see their evening ritual. A tag like that takes up ninety seconds of time, but it covers miles of emotional ground."

Nearly as sweet are the contents of Karen's letter to Leland, which the Captain discovers in the time capsule. Although it was only seen on-camera for a second, and thus probably not meant for the audience to actually read, here it is, courtesy of freeze-frame technology:

Dear Leland,
You are the most important person in my life!
I love you with all of my heart and soul!
No one will ever fulfill my dreams like you do!
You are my world, you are my everything!
There would be no life without you!
No man compares to you!
I will be forever yours!
                                              Love, Karen

The Quotable *Monk*

"Monk, I'm going to say something I've wanted to say for a long time. I just solved the case."
—Stottlemeyer

The Weirdest Clue: The security guard at the nursing home misspelled his name on the sign-in sheet.

Idiosyncrasy of the Week: We learn the whole hierarchy of Monk's fears, or at least the first eight, as he rattles them off for the Captain: Germs, needles, milk, death, snakes, mushrooms, heights, and crowds. Unfortunately, Stottlemeyer cuts him off before he can complete a definitive list.

The Clue that Breaks the Case: Karen Stottlemeyer's documentary clues Leland in to the fact that Dennis Gammill drove a rental car to the time capsule ceremony—because Gammill's own car would have implicated him in a hit-and-run accident.

"Mr. Monk Goes to the Theatre"

Episode 2-06
Teleplay by Tom Scharpling; story by Wendy Mass & Stu Levine
Directed by Ron Underwood
Original Airdate: August 1, 2003

GUEST CAST

Mrs. Cheryl Fleming	Betty Buckley
Jenna Ryan	Melissa George
Sebastian	Simon Templeman
O'Dell	David Doty
Benjy Fleming	Kane Ritchotte
Doorman	Mark Phinney
Hal Duncan	Marc Vann

Judge	Gwen McGee
Kathleen	Susan Chuang
Salon Manager	Jorge Luis Abreu

SPECIAL GUEST STAR

Gail Fleming	Amy Sedaris

Sharona's sister Gail has hit it big, starring in a hot new play that's bound for New York. But as Monk and Sharona sit in the audience watching her performance, they realize something is amiss onstage. During her big scene, Gail uses a fake knife to stab her costar, Hal, who falls to the floor, wheezing, and doesn't get up. When the director asks if there's a doctor in the house, a man rushes up from the audience and leans over Hal to take his pulse. "He's dead," he pronounces. "He's been stabbed."

Sharona is positive her sister is innocent, but things look bad for Gail. She's the only one who had access to a knife onstage, and the police know that she and the victim dated until Hal broke it off. As if things aren't stressful enough for the Fleming sisters, their mother arrives for a visit. After hearing the details, she asks Monk and Sharona to clear Gail's name, because, after all, that's what they do, right?

Monk and Sharona quickly learn two important facts: that Hal had a severe food allergy, and that Gail's understudy, Jenna, wanted Gail's role very badly. When Jenna dodges an appointment with the investigators to attend a singles speed-dating event, Sharona gets Monk to sign up so he can question the actress. Monk manages to gather only a bit of information before Jenna grows suspicious of his line of questioning, so he and Sharona do some additional research at the theatre. Monk suggests they reenact the fatal scene from the play, with him playing the role of the deceased man. He does such a good job that the director decides to hire him as a temporary replacement for Hal.

On the night of Monk's first performance, however, the detective begins to regret the decision. Performing in front of a real audience? What was he thinking? Stricken with stage fright, Monk begins to hyperventilate and Sharona takes his pulse. But as Monk watches her, he suddenly cracks the case!

Hal had food allergies, he reminds Sharona, and he had to eat an apple onstage—an apple that Jenna had access to before the performance. Monk sends Sharona to Jenna's dressing room to hunt for something that would have caused an allergic reaction if put on the apple.

The nervous Monk is shoved onto the stage, where he struggles to deliver his lines to Jenna. When Sharona returns brandishing the bottle of peanut oil she found in Jenna's bag, the actress realizes the jig is up. As the infamous knife scene arrives, Jenna grabs a real knife instead of the prop one and lunges toward Monk . . .

. . . Only to be tackled by Sharona and injured during the subsequent struggle. A man in the audience asks if there's a doctor in the house, and rushes onstage to tend to Jenna. Monk recognizes him at once. He's the "doctor" who examined Hal during the previous performance—the man who actually stabbed Hal when he pretended to examine him. Monk realized that he was a phony M.D. when he observed Sharona take his pulse the correct way. As the police arrive to arrest Jenna and her assistant, Monk reveals the assailant is Jenna's father, a man who'd do anything to see his daughter succeed as an actress, even help his daughter commit murder!

*   *   *

"In the Olympics," notes Andy Breckman, "the judges assign a degree of difficulty to the events. They factor in how hard something is before they judge it. And I would say that 'Goes to the Theatre' had a high degree of difficulty. It involved having an on-screen audience, it had a complicated mystery, and it had a complicated summation."

"It's like ironing; you just keep going over the thing," Tom Scharpling adds with a shrug. "Eventually we just had to trust that if we got Monk on that stage, the character was going to take you where you want to be. And Tony knocked it out of the park. He did things we never could have conceived of [in the writers' room]."

The pitch, that someone is killed on stage in front of an audience, had come from children's book author Wendy Mass and her friend Stu Levine. "I was very excited by that idea," says Breckman. "It gave us a chance to give Monk stage fright."

"That was really fun for me," Tony Shalhoub says. "I love playing actors because it's a chance to draw on every actor's demons and insecurities. You get to illustrate and act out all of the bad things you've either done or seen onstage. One of my favorite moments is when Monk forgets to breathe as he delivers a line and he gradually runs out of breath and kind of faaaades ouuuut," Shalhoub demonstrates, his voice becoming fainter and fainter. "And I love it when Monk is thrown into the room and he knows he's supposed to lean back against the door and put his foot up against it. He gets thrown too deeply into the room to do that, but he still puts his foot

up . . . even though the door is six feet behind him. Those are homages to all the times actors—myself included—have not been able to roll with the punches when something goes wrong onstage, and they stay tied to their rehearsed choices. We've all done that. So the episode presented a chance for me to be a really bad actor," he concludes proudly.

The episode featured the second appearance of Sharona's sister, Gail, who first showed up in "Mr. Monk and the Earthquake." Gail is played by the talented and very busy actress Amy Sedaris, who's appeared in a slew of comedies, including *Strangers with Candy, Elf, Maid in Manhattan,* and the recent cinematic remake of *Bewitched.* "Frankly, I wish Andy would write more roles for guest stars," David Hoberman sighs. "But Monk is not like *Columbo,* where they had a juicy role every week for some big name."

The Quotable *Monk*

"What if my character expresses his rage by putting away the groceries—roughly?"—Monk

The Weirdest Clue: The prop apples taste funny, probably because they've been coated with peanut oil.

Idiosyncrasy of the Week: Stage fright, of course.

The Clue that Breaks the Case: When Monk observes how Sharona takes his pulse, he realizes that the "doctor" who attended to murdered actor Hal Duncan is a phony M.D. and also the real killer.

"Mr. Monk and the Sleeping Suspect"

Episode 2-07
Written by Karl Schaefer
Directed by Jerry Levine
Original Airdate: August 8, 2003

GUEST CAST

Trevor .... Frank John Hughes
Agent Grooms .... Josh Stamberg
Ricky Babbage .... Chad Donella
Brian Babbage .... Matt Winston
Benjy Fleming .... Kane Ritchotte
Nurse Stempel .... Kathryn Joosten
Maria .... Michelle Krusiec
Mailman .... Shishir Kurup
Amanda Babbage .... Beth Skipp
Dwayne .... Jake Richardson
with
Dr. Kroger .... Stanley Kamel

Stottlemeyer and Disher are out on the street, questioning a wiseass kid, when a car screeches onto the scene and sideswipes Stottlemeyer's sedan. Before the captain can respond, the driver has smacked the car again. And again. And again.

Clearly, this isn't an accident. Infuriated, Stottlemeyer and Disher leap into the car, prepared to give chase. But before they can even turn over the engine, it's all over. An oncoming truck has wiped out the culprit's car, and the reckless driver is in a coma.

Months later, Amanda Babbage brings in the day's mail, noting a mysterious package. When she opens it, the package explodes, killing her instantly. Stottlemeyer brings Monk in to consult on the case, despite the fact that Federal agents are already on the scene. Monk immediately makes two pertinent discoveries: the killer has a

very distinctive style of tying knots, as evidenced by the recovered string that he used to secure the package; and the killer didn't know that Amanda Babbage had recently moved—the package was forwarded from her previous address.

The Feds immediately suspect Ricky Babbage, the victim's brother. He has motive; he and his two siblings have been squabbling over their late father's will for months. But Monk declares that Amanda's *other* brother, Brian, is the real killer. The Feds are amused by the accusation. Brian's been in a coma for four months. His car was creamed by a truck while he was fleeing from the cops. Yes, he was the lunatic who rammed Stottlemeyer's car.

Still, Monk is convinced. While investigating, he spots Brian's shoes in a closet, and notes that they're tied with the same careful knots as the string. And, having been in a coma for months, Brian wouldn't have known that Amanda had moved. But since he's not faking the coma, how could he have mailed the bomb? Monk reasons that it's just a matter of time till he figures that out.

Of course, that would be easier if he didn't have two troubling distractions in his life. His psychiatrist, Dr. Kroger, is out of town on a three-week vacation, leaving Monk with no one to unload on. Worse, Sharona's ex-husband, Trevor, has suddenly returned to woo her and Benjy—and it looks like they might want to return to New Jersey with him.

Struggling to focus on the case, Monk finds something peculiar in Brian's home. The coma victim had been gluing ketchup bottles to the ceiling prior to the accident. While Monk is puzzling out why he'd have done this, he sees Brian's maid opening a package tied with the same elegant knot he saw before. Monk snatches it out of her hands and tosses it into the toilet just before the package explodes! A few days later, he and Sharona pay a visit to Ricky Babbage's apartment, where Monk notices a piece of peeling wallpaper. After Ricky mentions that his landlord has repeatedly glued it down, but the glue just doesn't last, Monk realizes exactly how Brian set his murder plan in motion. And, after saving Ricky from yet another bomb, Monk reveals the solution to all.

Brian wanted his two siblings dead so that he could inherit *all* of his dad's money. He made three mail bombs—one would be sent to himself to avoid raising suspicion—and then glued them to the inside of three different mailboxes. He knew from his experiments with the ketchup bottles that the glue would deteriorate over a period of weeks, after which the bombs would fall into the stack of mail below and be delivered. To further turn suspicion away from his own door, he committed a crime that he knew would land him in jail for a few months—just long enough for Ricky and Amanda to be killed. He hadn't counted on being hit by a truck, however.

When Brian awakens from his coma, Monk tricks him into incriminating himself. The icing on the cake, however, is the news that Sharona will *not* be leaving town. She's discovered that her ex had some ulterior motives for wanting her back, and she has decided to stick around.

There are time-release medications and time-release pesticides, so why not a time-release murder? That's what Andy Breckman and his team wondered. "We started kicking around the idea of a bomb that goes off a week after it's delivered," says Breckman, "but that notion didn't become an episode until we realized that if the suspect were in a coma, it would be interesting for Monk to suspect him."

"Mr. Monk and the Sleeping Suspect" is one of very few *Monk* episodes that open with a teaser that *doesn't* focus on a murder. Although the audience will eventually realize that the crazed behavior of the malevolent driver is indeed connected to a murder plot, they're briefly caught up, like Disher, in the excitement of a prospective car chase—Disher's very first car chase, as it happens. "It's untraditional because it's just Ted and me," says Jason Gray-Stanford. And it's also funny as heck, with Stottlemeyer turning to his partner to deadpan, "Chase over—whaddya think?" before the car even gets out of gear. Gray-Stanford chuckles at the memory. "That's my all-time favorite teaser," he admits.

But it wasn't the desire for a funny scene that made the car chase so short—it was the previous episode. " 'Mr. Monk Goes to the Theatre' was so costly to produce that we were hamstrung for money," explains Tom Scharpling. "We had wanted them to at least go up the street and *then* stop, but the budget was so tight that we couldn't even let them move the car," he laughs. "It almost got to the point where they couldn't even get *in* the car."

Despite the tight budget, Tony Shalhoub counts the episode among his favorites. "Certain episodes stand out for me, and I loved 'The Sleeping Suspect,' " he says. "That was really fun. I loved that Monk's convinced the killer is the guy in the coma, and I loved the whole difficulty for him in buying a birthday present for Benjy, and that his shrink has gone away so he talks to the sleeping guy as if he's a shrink. And I loved the ketchup bottles on the ceiling.

It's a great crime, and I really enjoyed the way the writers solved it."

Why ketchup bottles? "We just wanted to have a demonstration sequence," notes Andy Breckman. "Ketchup bottles on the ceiling seemed like the right thing, because it was so visual."

Colorful, too. But how would the idea of crashing *condiment* bottles occur to the writers? "Well, we *do* tend to kick these things around at lunch . . . ," Tom Scharpling suggests.

"Sleeping Suspect" marks director Jerry Levine's first outing with the series. Levine soon would join Randy Zisk as the two most prominent directors in the *Monk* stable.

The episode is also notable for its strong Sharona subplot. "The plotline about Sharona's ex-husband wanting her to move to New Jersey with him gave us some great character material," says Gray-Stanford, including, he states, the fact that Disher—who'd bad-mouthed Monk's assistant since the series's pilot, was, well, kind of interested in her. Their repartee no longer seemed quite so antagonistic. It was actually kind of flirty—in a semi-insulting junior high kind of way—and it would become a staple of future episodes. Gray-Stanford was pleased that he was able to tell Sharona, "I'm glad you're gonna stay," a sentiment that is, of course, also endorsed by Monk.

While Sharona decides *not* to go to New Jersey here, her conversations about whether or not she should leave Monk behind foreshadow the character's ultimate choice a year later. It's clear that she still loves Trevor, and that she'd like to see her family together again. Her disappointment at Trevor's apparent financial motive is palpable, and one can only hope that when she finally reunited with him that he'd somehow managed to pull his act together.

The Quotable *Monk*

"There's something you don't see every day."—Monk

The Weirdest Clue: Brian Babbage was looking for a really incompetent lawyer.

Idiosyncrasy of the Week: Monk repeatedly blocks out the fact that Dr. Kroger is going on vacation.

The Clue that Breaks the Case: The peeling wallpaper in Ricky Babbage's apartment clues Monk in to the fact that glue deteriorates after a while.

"Mr. Monk Meets the Playboy"

Episode 2-08
Written by James Krieg
Directed by Tom DiCillo
Original Airdate: August 15, 2003

GUEST CAST

Dexter Larson	Gary Cole
Miss Luden	Fay Masterson
Amber	Erinn Bartlett
Danny Bonaduce	Danny Bonaduce
Noelle Winters	Lisa Thornhill
Benjy Fleming	Kane Ritchotte
Shawn Clemmons	Edward Edwards
Elliot D'Souza	Mark Tymchyshyn
Bethany Daniels	Jennifer Lyons

The atmosphere is festive at Sapphire Mansion, the legendary pleasure palace that is also the home of Dexter Larson, founder of *Sapphire Magazine*. Larson is about to throw an anniversary bash for his slick publication, but while the girls that grace its centerfold have never looked better, the magazine has seen better days. According to Elliot D'Souza, chief financial officer for the publishing group, the magazine is hemorrhaging money, and D'Souza plans to shut it down, much to Larson's dismay. But before D'Souza has the opportunity to proceed with his plans, he's killed in his gym. Since the room was locked from the inside, the police assume that he died in an accident: his barbell slipped and crushed his throat. But D'Souza's assistant thinks that someone murdered her boss, and she asks Monk to look into it.

When Monk and Sharona question Larson, they note several inconsistencies in his alibi for what he was doing the morning of D'Souza's death. Before they can probe any deeper, Larson confronts Monk with some nude photos of Sharona, taken when she was a young single mother trying to make ends meet. Larson says he'll publish them if Monk pursues the investigation. The threat works; Monk would rather drop the case than allow Larson to harm Sharona's reputation. But when Monk tells the captain he thinks D'Souza's death was accidental, Sharona can tell that he's lying and presses him for the truth. She's shocked to hear that the embarrassing photos have resurfaced, but after being urged by her son not to let "the bad guys" get away, she and Monk decide to find out the truth behind D'Souza's death.

Returning to the mansion, Monk meets Noelle, a former *Sapphire* Girl. Noelle has nothing but kind words for Larson who, she reveals, recently purchased an apartment for her. In the meantime, Sharona befriends Amber, Larson's alibi for the morning in question, and, coincidentally, the recently named *Sapphire* Girl of the Year. Instead of celebrating, however, Amber seems strangely contrite.

Investigating D'Souza's gym one more time, Monk is surprised to learn that Noelle lives directly below. However, she wasn't in the apartment the morning of the murder. Monk suddenly understands how D'Souza was killed. Larson had keys to Noelle's apartment, and he used them to enter while she was gone. When he heard D'Souza working out in the gym above, he turned on the powerful electromagnet he'd brought with him, causing D'Souza's barbell to clamp down on the CFO's neck and kill him. When Monk makes his accusation, Amber admits that she lied about being with Larson in exchange for being made *Sapphire* Girl of the Year. After Stottlemeyer books Larson, Disher finds the embarrassing images from Sharona's past and burns them so they won't ever resurface again.

Director Tom DiCillo is known for his ability to bring out the best in the characters on-screen. That's understandable. Following a successful career as the cinematographer of a number of independent films, DiCillo began to write and direct. And so, with films like *Johnny Suede, The Real Blonde,* and *Living in Oblivion,* he was directing characters that he'd actually created. While *Monk* didn't really fall in that category, the show's creative team was very happy to get such a good character director for "Mr. Monk Meets the Playboy." "It's a very character-driven episode," Tom Scharpling states. "All those scenes with Sharona were important. And the scene with her telling Benjy that she took some revealing pictures when she was young and stupid is one of the best performances in all of *Monk.*"

"That scene was right out of *Norma Rae,*" adds Andy Breckman. "Sally Field sat her kids down and told them about the past. This was our homage to that movie."

Tony Shalhoub's performance also excels here, particularly in an agonizingly prolonged wordless sequence where he tries to respond to Sharona's question about whether he actually looked at her nude photos. And then, of course, there's the scene where he makes all the Bunnies . . . er, *Sapphire* Girls, cry. "You know that Monk would be the ultimate buzz kill at *any* party," Scharpling laughs. "He finally gets inside the walls of the ersatz 'Playboy Mansion' and he brings everybody down."

It's a good thing that the character work was solid, because the plotting was a little shaky, starting with the crime. "It was insane!" Andy Breckman shouts. "It's an insane murder! Somebody said it was easy to make electromagnets, and we thought that if you made a bunch of magnets you could get underneath a man's gymnasium when he was working out and strangle him by attracting the barbell." Of course, knowing exactly *when* to turn on the electromagnet still would be a little iffy. And is it *honestly* that easy to make an electromagnet? Breckman shrugs. "I really don't know," he admits. "I just want to *believe* that it's easy."

The working title for the script had been "Mr. Monk at the Playboy Mansion," spoofing, of course, *Playboy*'s famous founder Hugh Hefner. Considering the subject matter, "It was about as tame a story as you could possibly imagine," says Hy Conrad. But that's as it should be, given the audience for the show. "Since the very beginning, we've been aware that families watch *Monk,* so we're more prudish than many shows," Conrad adds.

"We're prudish," agrees Randy Zisk. "We had the girls wearing *lots* of clothes. We tend to play a lot of different types of humor, but it's always humor for all ages. Whenever we get close to crossing the line, we pull back."

Actor Gary Cole, known more recently as the vice president on *The West Wing,* scored perfectly as the fictional killer (his performance followed that of another *West Wing* vet, Kathryn Joosten, who appeared in "Sleeping Suspect"). Former *Partridge Family* star Danny Bonaduce appeared as himself, playing the killer's guest at the party. The *Monk* creative team—mostly comedy writers, you'll recall— thought of his casting as a kind of spoof on themselves. "That's *our* version of a Playboy party," Scharpling chuckles. "With Danny as the biggest star in attendance, it's more like we're hangin' outside The Comedy Store than attending a very exclusive party at the Mansion."

The Quotable *Monk*

"Mom, you can't let somebody get away just because I might have a bad day at school."—Benjy

The Weirdest Clue: Monk notices that all of the metallic objects in the gym, including the hands of the clock, are facing the same way.

Idiosyncrasy of the Week: Monk is very anxious to use a wipe after touching an issue of *Sapphire Magazine.*

The Clue that Breaks the Case: The marks in the carpet of Noelle's apartment—which just happen to match the treads of a nearby ladder.

"Mr. Monk and the 12th Man"

Episode 2-9
Written by Michael Angeli
Directed by Michael Zinberg
Original Airdate: August 22, 2003

GUEST CAST

Kenny Shale	Jerry Levine
Stewart Babcock	Ed Marinaro
Ian Agnew	Billy Gardell
Mrs. Ling	Lauren Tom
Tommy Zimm	David Figlioli
Frank Pulaski	Jimmy Shubert
Lisa Babcock	Deborah Zoe
Trainee	Chris Owen

with

Dr. Kroger	Stanley Kamel

A tollbooth operator is murdered, the ninth victim of a peculiar rash of homicides that have struck San Francisco in two short weeks. Stottlemeyer barely has time to breath, let alone solve the individual crimes. He contacts Monk, hoping the detective can help him close at least one of the open cases. Monk wonders if this murder is connected to the other eight, but the captain assures him that the victims didn't have anything in common.

Not long after, a woman is strangled in a movie theatre: victim number ten. Monk accompanies Stottlemeyer to the scene and finds solid evidence that this murder is related to that of the tollbooth operator. Stottlemeyer grimly accepts that this is the work of a serial killer.

At the police station Monk reviews photos of the ten victims. Several of them bought insurance from the same person: Henry Smalls. Could Smalls represent the common denominator in the murders? Monk stakes out

Smalls' house, but just as the suspect arrives home, a man in a ski mask emerges from the shadows and stabs Smalls to death. Monk tries to stop the attacker, but he gets away.

Back at the station Monk notes that the eleven victims, despite being extremely different, all lived in the same county and were registered voters. Suddenly he realizes where a disparate group like that would come together: on a jury. Disher determines that six years ago they all served on the same jury for a personal injury case.

A twelfth member of the jury is still alive—could he be the killer? Wallace Cassidy—Juror Number Twelve—is a gambler who always needs money. A search of Cassidy's house turns up a human finger stashed in the freezer. Cassidy certainly seems guilty of *something*, and Stottlemeyer is anxious to close the case, as is Deputy Mayor Kenny Shale, Sharona's latest boyfriend. But Monk doesn't think Cassidy is the guy he encountered at Smalls' house—his fingernails are too long.

That's really not enough to convince Stottlemeyer, but he gives Monk another six hours to prove that someone else is the killer. Monk heads for the home of Charles Babcock, the defendant from the lawsuit six years earlier. On the surface it doesn't look like Babcock would have a motive; his insurance company paid the damages, so he wasn't on the hook for any money. But Monk catches Babcock and his wife in a lie, which leads him to conclude that the pair is somehow involved in the murders. And when he gets a good look at a piece of evidence from the crime scene of Henry Smalls, he knows how to prove his theory.

He lays out the whole case for Stottlemeyer— and the Babcocks. Six years ago, the jurors were brought to Babcock's house to see the scene of the accident. While they were there, one juror—Cassidy—found the body of Babcock's *first* wife in the freezer. He took a picture of it—and also one of Mrs. Babcock's fingers. He's been blackmailing Babcock ever since. Babcock knew his blackmailer was one of the jurors, but he didn't know which one. Finally, after years of paying, he got fed up and began killing the jurors, one by one.

It's a nice theory, but Babcock is sure Monk can't prove it. But, of course, he can. The police found part of the killer's shirtsleeve in Henry Smalls' hand. The stitching on the cuff button is unique, one-of-a-kind, and Monk recognizes it at once. It's the handiwork of Monk's own dry cleaner, Mrs. Ling. Summoned to the scene, Mrs. Ling identifies the stitching, the shirt, *and* the man the shirt belongs to: her regular customer, Mr. Babcock. That's enough for Stottlemeyer, who happily arrests Babcock for the murder of eleven jurors *and* his first wife.

"Mr. Monk and the 12th Man" begins with an unusually horrific murder: a tollbooth operator being dragged to his death on the highway. That's pretty grisly for a family-oriented show, and according to Andy Breckman, "That's why we didn't show it on-screen."

The episode is about a serial killer, and in itself represents something of an anomaly for *Monk*. "Andy usually wants us to shy away from that kind of story," Hy Conrad says. "We generally don't have more than two murders in an episode."

Ratings for the show indicated that viewership dipped during the second half hour. "That's very rare for *Monk*," Conrad comments, but the writers think they know the reason why.

"We tipped our hand too early," says Tom Scharpling. "We gave away the hook at the end of Act Two, letting viewers know that the victims had been members of a jury. That was the big reveal, and the rest of the show was just playing out the string by having Monk interview people."

And interviews, the writers have learned, seem to be another no-no for Monk—even if many police procedurals have had a great deal of success with the format. Call it *Law and Order* syndrome. "Nine-tenths of a *Law and Order* episode is someone interviewing someone else," Conrad explains, "and we really try to stay away from that. If we have an interview, we try to do something a little odd, like put a pipe in the interviewee's head."

For those viewers who stuck around for the second half of the show, that particular interview was a genuine highlight of "12th Man." Billy Gardell's twitchy performance as accident victim Ian Agnew, complete with the squirm-inducing pipe-in-head, was worthy of a veteran of the premiere comedy club circuit—which, by the way, he is. It may have been dark humor, but it was actually one of the lighter moments found between the rather grim series of murders Monk investigates. Call it a guilty pleasure.

"Guilty" is an adjective that also applies to the writers' feelings about the sequence with Monk's dry cleaner, Mrs. Ling. Ling, played by Lauren Tom, whose performances have graced such disparate entertainments as *The Joy Luck Club* and *Futurama*, is . . . well, no use beating around the bush—a stereotype. To be fair, a lot of elements contributed to that. If the writing started Mrs. Ling off on the wrong foot, then Tom's performance nudged it closer to the edge of political incorrectness, and the costuming pushed it right over the edge. "She looked like she was straight out of a Charlie Chan movie," sighs Conrad. Adds Dan Dratch, "Comedy has evolved, but this was like a Don Rickles routine from the nineteen fifties."

Nevertheless, Mrs. Ling's presence did have a useful payoff. "The Mrs. Ling runner seemed like it was just a soft-shoe to keep you entertained while the mystery was getting under way," Tom Scharpling says, "but it tied right into the mystery in the end."

In fact, it was Mrs. Ling's sartorial expertise with buttons that provided the key element, allowing Monk to prove his case against Babcock. "It's a great clue," enthuses Breckman.

Viewers who like to play detective may note that the movie theatre where victim number ten is killed is screening the same pair of Alfred Hitchcock films as the theatre in "The Billionaire Mugger." A closer look, in fact, confirms that it's an alternate take from the "Billionaire" shoot—and a clever way for the producers to stretch the budget for "12th Man."

By the way, actor Jerry Levine, who plays Kenny Shale, is indeed the same Jerry Levine who frequently directs *Monk* episodes. According to his coworkers, he performs both tasks with equal aplomb.

The Quotable *Monk*

"He's brilliant, but he's Monk. He's lost in Monkland."—Stottlemeyer

The Weirdest Clue: Monk notices that the serial numbers on the ten-dollar bill used by the perpetrator of the theatre murder are just one digit off from the bill given to the dead tollbooth operator.

Idiosyncrasy of the Week: Monk is compelled to roll Sharona's car backward and forward until he advances her odometer from 99,999.9 to 100,000.0.

The Clue that Breaks the Case: Mrs. Ling's unique stitching on the button of the perp's shirtsleeve.

"Mr. Monk and the Paperboy"

Episode 2-10
Written by David Breckman & Hy Conrad
Directed by Michael Fresco
Original Airdate: January 16, 2004

GUEST CAST

Kevin Dorfman	Jarrad Paul
Vicki Salinas	Nicole DeHuff
Boz Harrelson	Joe Sikora
Benjy Fleming	Kane Ritchotte
Captain Dupres	Endre Hules
Lt. LaFitte	Orlando Seale
Malcolm Cowley	Mark Totty
with	
Dr. Kroger	Stanley Kamel

In the wee hours of the morning Nestor and Jose Alverez deliver the daily paper to their most demanding customer, Adrian Monk. When Nestor spots a shadowy figure attempting to steal it, he tries to stop him. The two engage in a brief scuffle, during which Nestor is killed.

To Monk's dismay, his apartment soon becomes the focal point of the police investigation, complete with messy cops who bring disorder to his very meticulous abode. In the midst of all the chaos, Monk's nerdy upstairs neighbor Kevin Dorfman stops by to see what's happened. Disher interviews Kevin, hoping he might have overheard something, but Kevin assures him that when the crime happened he was *extremely* occupied with his hot new girlfriend Vicki. Vicki works at the Stop N' Go, the local minimart; that's where she met Kevin and apparently succumbed to his not very apparent charms.

Monk decides that the killer didn't want the investigator to see something in his morning news, so he and Sharona head over to the Stop N' Go for another copy of the stolen paper. When they check out, Boz, the store's other clerk, asks them if they'd like a lottery ticket. Sharona declines; there's just been a big winner, so what's the point?

With no obvious suspects, Monk, Sharona, Stottlemeyer, and Disher pour over the paper, looking for anything that might suggest the motive behind the crime. In the process, Monk manages to solve two completely unrelated murder cases, including one that took place in France! But there's nothing that seems to pertain to the crime that took place on his doorstep.

The next day, store clerk Boz is found murdered near the night deposit box of the neighborhood bank. Did someone kill him for the money? Monk thinks not and Sharona observes that the killer—who used a broken bottle to stab Boz to death—obviously was a woman. There's lipstick on the bottle.

After spending fruitless days on the newspaper, Monk at last decides that he isn't going find the clue. Defeated, he tosses it in the trash—but retrieves it a second later when he spots a headline displaying the winning numbers from the recent lottery. Monk recognizes the digits—they're Kevin Dorfman's "lucky numbers:" the numeric portions of his neighbor's previous addresses.

Suddenly Monk comprehends who killed the paperboy—and why! The killer was trying to keep the paper from Kevin, not Monk, because Kevin had just won the lottery, although he wasn't aware of it. Kevin bought all his lottery tickets at the Stop N' Go from Vicki. When Vicki and Boz realized that the $43 million winning ticket belonged to Kevin, the pair concocted a scheme for Vicki to seduce and marry Kevin. That would allow her to inherit the money— once Kevin was out of the picture. Somewhere along the way, Vicki decided that there was no reason to share the money with Boz, so she killed him.

Monk and Sharona are too late to prevent Vicki from marrying Kevin, but they figure out where the couple plans to spend their honeymoon. As they approach the locale, they find Kevin's car in the middle of a railroad crossing, with Kevin locked inside, alone and unconscious. As a train bears down on the car, Sharona struggles with the murderous Vicki while Monk pulls down the track switch and saves Kevin from certain death. A few days later, the newly flush Kevin gives Monk a whopping $400 for his trouble before he heads off to one of his several expensive new homes.

As much as audiences love him, it's probably hard for them to imagine a more annoying character than Monk. But it isn't hard for the writing staff to think of someone like that. Take Kevin Dorfman. Please.

To paraphrase the immortal words of Jessica Rabbit, Kevin's not bad. They just wrote him that way. His destiny is foretold by his description in the script: "He's the most boring man ever born."

"We created Kevin by working backwards

from a clue," says Hy Conrad, the man who co-wrote that script with David Breckman. "We thought, 'Wouldn't it be great if Monk realizes that the winning lottery numbers are the addresses where his neighbor had previously lived?' "

Well, yeah, that's pretty good, but how do you plant those addresses within the story so that Monk and the viewers at home get to hear them? Simple. Give the neighbor the type of personality that would lead to the disclosure. "We *had* to make the neighbor boring," says Conrad, "a guy who just goes on *and on and on.* By working backwards from that clue, we 'found' Kevin's personality. And when they cast Jarrad Paul," Conrad concludes, "Kevin Dorfman became a *great* character."

Considering the fact that he's already played characters known as "Zit Boy" *(Liar, Liar)* and "Pipsqueak" *(Men Behaving Badly),* it seemed like the casting department was on the right track when they invited actor Jarrad Paul in to read for the role. And Paul lived up to expectations, although he admits the writers were probably responsible for that. "It was a really funny part," says Paul, "and obviously written really well, so the audition *did* go well."

Maybe a little too well. The *Monk* producers generally attempt to keep the show from tipping too far into flat-out comedy by keeping the humor within certain parameters. "But I didn't really give Kevin any parameters," Paul laughs. "Maybe I should have, but I didn't. One day a team of about eight people from the network came to the set and said to me, 'You've gotta tone it down!' " He sighs. "I guess Kevin is better in small doses."

Clearly, the executives weren't *too* disturbed, because additional doses of Dorfman were ordered up for subsequent episodes "Mr. Monk and the Game Show" and "Mr. Monk and Mrs. Monk."

While Kevin Dorfman certainly gives Monk a run for his money in terms of who's the oddest duck in the episode, Monk, as usual, has no trouble coming out on top of that competition. Monk would rather sing show tunes than talk to Kroger about his physical relationship with Trudy, and he can't bear the thought that Sharona might be physically stronger than him. He goes to pieces when he inadvertently rubs his hands with a greasy rag instead of a hygienic wipe (Monk's plaintive cry of "Oh, the humanity!" is a steal from reporter Herb Morrison's famous on-air reaction to the Hindenburg disaster of 1937). And his favorite comic is one of the longest-running (fifty-one years and counting!) and corniest strips to be found in the daily paper.

"Monk has a total lack of humor," says Andy Breckman. "That's one of my favorite things about him. So I just *love* the idea that he thinks *Marmaduke* is the gold standard of comedy. It's the one cartoon he can get, because it's so obvious. Now, the truth is," Breckman confides with a grin, "that I find this a lot funnier than Tony [Shalhoub] does. I'm always pushing for more Marmaduke jokes."

The Quotable *Monk*

"I don't have to be the man. But I would like to be . . . man-ish."—Monk

The Weirdest Clue: Monk figures out Kevin and Vicki's honeymoon destination after he notices that only one travel brochure has been taken from an entire rack of brochures in the office of the Justice of the Peace.

"Mr. Monk and the Three Pies"

Episode 2-11
Written by Tom Scharpling & Daniel Dratch
Directed by Randy Zisk
Original Airdate: January 23, 2004

GUEST CAST

Ambrose Monk . . . . John Turturro
Pat Van Ranken . . . . Holt McCallany
Town Official . . . . Leslie Jordan

The town of Tewkesbury is celebrating its centennial anniversary. There are games, competitions, and raffles galore, including one for a homemade cherry pie. Pat Van Ranken is particularly interested in winning the pie, but he's out of luck—the cherry delight goes to Mrs. Dohan. As the happy winner climbs into her car, however, Van Ranken confronts her and demands the pie. Instead, Mrs. Dohan sprays him with Mace. Enraged, Van Ranken smashes her head against the dashboard, killing her. Then he jumps into the car and drives away with the body *and* the pie.

The next day, the police find Mrs. Dohan's body in her abandoned car. Stottlemeyer attributes the woman's death to a carjacking, but Monk is dubious. Before he has a chance to delve more deeply into the case, however, he receives a surprise phone call from his brother Ambrose. The estranged brothers haven't spoken in seven years; Monk has never forgiven Ambrose for failing to call after Trudy's death. But now Ambrose wants to see Monk on a life-or-death matter. After some prodding by Sharona, Monk goes to see Ambrose in nearby Tewkesbury.

Ambrose is a true Monk, confined by his chronic agoraphobia to the home where the two brothers grew up. In fact, surrounded by stacks of newspapers and file cabinets full of mail that he's saving for their father—who abandoned the family when Monk was eight years old— Ambrose is even more eccentric than Adrian ("the fearless one" in the family, according to Ambrose). But like Adrian, Ambrose has keen powers of observation, and he's 85 to 90 percent certain that his next-door neighbor has killed his wife.

Two nights earlier, Ambrose heard Pat Van Ranken and his wife Rita fighting, followed by the sound of four gun shots and a lot of odd behavior by Pat. Although Monk would like to dismiss Ambrose's suspicions, he can't. There are quite a few clues that lead him to the same conclusion as Ambrose—and Rita is nowhere to be found. Monk and Sharona tail Van Ranken to the Centennial festival, where they see him win a sack race and a second cherry pie, and moments later, tear the pie apart. He's obviously looking for something—but what?

After learning that Rita Van Ranken baked three pies for the festival—the first having been won by Mrs. Dohan—Monk concludes that Van Ranken killed the poor woman for her pie. He notes that the third pie will be given to the winner of a bingo tournament. And sure enough, Van Ranken attends the tournament and

wins the pie. But before he can get away, Monk
stops him and calls in Stottlemeyer. Monk
explains his theory: Van Ranken shot his wife
just as she finished baking the three pies. As he
cleaned up the mess, he realized that one of the
discharged shells from his gun was missing. He
figured it must be in one of the pies—which, by
that time, had been delivered to the festival.
Sharona thoroughly searches the third pie—but
there's no sign of the shell.

When Monk goes to tell Ambrose the news,
the two finally discuss why he's avoided
communicating with Monk since Trudy's death.

Trudy was running an errand for Ambrose on
the day she was killed by the car bomb.
Ambrose blames himself for putting her in
harm's way. Shocked, Monk tells his brother that
it wasn't his fault, absolving him of all those
years of self-torment.

Later that day, Monk and Van Ranken
simultaneously realize where the ammo shell
is: in a bag of flour that Rita borrowed from
Ambrose, and which Van Ranken has since
returned. Monk and Sharona race to Ambrose's
house, but Van Ranken already has set the
place on fire, hoping to destroy the evidence

within. The police show up in time to arrest Van Ranken, but it's up to Monk to save his brother, who's still afraid to leave the house. Finally the two emerge, smoky but otherwise unharmed, two brothers united for the first time in years.

As Andy Breckman periodically reminds us, *Monk* was inspired by Sherlock Holmes. And so, just as Holmes had Mycroft, the older, smarter brother who was a near recluse, moving about only in his rooms, his office, and the gentlemen's Diogenes Club, Adrian has Ambrose, one of the few men in the world who makes Adrian look normal. Breckman had always planned to bring Ambrose into the series at some point, but he was in no hurry. "Mr. Monk and the Three Pies," provided the opportunity, but Ambrose's involvement wasn't the inspiration for the episode. No, it was a rather more slapstick impulse. "I've always wanted to construct a story where it became a matter of life or death for someone to win a potato sack race," Breckman says with a chuckle.

By the middle of Season Two, the production staff had decided it was time to do some reverse engineering on Monk, to establish how the character had become the very odd duck he is today. Introducing viewers to his brother seemed like a good place to start. Using Mycroft's reclusiveness as a starting point, they began to assemble a brother "even crazier than Monk," says Hy Conrad. But how do you work someone who doesn't leave his home into a mystery? The writers didn't need to look any farther than the classic film *Rear Window* for their inspiration. "When Tony Shalhoub came to visit us in New Jersey," laughs Conrad, "he asked, 'What are you going to do when you run

out of Hitchcock movies [to borrow from]?'"

The talented actor John Turturro created a sympathetic flesh-and-blood character out of a part that in the wrong hands easily could have become a joke. Shalhoub was instrumental in pulling the busy Turturro into the mix. "Years ago, we did a film together called *Barton Fink*," Shalhoub relates. "And then around nineteen ninety-nine we did the play *Waiting For Godot* on Broadway. Normally John doesn't do television, but fortunately he was available for the part. And he won an Emmy for it," he concludes proudly.

While the episode retains many of the comic elements the audience expects in a *Monk* episode, "Three Pies" is also very much a psychological drama, with tangible pathos. Viewers learn how both brothers have learned to cope with the frightening inner world they obviously face on a daily basis. But their fears aren't identical. "We gave Ambrose the traits that we've always refrained from giving Monk," explains Tom Scharpling. "Monk wouldn't be as much fun if he was a walking encyclopedia, so we've always reined in the tendency to have him regurgitating statistics. But we figured we could do that with his brother."

Television production is often art by committee, prone to discussion and negotiation. And sometimes, even amidst a group as tightly knit as the *Monk* staff, there are disagreements. A case in point: "Tony likes us to give Monk a trigger," says Andy Breckman. "For that 'clue that breaks the case,' he likes there to be something to help Monk make connections in his head. In 'The Three Pies,' it was important to Tony that Monk see the bingo chips flipping through the air to help him think of the bullet shells. But personally, I believe Monk *doesn't* need a trigger," he adds. "I think Monk can be doing something completely unrelated, like vacuuming, and suddenly solve the case." Sometimes Breckman wins these disagreements, sometimes Shalhoub. In this case, the flying chips were added to the scene.

Another disagreement occurred when the script required Sharona to refer to Monk as "a regular Evel Knievel." The scene occurs after Ambrose tells Sharona how fearless Monk is. While shooting the scene, Bitty Schram insisted that the reference to Knievel was too obscure for the show's audience. After a brief discussion, director Randy Zisk convinced her that the public would get the joke and the dialogue went on as written.

The Quotable *Monk*

"I don't understand. Usually when he does that whole summation thing, it's all over . . . we get to go home."—Disher

The Weirdest Clue: The yellow acorns in the back of Van Ranken's truck reveal where he buried his wife.

Idiosyncrasy of the Week: Apparently the rest of the Monk family was as dysfunctional as Adrian. Ambrose's agoraphobia keeps him a prisoner in his own home. No one in the family liked to touch. Mom numbered all the coffee mugs so they could be put back into the cupboard in order. And Dad . . . well, we're not sure if he was being quirky or if he was attempting to salvage his sanity when he went out for Chinese food and never came back.

The Clue that Breaks the Case: Bingo chips flipping through the air remind Monk of bullet shells being ejected from a gun—and Monk realizes what Van Ranken's been looking for.

"Mr. Monk and the TV Star"

Episode 2-12
Written by Tom Scharpling
Directed by Randy Zisk
Original Airdate: January 30, 2004

GUEST CAST

Brad Terry	Billy Burke
Benjy Fleming	Kane Ritchotte
Susan Malloy	Nicole Forester
Laurie	Stacey Scowley
TV Reporter	Brooke Burke
Dustin the Bartender	Jeff Parise
TV Director	Charles Dougherty
Lee	Vic Chao
J	Lara Boyd Rhodes

with

Dr. Kroger	Stanley Kamel

And

Marci Maven	Sarah Silverman

Sharona is thrilled when she and Monk are summoned to the home of Susan Malloy, the murdered ex-wife of actor Brad Terry, star of the hit TV show *Crime Lab S.F.* Sharona's hoping to catch sight of Terry and she's not disappointed. Terry was at the house when the murder occurred, or rather, he was out front dealing with the journalists and paparazzi who'd managed to track him there. When Susan's bloodcurdling screams filled the air, Terry raced inside, only to find that she'd been stabbed to death.

The evidence points to a break-in, but there are things that don't make sense to Monk, including the fact that Terry parked out in the open where anyone could spot his car, even though Terry had previously stated that he was trying to avoid the press. Sharona, Stottlemeyer, and Disher, however, are so charmed by Terry that they shrug off Monk's qualms.

When Monk and Sharona pay a visit to the set of *Crime Lab S.F.*, they learn that the production is filming its one-hundredth episode, making it eligible for syndication and a very big payout to Terry. Monk observes that half of that money would have had to go to his ex, Susan, which could be a motive for murder. Terry laughs off the comment and volunteers to take a lie detector test, which he passes with flying colors. That night, Sharona, Stottlemeyer and Disher are invited to the cast party celebrating the one-hundredth episode—while Monk spends the night at home, alone.

At the party, Terry is approached by Marci Maven, an obsessed fan who is desperate to talk to the actor. Sizing her up as the kind of stalker who may have killed Terry's wife, Stottlemeyer and Disher take her down to the station for questioning. By morning, Marci has confessed to Susan Malloy's murder, claiming that she did it because she loves Terry. Monk doesn't believe Marci, but Sharona, Stottlemeyer, and Disher, all clearly enamored with the actor, convince Monk to call off his pursuit. Yielding to peer pressure, Monk capitulates. He visits Terry in his trailer while the actor is working out and tells him that Marci has confessed. But when Monk notes that the pulse monitor hooked up to Terry never changes while he tells a blatant lie to a production assistant, the detective realizes that the actor could fool a lie detector just as easily.

Now Monk's back on the case. He quickly figures out that Marci confessed to killing Susan because she *does* love Terry—and she knows he's guilty. But how would she know that? Returning to the murder scene, Monk notices two details that tell him everything he needs to know: the volume on the television has been turned all the way up, and the workout tape that

Susan had been exercising to on the morning of her murder is missing.

With Stottlemeyer, Disher and Sharona at his side, Monk confronts Terry with the facts. The press provided Terry's alibi for the time of Susan's death; they all heard Susan scream *inside* the house while Terry was *outside* talking to them. But it was a prerecorded scream, from a B horror film that Susan had made years before. Terry had dubbed the scream onto Susan's workout tape and turned the volume on the TV up so that everyone outside would hear it. When Terry came in, allegedly to save Susan, he stabbed her. Marci, being the rabid fan she was, recognized that scream, and realized that Terry was guilty. Of course, being crazy, she opted to cover up his guilt rather than telling the police the truth.

Once Terry is jailed—and his show cancelled—Marci shows up at Monk's door to thank him for solving the case and getting her out of jail. She confides that she doesn't like Terry anymore . . . but she *does* think that Monk is wonderful.

Imitation may be the sincerest form of flattery, but parody is certainly funnier. Even self-parody. Which is why, when the *Monk* writers decided to spoof police procedurals, they didn't hesitate to include their own show in the mix.

"We really take pride in the fact that no one in *Monk* relies on technology," David Breckman says. "*CSI,* on the other hand, is largely about the use of technology."

"We consider ourselves the anti-*CSI*," chimes in brother Andy. "I'm just not into that forensic stuff, and creating *Crime Scene S.F.* was a way to have fun with that."

An easy target for that fun was the gizmo-heavy nature of current crime-scene dramas, epitomized in *Crime Scene S.F.* by the "SpectroScope," a clumsy-looking device that's described in the script as "a huge, futuristic infrared crime-scene analyzer. It straps to Lee's body like a SteadiCam. It projects infrared beams. It has whirring cameras. And a robotic arm. It hums loudly. It's insane."

The dialogue, too, was ripe for ribbing. As J, the crime show's sexy female computer tech, scans the room, she makes an astute discovery that will eventually lead Special Agent Rusty Clark to the killers: "It looks like a fiber." That's one single fiber, of course, and she wouldn't dare guess the type without the trusty SpectroScope.

"We were emphasizing how retro our own show is," comments Tom Scharpling, the episode's writer. "Computers are the absolute last resort on *Monk,* while they're kind of the first place other shows go. *CSI* is working with two-thousand-eight technology, while we're working with nineteen-seventy-three technology."

"Of course," Dan Dratch relates, "it isn't as if *CSI* isn't kicking our butts in every which way."

"They could crush us," Scharpling agrees. "With one flick of the wrist."

But while *Monk* may not have the ratings of shows like *CSI,* it does have a devoted fan base—which is where the writers got the idea for Marci Maven.

"Marci was a tribute to our fans at the online sites," explains Scharpling. "We named her after a guy who posts on the message boards using the name Monster Monk Maven. It was fun to name a character for him."

Marci's biggest obsession—besides Brad Terry—was also drawn from the message boards.

"There was so much talk on the boards about the new theme song," moans Dratch. Apparently, a goodly percentage of the fans thought that dropping the old theme just because a big name might draw more attention to the show was . . . well, kind of fickle. "There were all these jokes about it, like 'If you have the chance to get Led Zeppelin . . .'"

Jeff Beal, the composer of the original theme song, was surprised by the in-joke. "Seeing it for the first time was one of the strangest experiences I've ever had," Beal says, shaking his head. "I hadn't read the script, so I didn't know about this running joke until I went to spot music for the edited cut. Suddenly I realized that something that happened in my life had made it into the show." The episode closes with the original Monk theme, as dictated by this notation on the script's final page: "Roll our end credits . . . as we play Jeff Beal's Emmy Award–winning theme song from Season One." As you might expect, "TV Star" is one of Beal's favorite episodes.

Comedy writer/performer Sarah Silverman, another vet of the *Saturday Night Live* writing team, and star of *School of Rock* and *Jesus Is Magic,* is perfectly cast as Marci. The *Monk* writers were so taken with her performance that one of the cards pinned to the writers' room bulletin board—a repository for one-line story ideas and cool clues—states simply, "The return of Sarah Silverman."

Self-parody was the name of the game for several lines of dialogue in "TV Star." Monk is very excited when he sees that Brad Terry has a large supply of Sierra Springs bottled water in his trailer. Terry explains that the production gets it free because he drinks it on the show. "You gotta love them perks," he adds. Astute viewers may note that, in fact, Sierra Springs is a *real* brand, and gather that Monk's affection for the beverage may have something to do with similar . . . scenarios.

While actors and high-rated shows certainly received their due, the writers proved that they were equal-opportunity offenders when they stooped to skewering the lowliest man on the Hollywood totem pole. As a man walks past her near the set of *Crime Scene S.F.,* the star-struck Sharona asks, "Is he somebody?" "No," responds the seasoned production assistant. "He's just a writer."

The Quotable *Monk*

"I think I'm finally getting the hang of sixth grade." —Monk

The Weirdest Clue: Brad Terry's pulse is as steady as a metronome when he lies.

Idiosyncrasy of the Week: Monk has never gotten over the fact that everyone in his sixth grade class was invited to Robbie Walover's birthday party— except him. Even Dr. Kroger attended the party.

The Clue that Breaks the Case: Susan Malloy's workout tape is missing and the TV volume is turned all the way up.

"Mr. Monk and the Missing Granny"

Episode 2-13
Written by Joe Toplyn
Directed by Tony Bill
Original Airdate: February 6, 2004

GUEST CAST

Julie Parlo	Rachel Dratch
Nana Parlo	Pat Crawford Brown
Harold Maloney	Currie Graham
Carol Maloney	Eden Rountree
Ron Abrash	Michael Shalhoub
Jeff Burton	Scott Nankivel
Sasha Gordon	Jenni Pulos
Edie Rusher	Christina Huntington

Old Mrs. Parlo sits in her rocker and talks to the stray cat she recently took in. Suddenly two hooded intruders break into the house, strap Parlo to her chair, and tape her mouth closed. In a matter of seconds, they've kidnapped the old woman, leaving a message on the wall, indicating they will call at 4 P.M.—presumably with a ransom demand.

Mrs. Parlo's granddaughter Julie, a law student, is beside herself. Stottlemeyer and his team do their best to assure Julie that they know how to handle kidnappings, but Julie wants Adrian Monk, the "brilliant detective" she's read about. Although she can't afford to pay him, Julie promises Monk that if he helps recover Nana, she has a strategy to get him reinstated to the police force. Monk eagerly joins the investigation.

At 4 P.M., the kidnappers call, identifying themselves as members of "the Lightning Brigade," which Stottlemeyer and Disher recall as a 1970s group of radicals. They make their ransom demand: Julie must buy every homeless

person in San Francisco's Mission District a turkey dinner. After that, her Nana will be returned.

Julie complies, arranging for the soup kitchen at a Mission District church to serve a big turkey dinner that very night. And sure enough, before the meal is over, Nana Parlo wanders in, disheveled and exhausted, but otherwise unharmed.

The next day Stottlemeyer locates Ron Abrash, the former leader of the Lightning Brigade. As the Captain and Monk interrogate him, it becomes obvious that neither Abrash nor the Lightning Brigade was involved with the kidnapping. Stottlemeyer has no other leads, and with Mrs. Parlo safe, the case is on the back burner as far as he's concerned. But Monk will continue to pursue the culprits, whoever they are.

True to her word, Julie tells Monk how he can get reinstated. She'll file a suit against the police department, saying they've discriminated against Monk under the Americans with Disabilities Act. His obsessive behavior is well documented so they can't deny that he is, indeed, disabled. All he'll have to do to get his job back is pass a written test regarding department protocol.

Monk and Sharona return to the Parlo residence, with the hopes that Nana can remember enough about the kidnappers' route for Monk to track them down. Nana provides just enough input for Monk to pinpoint the residence of Harold and Carol Maloney, owners of a local antique shop. When Monk shows Mrs. Parlo photos of the couple, she immediately recognizes them. They came to her home two weeks ago, in response to the fliers she'd put up in the neighborhood regarding the stray cat she found. The Maloneys indicated

the stray wasn't theirs and left quickly.

Did the Maloneys have something to do with her grandmother's kidnapping? Julie wonders. Monk isn't sure yet. Should they call the captain? asks Sharona. Wait till tomorrow, says Monk. He has something to do first.

The next day, Monk takes—or rather *tries* to take—his reinstatement test. But although he knows the material cold, he gets so caught up in filling in the answer sheet correctly (using neat pencil marks that fill the circles precisely) that he never really starts the test. Humiliated, Monk locks himself in Stottlemeyer's office, propping a chair against the door. In the process, he suddenly solves the case.

Monk takes the police and Julie Parlo to the Maloney home, where they find Nana Parlo's rocking chair. The Maloneys claim that it's theirs—and that it's worth over $2 million. It's obvious to all that the Maloneys kidnapped Nana in order to get her chair. But how did they know she had the chair? And how can Monk prove it belongs to Nana?

The answers are one and the same. The lost cat flier included a picture of the kitty sitting on the rocking chair. When the Maloneys saw it, they went to Parlo's house, confirmed the chair was there, and then came back to steal it. They used the kidnapping as a cover for the theft.

The case solved, Monk goes home and removes his police dress uniform from his armoire. It looks like he won't be needing it. But Sharona quickly retrieves it and hangs it back in the armoire. She's sure he'll need it . . . eventually.

"Mr. Monk and the Missing Granny" has the distinction of being the only *Monk* episode to date in which the central crime is *not* a murder. "It was an experiment," says writer Joe Toplyn. "You don't have to be a mystery buff to know that the crime was a classic 'misdirect'"—a term often applied to the kind of sleight of hand employed by magicians and conmen to draw the audience's attention away from the actual manipulation that will make a trick appear to work. The episode was Toplyn's first—and only—freelance script for the series; he would become a staff member in Season Three.

Why a chair? That aspect of "Missing Granny" was inspired by a Roald Dahl story about a man who sees a valuable chair and—hoping to keep the price low—tells the owner that he'd like to buy it for firewood. Alas, his plan backfires when the owner does him the favor of chopping the chair into firewood for him! "That's where we got the idea of the valuable chair," Toplyn says.

While figuring out the clues that would help Monk retrace the route taken by Granny Parlo's kidnappers, Toplyn consulted with his "San Francisco expert," his wife Sherry. "We used a map of San Francisco and found an audible and olfactory route to a residential neighborhood where lawn sprinklers would be used. There's a drawbridge down by the Embarcadero, and that's where a bakery could have been. It's all plausible, although I simplified it," Toplyn laughs. "At one point I thought that they could have taken her past Pan Pacific Park, where there's a paddock with buffalo. She could have said, 'I smelled wet buffalo.'"

The buffalo didn't make the final episode, nor did a fun bit involving a crossbow. "The kidnappers had started out as museum curators," Toplyn explains. "So they had access to things like crossbows, which provided a clue for Monk." The crossbow would have been used in the library scene; instead of Monk almost being crushed by books, "the kidnappers shot an arrow at him," Toplyn notes. "It was an act break, so when the show went to commercial, we had a close-up of Monk looking as if he'd been shot. Then when the commercial was over, the audience saw he was actually holding a book on self-defense with an arrow sticking out of it." Toplyn chuckles at the image. "Somewhere along the line, somebody said no to the crossbow. I never knew who or why."

If actress Rachel Dratch, who plays Julie Parlo, is familiar to viewers, it's probably because she's been a regular cast member of *Saturday Night Live* since 1999. She's also done comedic turns on such shows as *Frasier* and *The King of Queens*. When Dratch, sister of *Monk* staff writer Dan Dratch, was initially cast in the role of Julie, her character was played more for laughs—she was a *really* bad law student. But somewhere along the line—probably the same line that led to the removal of the crossbow—it was determined that her character should have more depth and fewer funny lines, so Julie developed a newfound interest in running a bakery.

And if Michael Shalhoub, who plays former radical Ron Abrash, looks and sounds like someone you've met before, you may be responding to his familial resemblance to his brother Tony.

For the first time since "Mr. Monk Goes to the Carnival," Monk gets *this close* to being reinstated. But for now, that's something that neither the producers nor the man who plays Monk want to happen. "*He* wants to be reinstated," says Tony Shalhoub. "But I don't want him to be. It's better [for the character] that he's always on the fringe."

"Mr. Monk and the Captain's Wife"

Episode 2-14
Teleplay by Andy Breckman; story by Andy Breckman &
    Beth Landau
Directed by Jerry Levine
Original Airdate: February 13, 2004

GUEST CAST

Karen Stottlemeyer . . . . Glenne Headly
Evan Coker . . . . Daniel Goddard
Harry Bolston . . . . Geoff Pierson
Jared Stottlemeyer . . . . Jesse James
Frank Wicks . . . . Paul Gutrecht
Dr. Malding . . . . Rif Hutton
Detective . . . . Rick Ravanello
with
Dr. Kroger . . . . Stanley Kamel

A sniper's bullet kills a tow-truck driver, sending his vehicle careening into Karen Stottlemeyer's car as the captain's wife heads to a film shoot. When the captain finds out about the accident, he's beside himself with grief, fear, and anger. Karen's condition is stable, but she has a fractured skull. The doctors may be able to operate on her—*if* the swelling in her brain subsides. Leland can't face the thought of life without Karen; only Monk, who's still trying to get past the loss of his own wife, can truly empathize.

As Disher and Monk investigate the scene of the accident, they find the footprints of the sniper, and are surprised to see that he was barefoot. Strangely enough, so was the driver of the tow truck. The police task force speculates that a local union dispute may have led to the shooting; the tow truck belonged to a union shop and the driver was a scab.

When Stottlemeyer gets wind of the theory, he immediately confronts union leader Harry Bolston, who denies any involvement. But although Bolston is a shady character, Monk doesn't think that anyone connected to the union was responsible for the attack. However, Stottlemeyer, who's not thinking too clearly, is convinced Bolston's his man.

Later that day, Sharona and Monk return a lost dog found near the crime scene to the home of Evan Coker, the pup's owner. Sharona is attracted to Coker, and she dawdles to flirt with him, while Monk occupies himself by fiddling with a neighbor's miscalibrated sundial. When Sharona idly mentions that her boss is working with the police on the sniper case, and that Monk doesn't think it was a union thing, Coker takes notice. The next night, Coker surreptitiously approaches a truck depot and shoots a random driver.

As Coker had intended, the incident leads the police to be more convinced than ever that the killings are related to union activities, but Monk has a flash of insight that leads him in an entirely different direction. Summoning Stottlemeyer and Disher to the police impound lot, Monk points out the car that was being towed the day of Karen's accident. It belongs to Evan Coker, and Monk believes that Coker shot the driver because he needed to get something out of the car before anyone saw it. But what? Finding traces of gun oil in the glove compartment, Monk speculates that Coker was retrieving a handgun, probably one tied to a crime. The tow truck came to get his car early in the morning. Coker leaped out of bed, grabbed his rifle, and ran after the truck in his bare feet, knocking his neighbor's sundial off-kilter as he passed it. (It was at this point, Monk explains, that Coker's dog got out of the yard and followed his master to the scene of the crime.) When Coker got to a good vantage point, he shot the driver, retrieved the gun from his car—and stole the dead tow-truck driver's shoes so he wouldn't have to make the trip home in bare feet.

The police task force searches Coker's house but fails to find either the handgun or the shoes. Just then, Monk spots a garbage truck and chases it down. Sure enough, Coker had disposed of the incriminating evidence in the garbage—which is now safe in the hands of the police, thanks to Monk.

Not long after, Karen Stottlemeyer comes home from the hospital to her two boys and her very grateful husband, who now has some firsthand insight into Monk's own emotional underpinnings.

A Touch of Creativity

Perhaps Adrian Monk's most puzzling idiosyncrasy is his inexplicable habit of "touching lamps." If the habit doesn't seem to be explainable as a normal OCD symptom—it's because Tony Shalhoub invented it on the set.

"It was during the first scene of the pilot, which happened to be the first scene that we shot," Shalhoub explains. "We were on the crime scene set, and I was just moving around the room, when the director, Dean Parisot, said, 'Hey, what do you think about that lamp?' I looked up and noticed this goose-necked lamp on a desk, and I reached out and touched it. And with that one tiny gesture, a sort of ripple went through my body and my mind about

touching and becoming fixated and preoccupied with mundane things in what normally would be high-stake situations.

"Dean had asked kind of a silly question," Shalhoub admits with a chuckle, "and obviously I already had done some work on the character, but that really jump-started Monk. In terms of a real life in an environment, Monk is tugged at by the mundane. That opened up a whole new thing for me and for the character. It helped a lot."

So much so, that the actor still touches every lamp that his character sees.

"The show is about all the characters, this eclectic group of people that function around this phenomenon known as Monk," Ted Levine says. "We support that. It's a good thing."

But while Monk is clearly the focal point of the series, the writers periodically try to give each character his or her due. "We showcase each actor in at least one episode each season," states Hy Conrad. "Captain's Wife" was Ted Levine's turn in the spotlight for Season Two.

With Karen Stottlemeyer seriously injured in a car accident, the episode couldn't help but deliver a higher quotient of pathos than patter. "The story wasn't a lot of fun," admits Tom Scharpling. "It was kind of a downer." The writers attempted to lighten the episode by adding scenes like Monk's hellish trip to the 1950s diner with the Stottlemeyer kids, complete with rock-'n'-rolling waiters and waitresses. The scene certainly emphasized Monk's "fish out of water" status—not to mention giving him the clue that broke the case—but it didn't do much to up the mood overall. "It seemed like we were shoehorning fun into it." Scharpling sighs.

Despite the lack of fun, however, "The Captain's Wife" did a nice job of finally bringing the character of Stottlemeyer to the point where he truly understood the emotions driving Monk. He would, of course, continue to be irritated by Monk's innumerable shortcomings—who wouldn't?—but he no longer could say he didn't have a clue as to what was going on in Monk's head at any given time.

Beth Landau shares story credit with Andy Breckman on the episode. Call it part three to the *Monk* part of their courtship. He'd named a character for her in "Mr. Monk Goes Back to School," and given Stottlemeyer's wife her profession in "Very, Very Old Man." It seemed only natural to collaborate with her on a second story about the captain's wife. "At that point in our relationship, I was pulling out all the stops," admits Breckman with a chuckle. "I even named the two garbagemen after her brothers, Ronnie and Mo!" Not that the audience ever really hears their names—they're not Monk's regular garbagemen, after all. But they're in the script, plain as day. You can't say Breckman wasn't trying!

He must have done something right, because not long afterwards, he and Landau became Mr. and Mrs. Breckman, and today are the parents of a toddler named Molly.

The Quotable *Monk*

"The place you're in now—that's where I live."
—Monk.

The Weirdest Clue: Both the sniper and the victim were barefoot.

Idiosyncrasy of the Week: Monk is irritated by the sound of Kroger's new white-noise machine—which is half an octave higher than the old machine.

The Clue that Breaks the Case: When Monk straightens the round table that the dancing waiter has bumped, he realizes that the sundial was knocked out of alignment the same way—when the sniper next door bumped into it.

"Mr. Monk Gets Married"

Episode 2-15
Written by David Breckman
Directed by Craig Zisk
Original Airdate: February 27, 2004

GUEST CAST

Dalton . . . . Nestor Carbonell
Maria Disher . . . . Susan Kellermann
Jeffrey . . . . Patrick Breen
Rachel . . . . Jessica Lundy
Sheriff Mathis . . . . Jim Beaver
Joshua Skinner . . . . William Sanderson
Raymond Toliver . . . . Michael Ensign
and
Dr. Waterford . . . . Jane Lynch

Raymond Toliver figures it's his lucky day when he finds an old letter stuck behind the drawer of the nineteenth-century desk he's restoring. The letter, written by prospector Joshua Skinner before he died, reveals how he and mining partner Gully Watson found a rich vein of gold in 1849. Not long after, Skinner killed Gully and became the sole owner of a fortune in gold, part of which he used to build a large house near the mine. The rest he hid, and the secret of the hiding place seemed to have died with him . . . until now. According to the letter, the location of the gold is in Skinner's journals.

Toliver excitedly shares this tale with Dalton Padron, co-owner of their San Francisco antique store. "He killed his own partner over some gold," laughs Toliver. "Can you believe it?" Dalton can indeed, as he proves when he bludgeons Toliver to death.

A few days later, Lt. Disher entreats Monk and Sharona to look into the whirlwind nuptials of Maria Disher, his unglamorous middle-aged mother, to Dalton Padron, a young handsome

antiques dealer. It was an unlikely match to start with—and now Maria's husband says that the marriage isn't working. He wants her to accompany him to a therapy clinic. It all seems very fishy to Disher.

Monk and Sharona agree to check the guy out and go to Dalton's store. While they're there, Monk learns that Dalton's partner has recently gone missing, and Dalton is in the process of applying for a visa to travel out of the country. Monk notes that under "marital status" he's checked off "single." It looks like Disher's suspicions were on the mark—but how can Monk find out what Dalton is planning?

Sharona talks Monk into a bizarre idea. She and Monk will pose as man and wife and enroll in the same marital therapy clinic that Maria and her new husband are attending. The clinic is being held at the Waterford Institute, located at the former estate of millionaire Joshua Skinner. In between therapy sessions, "Mr. and Mrs. Monk" observe Dalton closely, and notice his inordinate interest in the many leather-bound journals that line the bookshelves in the Institute library. The journals are filled with pages and pages of Skinner's handwritten gibberish. When Sharona steals an old letter from Dalton's pocket, she and Monk figure out why Dalton is so interested in the journals. It's the same confession letter that Dalton's partner found—the one that indicates that the secret to where Skinner hid the gold is in his journals.

Clearly, Dalton's marriage to Maria was just a pretext that would allow him to come to the Institute and look for the treasure. But before they can use the letter to prove the truth to Maria, Dalton snatches it back and destroys it. Now aware that Monk and Sharona are on to him, Dalton lures the pair to an abandoned mineshaft and triggers a cave-in with them inside. Although they're quickly rescued by Mathis, the local sheriff, they have no proof of Dalton's malignant activities.

Back in San Francisco, Disher investigates Dalton's store and finds Toliver's body hidden in an armoire. He hastily calls his mother to warn her that she's married a murderer. Unfortunately, Dalton overhears the call. He quickly binds and gags the frightened Maria, then continues searching for the gold. But Monk has already figured out the hiding place. When Sheriff Mathis—contacted by the panicky Disher— arrives on the scene, he puts Dalton in handcuffs and releases Maria. Then Monk reveals where the gold is. It's actually *in* the journals—Skinner melted down his gold, mixed it with some ink, and wrote his journals with the precious substance. All someone needs to do to regain the fortune is burn the pages of the journals and retrieve the molten gold.

Making one last desperate attempt to get that fortune, Dalton steals Mathis's gun and forces the group into a walk-in closet. But before he can spirit away the journals, Disher arrives, arrests Dalton, and frees the others. Before they depart, Monk and Sharona confess to the marriage counselor that they're not really married. The counselor is greatly relieved— they're the least compatible couple she's ever worked with!

It plays almost like a *Monk* scenario. Andy Breckman and his daughter Rachel, then seventeen, are out on the town, having a good time. They have tickets to a Broadway show, but first they go to dinner. Rachel innocently suggests that it would be fun to see an episode of Dad's TV show where Monk and Sharona

pretend to be married. And suddenly, for Breckman, the whole thrust of the evening changes. Instead of filing the idea away for consideration at a more appropriate time, Breckman's brain goes into overdrive, latching onto the idea like Monk onto an unbalanced bookshelf. "I spent the entire time we were at the Broadway show thinking about the plot for the episode," sighs Breckman. "And I missed the show—the whole show."

Such is the life of a writer. On the positive side, notes David Breckman, who ultimately wrote the script for "Mr. Monk Gets Married," it did lead to a pretty good—if somewhat far-fetched—episode. "Andy walked into the writers' room with the entire story already formulated in his head," says David. "Rachel's idea inspired the whole thing."

If the previous episode ("Mr. Monk and the Captain's Wife") put a spotlight on Stottlemeyer, "Gets Married" shifts the focus to Randy Disher. (Stottlemeyer, in fact, isn't even in the episode.) It's Disher's predicament—or rather, his mom's predicament—that inspires Monk and Sharona's charade, as they book themselves into a marriage retreat to spy on Mom and her shady new husband. But all of that activity is just the backdrop to the true mystery at the heart of the story: the secret of Joshua Skinner's gold.

"Sometimes Andy and David's plotting can get a little far-fetched," Dan Dratch says with a smile. "When that happens, someone will rib them a little and the rest of us will join in. But they had it down with 'Gets Married.' The mystery they came up with was too good to pass up."

Who doesn't like a story about a treasure hunt? Especially one with such a novel—or rather journal—twist? It was a great idea, and the sepia-tinted historical section, featuring character actor William Sanderson (best known as Larry, brother to the two silent Darryls in *Newhart*), made for an extremely distinctive summation. However . . .

"There *is* one flaw in the episode," David Breckman admits. "In order to use up the amount of ink all of that melted gold would have produced, Skinner would have had to write journals for about a billion years! After all, you could probably write out *Crime and Punishment* and *War and Peace* with a single ballpoint pen—and that's what? Four grams of ink? The gold in our nine hundred forty-seven volumes probably would have amounted to about eleven dollars' worth!"

"Yeah," Andy Breckman agrees with a good-natured shrug. "I guess we weren't very careful."

The Quotable *Monk*

"I don't know how not to worry."—Monk

The Weirdest Clue: Monk knows that a map in Dalton's antique shop is a fake because there was no West Virginia until after the Civil War.

Idiosyncrasy of the Week: Monk won't sit on the ground, because "animals do terrible things on the ground."

The Clue that Breaks the Case: When Monk puts a skinny journal on an unbalanced shelf, he notices that it weighs far more than another, much larger book.

"Mr. Monk Goes to Jail"

Episode 2-16
Written by Chris Manheim
Directed by Jerry Levine
Original Airdate: March 5, 2004

GUEST CAST

Sylvia Fairbourn . . . . Kathy Baker
Spyder Rudner . . . . Danny Trejo
Warden Christie . . . . John Cothran
Lody . . . . Patrick St. Esprit
Second Nazi . . . . Rick Cramer
Talk Show Host . . . . Jim Moret
Rastafarian Cook . . . . James C. Mathis III
Medical Examiner . . . . Joe Narciso
And
Dale the Whale . . . . Tim Curry

Just forty-five minutes before his scheduled execution, Ray Kaspo dies in his cell. Someone has poisoned his last meal. But why bother? The man was going to die anyway. Stottlemeyer asks Monk to investigate, but Monk—who doesn't like being inside prisons—initially turns down the case. Then he receives a call from his old nemesis, Dale Biederbeck, a.k.a. "Dale the Whale." Biederbeck is locked up in the same prison as the murdered man, and the police consider him their primary suspect. But Dale says he had no real motive to kill Kaspo—and he wants Monk to find the real killer so that the Warden will make good on his promise to install a window outside Dale's cell. In exchange for Monk's help, Dale promises to provide information related to Trudy's death.

Monk can't turn down that offer. While he interviews the prison cook, the guards find a dead kitchen employee with a wad of hundred dollar bills in his pocket. Now Monk knows *how* Kaspo was poisoned but not who was

Setting the Scene—
The Music of *Monk*

The jazz-influenced temporary soundtrack that the producers had used while editing the pilot suited composer Jeff Beal just fine. "Getting into jazz is what spurred my interest in composition," Beal says. "Jazz is very intelligent music, and yet it can support the playfulness of this show, of Monk's need to solve puzzles." Beal applied both of those musical values from the very beginning, even as he scored the first scene of the pilot, when Monk holds up the investigation to fret about whether or not he left his gas turned on. "For that moment, I brought a kind of 'plunky' sound in, and I changed the key several times to build in surprises and work up to an expectation, but then not let the music resolve it in a conventional way," he says.

Beal also gives his rhythms a motif of halting rather than regular beats, and those rhythms translated dramatic ideas as if the music, like Monk, is thinking. "We've had some really fun thinking scenes," Beal says. "Like those Zen-like moments when Monk is silently doing something unfathomable for three minutes, and almost, but not quite, torturing the audience. At those times, Tony Shalhoub's performance is like a throwback to the great silent comedians. Music can heighten the severity of those scenes. And," Beal admits, "I use those moments. If Tony is miming something—enter composer!"

Beal had a great deal of fun composing the very distinctive "Monk Main Title Theme" that was featured throughout the first season and that he periodically reprises under the action of closing scenes. "Writing a theme song is as big as a composer gets," he relates. "It actually becomes a little pop culture icon that people relate to a show." Beal's *Monk* theme song is surprisingly simple, consisting of two acoustic guitars (both played by the guitar virtuoso Grant Geissman) and what sounds, for all intents and purposes, like an acoustic bass. "That's me playing, using a sample of an acoustic bass on the

behind the murder. A few minutes later, Sylvia Fairbourn, the prison social worker, asks to speak to Monk. Sylvia confides that she overheard Kaspo tell another inmate, Spyder Rudner, that right before they injected him, he was going to reveal what happened in Calgary. Spyder, she says, swore he'd see Kaspo in hell first.

Realizing that Spyder will never talk to a cop, Monk arranges to go undercover and share a cell with him, even though Spyder is considered the most dangerous man in the prison. Oddly enough, the two men hit it off, and Spyder eventually tells Monk that he never even met Kaspo.

Monk realizes that Sylvia set him up, hoping that Spyder would kill the investigator. But why? When he sees her watching a television interview with the author of an unauthorized biography about reclusive billionaire Lambert keyboard," Beal reports. "It's fooled a lot of people."

Although Beal's catchy theme song was popular with fans, the producers opted for something that they hoped would draw a little more attention to the series as they launched the second season. "We wanted to try something different that would promote the show and step it up a bit," explains David Hoberman. "And I thought of Randy Newman because he's such a genius and his sensibility would be so right for *Monk*. I called his agent and asked if Randy would be interested in writing and singing a new theme song for *Monk*. By the time Tony [Shalhoub] and I went over to Randy's house, he'd already had formed an idea for this song he called 'It's a Jungle Out There.' "

"I was perfectly happy with Jeff's theme song," admits Andy Breckman, "but I had started out as a singer/songwriter, and I idolized Randy Newman. He was

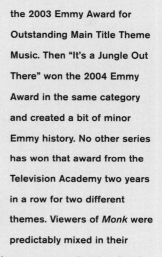

my hero. So I was thrilled with David's idea. And I was thrilled to be in L.A. when he recorded the song. It was one of the greatest days of my life."

Ironically, after the shift in themes, Beal's version won the 2003 Emmy Award for Outstanding Main Title Theme Music. Then "It's a Jungle Out There" won the 2004 Emmy Award in the same category and created a bit of minor Emmy history. No other series has won that award from the Television Academy two years in a row for two different themes. Viewers of *Monk* were predictably mixed in their reaction to the change in theme songs, a situation that the writers tapped into when they sat down to write "Mr. Monk and the TV Star." And even though Beal's main theme no longer backs up the opening credits, he continues to remain a vital presence on the show, scoring each episode and providing Monk with his weekly jazz infusion.

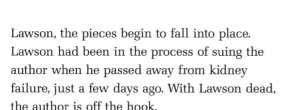

Lawson, the pieces begin to fall into place. Lawson had been in the process of suing the author when he passed away from kidney failure, just a few days ago. With Lawson dead, the author is off the hook.

Monk thinks he knows who was behind Kaspo's murder and why—but he needs proof. As he and Sharona wait for some phone calls to be returned, Monk receives word that the warden wants to see him in the rec room. But

when he gets there, the only people waiting for him are a bunch of neo-Nazis, eager to take Monk apart. Mrs. Fairbourne has set him up again!

Back in the prison administration office Sharona gets the call she's been waiting for: the late Mr. Lawson had an extremely rare blood type. He needed a kidney and there was an organ donor with that same blood type who was about to die. Unfortunately, the poison that killed that donor—Ray Kaspo—was so powerful that it destroyed all his internal organs. So Lawson died—and with him, his lawsuit against author J. T. DeMornay, son of Sylvia Fairbourn.

Realizing that Adrian is in danger, Sharona and the warden rush to find him, only to learn that Spyder has already taken care of the neo-Nazis. Now that Monk has fulfilled his end of the bargain, Dale the Whale provides the information Monk risked his life for. The car bomb that killed Trudy was not intended for Monk; it was meant for Trudy. A man named Warrick Tennyson was involved in her death—and he's in New York City.

It looks as if Monk and Sharona are about to head for the Big Apple.

"Sherlock Holmes had Moriarty, his archenemy, his nemesis," Andy Breckman says. "We liked the idea of Monk having a recurring all-powerful nemesis, too. So we brought back Dale the Whale," last seen, appropriately enough, in "Mr. Monk Meets Dale the Whale."

At least, they brought back the *character* of Dale the Whale. But the actor beneath those eight hundred pounds of flab this time was Tim Curry, perhaps best known as the legendary Dr Frank-N-Furter of *The Rocky Horror Picture Show,* but more recently the regal King Arthur in the Broadway hit *Spamalot.* What happened to Adam Arkin? "We had casting conflicts," Breckman explains. Arkin's schedule didn't jibe with the *Monk* production schedule. It happens all the time. Such is the life of a busy actor.

Replacing a character—even a memorable character—isn't unusual on TV. As Stanley Kamel observes, "It's sort of like the Darrins in *Bewitched* (played, in different seasons, by Dick York and Dick Sargent)." The producers were happy with Arkin, and equally happy with Curry, who gave the character a somewhat more jovial (although still threatening) demeanor. But if Dale returns to the show, there's no telling who'll be inside the fat suit. "With Tim working on Broadway, who knows if we'll be able to get him next time," comments a resigned Breckman.

While Dale's role in the story, whoever played him, was consistent throughout the writing process, the motive behind the murder of the death row inmate was not. "Originally, the guy was going to be electrocuted, not lethally injected," Hy Conrad explains. "And it turns out that when he was a baby, his parents had tattooed a Swiss bank account number on his head—so he was killed before his head could be shaved, revealing the number. That was kind of an odd idea. I think we're better off with what we ultimately did."

Although Dan Dratch, who had pitched the tattoo idea, can see the point, he doesn't quite agree. "I thought the head-shaving idea was more refined than *liquefying his organs,*" he says with a shudder.

Taking note of Monk's surroundings, composer Jeff Beal took a break from the usual jazz emphasis of the soundtrack to work in some hip-hop musical loops. "It's fun to vary the use of the music to fit the specifics," he says. The episode was shot in an actual prison, the Lincoln Heights Jail located just a few miles north of downtown Los Angeles. Filming in California prisons is not allowed, but the Lincoln Heights Jail has been closed since 1968. The location has been seen in uncountable movies and television shows. But beyond that obvious use, various rooms in the facility house a youth club, a theatre group, and a cultural center.

As the Season Two finale, "Mr. Monk Goes to Jail" was written as a cliffhanger, with Monk and Sharona making plans for a trip to Manhattan in search of Trudy's killer. That episode would open Season Three. "The mystery itself was self-contained," Andy Breckman says. "But we wanted to end the season on a mysterious note, teasing the audience with something that would come later," he adds. The director attempted to enhance that sensation by having Dale turn his ominous gaze directly toward the camera (and the audience) in the last shot, "breaking the fourth wall," so to speak.

Did the tactic work? Not so much. "I was hoping to get a 'Who shot J. R.' sort of buzz going," Breckman sighs, "but we couldn't get arrested."

The Quotable *Monk*

"There's the Adrian Monk we know and love. Your fear is huge. But your curiosity is huger."—Dale the Whale

The Weirdest Clue: Monk pegs the tallest prisoner in the yard with his shirtsleeves rolled down as the man who stole Spyder's watch.

Idiosyncrasy of the Week: Monk frisks himself because he can't bear to let the guard pat him down.

The Clue that Breaks the Case: Monk's realization that Mrs. Fairbourn hid the TV remote during the interview with the author of the Lambert Lawson tell-all book leads him to the motive behind Kaspo's murder.

Season Three

"Adrian, Sharona is moving on with her life, and if you loved her, you'd be happy for her"

By the time *Monk* began gearing up for Season Three, the idea of producing original programming for basic cable was becoming commonplace. Still, *Monk* managed to stand out from the crowd as unique. Elsewhere on USA, ongoing genre hits like *The Dead Zone* and newcomer *The 4400* were gauged for a specific sci-fi audience. Across the dial, intelligent but cynical and often dark fare such as *Nip/Tuck* and *The Shield* were produced for an adult audience. But *Monk* was a family show, with its characters, plot twists, and even its *violence* somehow permeated with an aura of fun and good will that viewers, both young and old, responded to. "When people found out I worked with *Monk*, they just wanted to rhapsodize about it," Paolo de Oliveira says. "That's really gratifying. It was the first show that I'd done in recent years that people wanted to see go on forever. I refer to it as the crown jewel."

And yet, in spite of all that good will, the third season got off to a bumpy start. Reviews for the premiere episode, "Mr. Monk Takes Manhattan," were mixed at best. Critics and viewers weren't thrilled about taking Monk out of his natural (so to speak) environment. And yet, Andy Breckman doesn't feel the episode would have made such a negative impression on the audience if it hadn't been the first one up to the plate. "The biggest mistake we made was airing 'Manhattan' as the season premiere," Breckman says. "If we'd aired it fourth or fifth, I don't think anyone would have remarked on it. Airing it first was like claiming we were putting our best foot forward, so it was judged differently."

Unfortunately, they stubbed their metaphorical toes the following week as well. "The second biggest mistake we made was airing 'Panic Room' right after 'Manhattan,' " Breckman notes with a sigh. "Both of those shows had very silly elements, and to the casual viewer, they seemed to mark a change of tone. But that was misleading, because the rest of the season didn't follow that example at all." In fact, by the third episode, the critics were back in the *Monk* camp, and by the fourth, the ratings had risen, and the series was back on track.

Unlike many hour-long shows, which often include running story lines, each Monk episode is written and produced to stand alone, for the most part self-contained, with very few plot points carrying over from week to week. It's been that way since the pilot. "The concept was that TV stations could rerun any episode from any season, and viewers wouldn't notice if they weren't in order," Tom Scharpling explains. "Of course, that's assuming there are no cast changes," he adds with a wry smile.

No one wanted changes among the principal characters, but as Robert Burns so poetically observed, "The best laid schemes o' mice and men, gang aft a-gley." And by the middle of Season Three, "a-gley" was the order of the day. Bitty Schram would no longer be with the show, so the character of Sharona Fleming, too, was suddenly gone. And Monk wasn't the only one rattled. "It was scary and risky to have such a big change," Randy Zisk admits. "We didn't know what would happen to the chemistry of the show."

"We'd had the dynamic down cold," Tom Scharpling says. "And we could have done it forever, but then Monk's assistant changed in midstream." The change had an impact on all the characters, not just Monk, he explains. "It was different for Disher. It was different for Stottlemeyer. Suddenly, we had a whole new set of equations to play with. And because Natalie is a different person than Sharona, we could get some surprises from her. That was a benefit we hadn't expected. It gave us a shot in the arm."

Still, the filmmakers found themselves worrying about how fans of the show would react to the change. The pressure involved in crafting the first Natalie episode was intense. "I knew it was going to be very important," Breckman says. "Writing it was like pitching a championship game. The series was on the line."

Even if Breckman's initial script with Natalie worked, the pressure would continue. Several scripts already had been written that featured Sharona, and half a dozen others had been formulated with her in mind. The new character would have to fit into those scripts—which meant extensive revisions were in order.

"We started retrofitting Sharona episodes for Natalie," Hy Conrad notes. But not every bit of Sharona-like behavior was excised. Monk is Monk, after all, and some of the traits that bugged Sharona were bound to bug a new assistant. Sometimes this worked fine. Other times, not so much. "When Natalie complains about needing to get her expenses paid (in "Mr. Monk vs. the Cobra"), the lines would have seemed more natural coming from Sharona's mouth," Conrad says. "Coming from the new assistant, it seemed harsh."

As the writers struggled with creating a new character on the page, the casting department struggled to find that new character in the flesh. When actress Traylor Howard's manager told her about a casting search at USA Network, she was busy developing her own show and initially didn't wish to be involved. "Writing and producing my own show was my next move, and I didn't want to get distracted," Howard says. "But I had known Randy Zisk from a long time ago (she'd worked with him on an episode of *Lois and Clark*), so I went in."

Howard had extensive experience at interviewing and reading for roles, so she wasn't the least bit anxious about this one. At least not until she got some last-minute advice from the director. "Just before I stepped into a room filled with suits," she relates, "the director came out and said to me, 'Don't get too sitcommy.' And I said, 'What does that mean?' It was literally just before they opened the door!"

Despite that sudden injection of doubt, the suits liked what they saw and offered her the role. "They were very open," Howard says. "It went well." So well, in fact that she set aside her other plans and accepted the part of Natalie Teeger, Monk's new assistant. Her first appearance would be in "Mr. Monk and the Red Herring."

The critics liked her, too. Writing for *Daily Variety,* columnist Brian Lowry enthused, "Howard's addition brings an infusion of creative energy, enabling Monk to be seen

through a fresh set of eyes." Thankfully the fans, too, were generous in their praise.

Obviously, with Sharona's character no longer a part of the series, her son, Benjy, played by Kane Ritchotte, also had to be set aside. "We still wanted Monk to have family, because that element had been working for us," Andy Breckman says. The creators knew that Natalie should be different from Sharona, but not too different, so they gave her a daughter, Julie. "We auditioned three girls," Traylor Howard recalls. "All three were wonderful, but Emmy Clarke just had a different energy from the others."

Emmy Clarke is a Connecticut native. Her previous credits include an HBO movie titled *My House in Umbria,* which starred Dame Maggie Smith. "I auditioned for *Monk* on videotape," the young actress says, "and then one night while I was doing my homework they called me and asked if I could fly to California *tomorrow!* The only thing I was worried about was if the person playing my mother would be some mean lady. But then I read with Traylor and Tony, and they were both so nice."

The production company experienced a few additional changes. Freelance writer Joe Toplyn joined the staff as story editor; Hy Conrad was promoted to story editor, Dan Dratch to executive story editor, David Breckman to producer and Tom Scharpling to supervising producer. And Randy Zisk moved from co-executive producer to executive producer.

When award season came around, Tony Shalhoub won his second Emmy Award for Outstanding Lead Actor in a Comedy Series, taking home the trophy to join its twin. To top it off, he also took home his second Screen Actors Guild Award for Outstanding Performance by a Male Actor in a Comedy Series, and received his third Golden Globe nomination for the role.

Randy Newman won the musical ASCAP Top TV Series Award; Hy Conrad received his second Edgar nomination, Best Television Episode Teleplay, for "Mr. Monk and the Girl Who Cried Wolf;" and Randy Zisk was honored with his first Emmy nomination, Outstanding Directing for a Comedy Series, for "Mr. Monk Takes His Medicine."

"Mr. Monk Takes Manhattan"

Episode 3-01
Written by Andy Breckman
Directed by Randy Zisk
Original Airdate: June 18, 2004

GUEST CAST

Captain Cage	Mykelti Williamson
Steven Leight	Jeffrey Dean Morgan
Hotel Clerk	Ajay Naidu
Elmer Gratnik	Olek Krupa
Vladimir Kazinsky	Vincent Riotta
Warrick Tennyson	Frank Collison

Following up on the tip provided by Dale the Whale ("Mr. Monk Goes to Jail"), Monk, Sharona, Stottlemeyer, and Disher arrive in New York City, ready to interrogate Warrick Tennyson, the man who allegedly planted the bomb in Trudy's car. But even before they can check into their hotel rooms, the Latvian ambassador to the United States is murdered in the hotel's elevator. The murderer knocks Monk down as he flees from the scene of the crime—but all Monk gets is a glimpse of the man's left ear.

Although Captain Cage, the NYPD's lead detective on the case, initially thinks the killing was a political assassination, Monk sets him straight. The clues indicate the killer didn't even know who his victim was. The murder wasn't planned—it just happened.

And something else seems to have just happened. Monk came to New York because the district attorney had promised to put him in touch with Tennyson. But now the D.A. has changed her mind. Tennyson's agreed to testify in a Federal racketeering case and has been put in protective custody. The D.A.'s office won't let *anyone* talk to him.

Stottlemeyer negotiates with the D.A. and works out a deal: if Monk helps them solve the Latvian ambassador's murder, the D.A. will let Monk talk to Tennyson. With no other choice, Monk agrees. Following a lead provided by Cage, Monk goes to Brooklyn to interview Elmer Gratnik, a Latvian expatriate who had a political grudge against the ambassador. The lead is a dead end; Gratnik is innocent. But the trip to Brooklyn wasn't a total loss; he and Sharona learn that the ambassador's last words were Latvian for "This is not my coat."

On the way back to Manhattan, Monk gets lost on the subway and winds up in Times Square. By the time Stottlemeyer, Disher and Sharona find him, he's disoriented and exhausted. His instincts, however, are still intact. Looking up, he notices the image of a man on the JumboTron screen above Times Square. After studying the man's left ear, Monk realizes he's the killer.

The man on the JumboTron is Steven Leight. His wife was killed in Central Park a few days earlier. But what's the connection with the Latvian ambassador?, asks Stottlemeyer. Monk doesn't know . . . yet. But after tracking down Leight, Monk notices the suspect has a gold-wrapped mint that's identical to the ones served at a bar the ambassador frequented. And at that bar, Monk observes the ditsy coat-check girl giving the wrong coat to a customer. Suddenly, he cracks the case.

According to Monk, Leight murdered his wife in Central Park and took her jewelry to make it look like a mugging. Then he went into a bar and had a drink. Coincidentally, the Latvian ambassador was having a drink at the same bar. When the ambassador left, the coat-check girl inadvertently gave him Leight's coat. Realizing his wife's jewelry was still in the coat pocket, Leight raced from the bar and ultimately caught up with the ambassador at the hotel elevator. He shot the ambassador and then swapped coats to prevent anyone from finding the incriminating evidence.

With that case solved, the D.A. allows Monk to meet with Warrick Tennyson, who is gravely ill. Tennyson admits to Monk that he was paid $2,000 to build the bomb that killed Trudy. Unfortunately, he doesn't know the identity of the man who paid him, and he never saw his face. However, he *did* see the guy's hand . . . which had *six* fingers.

It's not much to go on, but at least it will give Monk something to think about on the flight home to San Francisco.

"We wanted a big event, but Manhattan overwhelmed us," Andy Breckman says ruefully. "We learned the same lesson that Dorothy Gale learned in *The Wizard of Oz*, that *Monk* works best in his own backyard. We don't need to have big events, and we don't need to leave Monk's turf to make the show work."

On paper, the idea of dropping Monk into the biggest, bustling metropolis in the entire world seemed like a "can't miss" idea. All of the elements that would make Monk utterly miserable (which generally translates as utterly

hilarious to the viewers) were right there: jostling pedestrians, ear-splitting jackhammers, vermin-infested pigeons, urinating subway passengers, and so forth. And yet for some reason, the episode wasn't well received, and, as generally happens when a show misses the mark, it impacted on the ratings of the episode that aired a week later, "Mr. Monk and the Panic Room."

In hindsight, the writers could spot the problems. Seeing Monk suffering in a rattling subway or being pushed along with the madding crowd just wasn't funny. After all, ordinary people *without* OCD symptoms suffer under such circumstances. Monk is funniest when he's reacting to something that no one else would think twice about.

But if some of the Big Apple zaniness misfired, the penultimate scene, where the episode finally gets around to paying off on the cliffhanger from the previous season, was a gem. When Monk turns off Tennyson's morphine drip, he's anything but funny—and the look of horror on Tennyson's face is chilling. Monk's behavior here is shocking, and yet, somehow, the audience is right there with him. *This guy killed Trudy. Make him suffer.* A few heartbeats later as Monk turns the drip back on—crediting Trudy for that small act of pity—viewers breathe a collective sigh of relief. They were okay with him torturing the jerk, but they're thankful that the memory of Trudy has kept Monk from doing something he'd regret later on.

Even though the trek to New York didn't pay off in rave reviews, the filmmakers earned their props for making great use of the location. The beautiful Art Deco locale where Monk witnesses the murder of the Latvian ambassador is the Waldorf Astoria Hotel, a century-old Midtown landmark. The small park where Monk and Sharona find the old men playing chess is on the Brooklyn Heights Promenade, near the base of the Brooklyn Bridge. The rest of the street scenes were shot in Times Square, home to the glitzy theatre district, dozens of tacky souvenir shops, and of course, the world famous JumboTron. Once considered a high-crime district, the area today is safe even for the likes of Monk, thanks, in part, to a very active police presence. Just ask director Randy Zisk.

"We set up five different scenarios in Times Square," Zisk says, "so we had the camera leapfrogging from one set to the next. The crew and I were down the street filming Monk trying to hail a cab while the three-card monte guys were rehearsing their scenes, and they looked so realistic that the police busted them!" Zisk laughs. "I guess we did a really good job at casting those guys."

The clue about the six-fingered man was inspired by an indelible memory from Andy Breckman's past. "I once worked in a place in New York where my coworkers kept talking about a restaurant up the street that had a six-fingered busboy," Breckman relates. "We were so excited about it! A few years later I went back to that restaurant and that's where I started to think about clues to Trudy's murder."

The Quotable *Monk*

You're going down, Mister Pee!"—Monk

The Weirdest Clue: Monk recognizes the killer by the mole on his ear—a task made easier when that ear is supersized on the JumboTron.

Idiosyncrasy of the Week: Monk can't stand the fact that a young skater is missing one glove.

The Clue that Breaks the Case: Monk realizes that the bar's ditzy coat-check girl gives out the wrong coats on a regular basis.

"Mr. Monk and the Panic Room"

Episode 3-02
Written by David Breckman & Joe Toplyn
Directed by Jerry Levine
Original Airdate: June 25, 2004

GUEST CAST

Chloe . . . . Carmen Electra
Leo Navarro . . . . Willie Garson
Ian Blackburn . . . . Stewart Finlay McLennan
Kurt Wolff . . . . Brad Hawkins
Benjy . . . . Kane Ritchotte
and
Dr. Kroger . . . . Stanley Kamel

It's the middle of the night at the estate of eccentric record producer Ian Blackburn. In his home studio Blackburn works on the latest recording of his wife, pop superstar Chloe, who's out of town. When Blackburn hears an alarm go off, indicating that an intruder has broken into the house, he grabs his pet chimpanzee Darwin and heads for his fortified panic room. Sometime later, the police arrive on the scene and force their way into the locked room. There, to their surprise, they see Blackburn lying on the floor, dead of several gunshot wounds and, hovering over him, a chimp holding a gun.

While it looks like an open and shut case to

Stottlemeyer and Disher, they solicit Monk's input. Monk admits that Darwin certainly appears to be the only likely suspect, although a few details don't jibe with that theory. Sharona, however, is certain the gentle ape is innocent and she convinces Monk to keep investigating. The two of them check out Kurt Wolff, the security expert who installed Blackburn's panic room, and also Blackburn's widow, Chloe, who appears to have wasted no time in finding some new male companionship.

There's not enough evidence to clear the chimp, whose likely fate is euthanasia. Unwilling to let that happen, Sharona breaks into the animal shelter and rescues Darwin from "death row," then hides him in Monk's apartment. Monk responds to his new roommate by calmly contacting his psychiatrist—and then he puts a sign out front, indicating that his building is for sale! Dr. Kroger and Monk's landlord, Leo, arrive at approximately the same time. Kroger is impressed; Monk seems to be holding up pretty well considering the mess the chimp is making of his neurotically tidy living space. But Leo isn't happy at all. Monk can't sell the place—he doesn't even own it! And why has he brought a chimp into a "No Pets" building?

When Leo takes off his cap to shoo the chimp off the furniture, Darwin goes bonzo. Suddenly, Monk recalls that the ape acted the same way when he met the animal control officer—who was bald, just like Leo. And, he realizes, just like Kurt Wolff.

In spite of the mess surrounding him, Monk smiles; he's cracked the case. Working with Stottlemeyer, he lays a trap, mentioning in Wolff's presence that there's a damaged digital recorder in the panic room that may have recorded the murder. Unfortunately, they won't be able to access it until the tech guy comes in to repair it tomorrow. That night, Wolff enters the Blackburn house through the secret entrance he put in when he installed the panic room. But instead of finding the damning evidence, he finds Monk and the police waiting for him. Monk's already figured out that Wolff was having an affair with Chloe and that the two of them had been plotting to kill Blackburn for a long time. Darwin witnessed the murder, which left him with the indelible impression that all bald men are bad. And although Wolff made it look like Darwin killed Blackburn, thanks to Monk's incomparable sleuthing skills, it seems the chimp has made a chump of the killers.

Sometimes a delicate sentiment can get buried beneath the fun of an episode. "Mr. Monk and the Panic Room," certainly seems to be about Monk's misadventures with a chimp that allegedly killed its owner. But another story lies in the episode, a pretty strong one, in fact. "Panic Room" begins with Sharona chiding Benjy for getting into a fight to protect a friend who couldn't defend himself. But before the episode is over, Sharona finds herself in Benjy's shoes, defending little Darwin against authorities that want to punish him for something she's sure he didn't do. When Sharona finally tells her son that he was right to protect his friend, it's a tender moment, maybe even the emotional heart of the episode.

Unfortunately, it's the monkey that got all the attention.

"The chimp became the star," Randy Zisk comments. Not that anyone really minded. By all accounts, Darwin (played by a chimp named

Mowgli) was a well-behaved guest star, and his interactions with the regulars weren't a problem. "Bitty Shram just loved him," recalls Zisk. "She was always holding and playing with him. And he was very receptive to her."

Ted Levine, too, seemed to bond with the chimp. Although the script didn't call for it, Levine brought in his own props for the scene where he "interrogates" Darwin, trying to get him to fire the supposedly unloaded gun. The first that the New Jersey–based writers heard of it was when the telephone rang. "We got a call from the set saying that Ted had brought in a fez and cymbals for his scene," says Hy Conrad, "and we said, 'Oh, my God, shoot it—*shoot it!*'"

The episode began with a second-season pitch from Joe Toplyn, then a freelancer. Toplyn offered up the idea that a contractor could build an addition onto a house, but not bolt it down. Then, later on, he could return to the place, jack up the whole addition and sneak back in. That rather absurd idea was quickly distilled to a secret passage into a panic room. "And that," recalls Toplyn, "was when Andy said, 'What if they bust down the door to the room and there's a chimp in there holding a gun?'"

The premise of the episode demanded two "must" scenes: (1) If Monk enters the panic room, there *must* be a scene where Monk panics in the panic room. (2) If there's a chimp, there *must* be a scene where Monk has to be alone with the chimp. The panic room sequence was one of those "fun train" moments that Breckman is so fond of, going on a little longer than you'd expect in order to boost the hilarity factor. But as long as it is, the scene as shot originally "went on for much longer," according to Toplyn, with Tony Shalhoub giving it his all.

As a counterpoint, Shalhoub actually underplayed the other "must" scene, to great effect. "It would have been too obvious if Monk just went, 'Ohhh, nooo, a monkey,' while freaking out," Tom Scharpling observes. "You can't go bigger and beat a chimpanzee at *that* game, so Tony performed underneath the chimp. It was great, and it played right into Tony's strengths."

Although the episode originally was called "Mr. Monk and the Monkey," the decision was made to give it a title that was less on the nose. "We gave it a gentler name," David Breckman says, "because we didn't want to hang a lantern on the fact that we were verging into Disney territory. It's 'Monk with a furry animal,' and despite the fact that *Monk* is often sentimental, we try not to make it too cute."

And yet, the writers couldn't resist forcing the poor detective to accept a kiss from Darwin. "But," Joe Toplyn asserts, "it's almost the last shot. We knew that the kiss could be seen as pandering to our audience's lowest sensibilities, but we gave it to them anyway and got the hell out of there!"

The Quotable *Monk*

"They call it a panic room. I know that's a difficult concept because to you *every* room is a panic room."—Stottlemeyer

The Weirdest Clue: The footprints outside the victim's home show that the intruder walked, rather than ran, away.

Idiosyncrasy of the Week: Panic rooms make the claustrophobic Monk very panicky.

The Clue that Breaks the Case: When Monk notices that Darwin the chimp is afraid of all bald men he realizes that Kurt Wolff killed Ian Blackburn.

"Mr. Monk and the Blackout"

Episode 3-03
Written by Daniel Dratch & Hy Conrad
Directed by Michael Zinberg
Original Airdate: July 9, 2004

GUEST CAST

Alby Drake	Judge Reinhold
Michelle Rivas	Alicia Coppola
Gene Edelson	Todd Stashwick
Benjy Fleming	Kane Ritchotte
Female Country Singer	Stacy Michelle
and	
Dr. Kroger	Stanley Kamel

It's a quiet evening in San Francisco, and Monk has joined Sharona and Benjy to watch a country-and-western special on TV. But mere seconds into the show's transmission, the power goes off—not just at Sharona's house, but also across the entire city. Fortunately for both San Francisco and Monk (who is afraid of the dark), the outage doesn't last long. The next day Monk and Sharona join Stottlemeyer and Disher at a power substation, where they learn the blackout was the result of a bomb. Someone *wanted* the power to go down—but why?

The bomber has left behind a note, deriding the energy industry for misusing the earth's resources. The language reminds Monk of that employed by an antimilitary radical named Winston Brenner in the 1990s. Brenner used to blow up recruiting stations. This latest bit of sabotage seems like something he *would* do—if he hadn't died in an explosion in 1995.

The FBI thinks Brenner might have faked his death, so Monk and Sharona join the police in looking up Brenner's old college roommate Alby Drake. Like Brenner, Alby is a former radical,

and the group catches up with him at the base of a large tree. Alby is on a high branch, waging a one-man protest against a condo developer. Although Alby refuses to cooperate with the investigation, he's troubled when Stottlemeyer informs him that three people died as a result of the blackout. After the group leaves, Alby phones his old friend and chides him for causing innocent bloodshed. He warns Brenner not to let it happen again. A short time later, Alby is murdered.

Monk concludes that Brenner, who undoubtedly wanted to keep his old friend from ratting him out, killed Alby. That evening, Monk nervously accepts a date with Michelle, the public relations officer for the power company. Things don't start out too well for the couple; Michelle has chosen a restaurant located on the fifty-second floor of a building, and when Monk balks at taking the elevator, they use the stairs—and miss their reservation. Hungry and exhausted, Michelle insists that they take the elevator back down. Meanwhile, Sharona attempts to watch a rebroadcast of the country-and-western special. But just as the special begins, the power goes out, leaving Sharona in the dark and Monk and Michelle trapped in the elevator. After his date, Monk's curiosity is piqued when Sharona mentions that the music special was interrupted again. Could someone be trying to prevent the viewers of San Francisco from seeing that show?

Monk obtains a tape of the special from a local TV station and he and Sharona finally watch it at his place. Monk quickly realizes why the power has been going out. At one point in the show, a female singer steps off the stage to flirt with a man in the audience. Monk recognizes the man as Gene Edelson, an engineer at the power company. Edelson, Monk deduces, is actually Winston Brenner. Edelson knew that anyone watching this special might recognize him as Brenner—and he'd do anything to stop that from happening.

Suddenly the power goes out again, but this time, only on Monk's block. Edelson/Brenner has cut the power and is coming after the detective! Fortunately, Monk manages to keep the killer at bay just long enough for Stottlemeyer to show up and arrest him. With the resolution of the city's blackouts, Monk bids good-bye to Michelle. Their date didn't go very well, but she's open to seeing him again—if Monk ever manages to get past his hang-ups.

Although the writers don't consider "Mr. Monk and the Blackout" one of their best ("It's an insane story," admits Andy Breckman), there is one aspect of it that they really like. "It's notable because Monk goes on a date," says Hy Conrad. "That was fun."

Fun? Walking up fifty-two flights of stairs to a restaurant only to find your reservation has been bumped? Sharing way too much time in an elevator with a claustrophobe who keeps murmuring, "Lobby, lobby, lobby"? It probably wasn't much fun for Monk *or* his date Michelle (played by Alicia Coppola). But no doubt most of the audience thought it was fun. For executive producer David Hoberman, however, the fictional experience resembled just another day at the office.

Hoberman readily admits to disliking elevators. In fact, he'll happily tell you all about the lengths he'll go to in order to avoid stepping into one. "I was going to go down an elevator," he says, referring to a memorable incident. "I waited for someone to ride down with me, because I'd rather have a companion in there, whether I know the person or not. I waited for five minutes, but nobody came. Then I saw a door to the stairs. I opened it, and I could see another door inside. I didn't know if that fire door would lock itself, and there was no way to test it, but there was a paper towel rack nearby. So I got a sheet and wedged it in the door, went to the inner door, found out there was yet *another* door, had to go back out, get another sheet of paper, and wedge it in that one. I had to do that four times. It took me fifteen minutes to get down to the floor I needed to be on. I could have taken the elevator and been down there in fifteen seconds.

"Now I think," Hoberman continues, "that if we were to film that, with Monk running back, getting a paper towel, thinking 'Oh, another door,' running back, getting another paper towel, it might play very Lucille Ball–like. But it was torture for me."

And how does the executive feel about people knowing this about him? "There was an article about me in the *Los Angeles Times* that said it all," Hoberman says with a shrug. And after all, it was his childhood phobias that helped to inspire *Monk* in the first place.

The date scene originally had been written for "The Captain's Wife," but the filmmakers ultimately decided that it wasn't appropriate there. The fluffy subplot of Monk's date just didn't seem to mesh with the captain's palpable anguish over his injured wife. "It was too much character stuff at the expense of the mystery," says Tom Scharpling, "But we knew the date idea was good and would find a better slot somewhere else."

"Mr. Monk Gets Fired"

Episode 3-04
Written by Peter Wolk
Directed by Andrei Belgrader
Original Airdate: July 16, 2004

GUEST CAST

Karen Stottlemeyer	Glenne Headly
Commissioner Brooks	Saverio Guerra
Paul Harley	Brennan Elliott
Larysa Zeryeva	Andreea Radutoiu
Ms. Lennington	Molly Hagen
Maintenance Worker	Todd Waring
Medical Examiner	Scott Adsit
and	
Dr. Kroger	Stanley Kamel

Paul Harley tells his lovely mistress Larysa Zeryeva that he has a surprise for her. After blindfolding her, he leads her into his garage, where (surprise!) he smashes her in the head with a tire iron. Then he proceeds to cut up her body with a chainsaw.

Over at police headquarters Stottlemeyer tries to crack an arson case that took place at a wig factory while his filmmaker wife Karen documents day-to-day activity in the precinct. However, when Stottlemeyer's new boss, Commissioner Brooks, arrives, the captain realizes it was a bad day for Karen to start shooting. Never a pleasant man, Brooks is on a real tear, criticizing Stottlemeyer and his team for wasting time on the arson when a far more pressing crime is at hand. A woman's torso has washed ashore in the San Francisco Bay—and Brooks wants *that* case given top priority.

Stottlemeyer brings Monk into the case, but before they can get started, they see someone steal the commissioner's hat right off his head. It's an odd crime, but Brooks tells Stottlemeyer to ignore it and focus on the torso case.

At the medical examiner's office, Monk immediately discerns some important clues about the identities of both the anonymous victim and her killer. But Monk's clever deductions are overshadowed when he makes a tremendous blunder, inadvertently deleting years of forensic records as he attempts to clean the M.E.'s untidy keyboard. Infuriated, the commissioner removes Monk from the case and yanks his detective's license.

With the devastated Monk out of the picture, Stottlemeyer and Disher hone in on Paul Harley as their prime suspect. Harley has all the characteristics that Monk had predicted about the killer *and* he was known to be involved with Larysa Zeryeva, a woman who fits Monk's profile of the victim. Unfortunately Harley's house and garage have been scrubbed clean; there's not an iota of Larysa's DNA left that will help the police to positively identify the torso.

Monk actually manages to land a job as a magazine proofreader, but he doesn't really want it. As he bemoans his fate to Sharona, a story in the newspaper catches his eye. Apparently someone has tried to steal the commissioner's hat *again*. As Monk considers the oddity of the crime, he realizes that the theft is connected to the torso murder and he solves the case!

The captain calls the commissioner to his office where Monk and Sharona explain what happened while Karen films the revelation. Paul Harley killed his girlfriend, Larysa, cut her up, and dumped her body in the bay. When her unidentified torso was recovered, Harley hurriedly wiped out any trace of Larysa in his home. But as he cleaned, he found a receipt indicating that shortly before her death Larysa had sold her long tresses to a wig maker. Harley was so desperate to get that hair, which was full of Larysa's incriminating DNA, that he burned down the wig place. Unfortunately, the hair already had been made into a toupee—for the Commissioner! The hat thief was Paul Harley, but he wasn't after the hat—he was after the toupee.

Brooks is reluctant to part with his hairpiece, but Sharona snatches it from his head, providing the police with the proof they need to bust Harley. And, since Brooks really doesn't want his "scalping" made public by Karen's documentary, it also gives Stottlemeyer the leverage he needs to get Monk's license restored.

Even when outside writers join Andy Breckman and his band of New Jersey in-house scribes, the writing process remains a group effort. Case in point: When freelancer Pete Wolk left the *Monk* writers' office after five days of story conferences, he was carrying a nine-page, single-spaced outline that would become the fifty-five-page script to "Mr. Monk Gets Fired." That document, Wolk says, "included the teaser, each act, every scene in each act, and the beats for each scene. It even had little pieces of dialogue. When I went home with it, I felt that I really had something to work with."

"Gets Fired," would be Wolk's first *Monk* script, but he wasn't a newcomer to the business. He'd cowritten numerous courtroom dramas dealing with subject matter that, as a practicing criminal defense attorney in Brooklyn, he was more familiar with. But while Wolk's scripts for *The Defenders* were worlds away from the ones he'd write for *Monk*, the lawyer already had a handle on the type of humor Andy Breckman likes. "Andy is my brother-in-law," Wolk notes. "I've known him for a long time."

The story for "Gets Fired" grew out of a rather hair-brained idea. "We thought it would be cool if the key missing piece of evidence was on someone's toupee," Wolk says. "So Monk would have to get it away from someone who denies being bald." That initially led the group to speculate on which of their regular characters would be "follicley challenged." After considering the ongoing impact that the revealed secret would have on a regular character, they took the story in a different direction and opted to create a new police commissioner.

Now they had a clue that breaks a case—but they didn't have a plot to go with it. "We were stuck in a rut trying to break that story," Tom Scharpling says. "It finally opened up when we hit on the idea of Monk getting fired. That's the last thing that came up, and it's what made the story work. It was the missing piece of the puzzle."

Much of the episode's humor springs from Karen Stottlemeyer's efforts to document her husband's work, a conceit that originated in Andy Breckman's fondess for the British TV show *The Office*. "At the time it was a little cult hit, and I thought it was brilliant," Breckman says. "But after we did 'Gets Fired,' it became very, very popular and I was a bit embarrassed by the thought that everybody could see where we'd pilfered the idea from."

Actress Glenne Headly loved becoming the show's de facto *cinema verite auteur*. "I think it would be really fun, and probably really hard, to be a documentary filmmaker," she says. "It would take a lot of training and determination." Of course, determination is a word that fits Karen Stottlemeyer to a tee, particularly when she's manipulating her husband into allowing her to continue filming in his station by telling him, "Leland, this is the most important thing I've ever done in my entire life, and to stop now would destroy me—but if you want me to, I will."

"The object is to be funny," Headly says of the soft-voiced, iron-willed woman she plays. "And in that scene, the object is to be *really* funny."

The Quotable *Monk*

"I had a great job. I was a cop. That's all I ever wanted to be. Couldn't fix the world—I knew that. But I could fix little pieces of it. One little piece at a time. Put things back together. I need it. I miss it so much."—Monk

The Weirdest Clue: The victim's torso: From one quick look Monk knows her approximate age, place of birth and that her killer was left-handed.

Idiosyncrasy of the Week: Monk's "germophobia" compels him to pelt a defenseless little boy with cough drops.

The Clue that Breaks the Case: When Monk reads that the "Mad Hatter" succeeded in stealing the commissioner's hat on his second attempt, but then just threw it away, he realizes what the thief was after.

"Mr. Monk Meets the Godfather"

Episode 3-05
Written by Lee Goldberg & William Rabkin
Directed by Michael Zinberg
Original Airdate: July 23, 2004

GUEST CAST

Salvatore Lucarelli	Phillip Baker Hall
Tony Lucarelli	Lochlyn Munro
Phil Bedard	Devon Gummersall
Agent Colmes	Rick Hoffman
Benjy Fleming	Kane Ritchotte
Jimmy Lu	Brian Tee
Norm	Jimmie F. Skaggs

After five members of the mob are gunned down in a barbershop by unknown assailants, Salvatore Lucarelli, the West Coast Godfather himself, asks Monk to find the killers and prevent a potential mob war. Monk doesn't want to have any dealings with Lucarelli, but the Feds want Monk to take the job and assist in bringing down Lucarelli's organization. Although

Stottlemeyer advises Monk not to capitulate, the detective agrees to take the case.

Monk is told there was a witness to the massacre; a man who says he saw three men enter the barbershop, and then heard gunfire from within. Monk heads to the crime scene first. There he finds some puzzling pieces of evidence. The barbershop's gumball machine is missing, and there's an unfinished crossword puzzle that Monk is certain belonged to one of the hit men. And Stottlemeyer notes that the bullets in all five victims came from one gun. Three killers, but only one gun? Another oddity.

Monk interviews the sole witness, Phil Bedard, an employee of the U.S. Mint. Bedard describes the jacket of one of the men he saw. It sounds like the type of garb that would be worn by the Tongs, a local Chinese gang. Monk pays a visit to Jimmy Lu, the Tongs' leader, but Lu denies being involved in the murders.

Returning to the barbershop, Monk again focuses on the missing gumball machine. If the killers only used it to break the window for their exit, why didn't they leave it behind? Suddenly he realizes that the crime had nothing to do with the mob or its enemies. Someone *wanted* them to think so, but it was really all about gumballs.

When Monk revisits Phil Bedard, he finds the Mint employee occupied with a crossword puzzle. Monk shows Bedard a surveillance photo of the front of the barbershop, taken by the Feds the day before the massacre. The photo shows Bedard exiting the shop and blowing a big bubble—the kind of bubble you can only make if you're chewing, say, five gumballs.

As Bedard listens nervously, Monk explains his theory of what happened. Bedard stole five rare pennies from the Mint, but as he left his place of employment, he noticed that he was being followed by one of the Mint's security guards. It was standard Mint procedure to randomly follow employees, but seeing as Bedard *did* have the purloined items on him, he panicked and ran into the barbershop, not knowing it was a front for Lucarelli's gang. He fed the pennies into the gumball machine and left. The next day, he returned to the shop and tried to retrieve the pennies. Unfortunately, one of Lucarelli's men spotted him, so Bedard grabbed the mobster's weapon and killed him, along with four other guys in the back of the shop. Then he grabbed the entire gumball machine and split. Although Monk doesn't have proof of what transpired, Bedard opts to confess and turn himself in rather than face the wrath of Lucarelli's men.

When producer Anthony Santa Croce joined the *Monk* staff during Season Two, he inherited a situation that might seem daunting to those with less stamina: extensive location shooting. "Given our eight-day shooting schedule," Santa Croce says, "we should be out [shooting on location] for five days and onstage for three. But we rarely do that. It's more like seven and one, meaning there are lots of locations to find, and all the locations are supposed to mimic San Francisco. That's hard to do."

"I don't know of another show that's out for seven or eight days an episode," Randy Zisk observes, "but *Monk* gets its strength from the location settings. Whether we're at a circus or a school or carnival or theatre, that's where the show really comes to life. Yes, some of our most touching scenes are onstage in Monk's apartment or the psychiatrist's office," he says, "but putting him outside, around 'normal people,' is where he really shines."

"Meets the Godfather" is an example of an episode shot entirely on location. Sal's restaurant, Palermo, was shot at the actual Palermo Italian Restaurant in Los Angeles's historic Los Feliz district. FBI Agent Colmes' office was in a warehouse not far from the auto shop where Sharona takes her car. It's a short move to the nearby location of Sharona's house, on a "San Francisco–like" hilltop. And the barbershop where the killings take place, along with the building doubling as the U.S. Mint, are adjacent to the famed MacArthur Park near downtown, the same park celebrated in Jimmy Webb's hit song of the same name, with its "sweet green icing flowing down."

"We used an office building right across from the park," Zisk reports. "That's why we chose it, so we could have the characters walk from the building and sit down on a park bench."

The idea for the story originated with that Mint—or, more accurately, with Tom Scharpling's experience with the U.S. Mint.

"Back in the days when I would write anything for anybody," he says, "I wrote a couple of commercials for the U.S. Mint. For research, I got to tour two actual mints." While talking to the employees, Scharpling became intrigued by the idea that "coins with any kind of an error on them don't get off the floor, but they can be worth tons of money because they're so rare," he explains.

Alert viewers, or those with a pause button, may be interested in the bit of Hollywood sleight of hand practiced while the filmmakers were shooting the scenes outside of Palermo. When Fat Tony first delivers Monk and Sharona to the restaurant, note that from the point when Sharona gets out of the car until she gets into the building, neither the camera nor the viewers see her face. That's because Bitty Schram wasn't available when the scene was shot, and a body double in appropriate wig and wardrobe stood in for her. The interior of the restaurant, with Schram as the delightful Sharona, was shot on a different day.

It's all in the magic of location shooting.

The Quotable *Monk*

"I haven't needed a babysitter since I was nine . . . teen."—Monk

The Weirdest Clue: The Feds have a surveillance photo of Bedard walking out of the barbershop blowing a bubble.

Idiosyncrasy of the Week: Monk insists that Jimmy Lu do one more crunch so that he'll hit an even 100.

The Clue that Breaks the Case: The killer could have used anything to break the rear window to make his escape, but he took the gumball machine from the front of the store, and then took the machine with him.

"Mr. Monk and the Girl Who Cried Wolf"

Episode 3-06
Written by Hy Conrad
Directed by Jerry Levine
Original Airdate: July 30, 2004

GUEST CAST

Varla Davis	Niecy Nash
Meredith Preminger	Emma Caufield
Denny Graf	Ed Kerr
Benjy Fleming	Kane Ritchotte
Trevor	David Lee Russek
Mr. Krenshaw	Tim Bagley
Billy	Victor McCay
Max	Todd Allen
and	
Dr. Kroger	Stanley Kamel

Working for Monk is enough to drive anyone a little crazy. Resilient Sharona is usually immune to the high level of stress that accompanies her job, but lately things have gotten strange. In the past few weeks, she's lost her ATM card, misplaced her car keys, and found her TV remote in the freezer. But when she thinks she sees a blood-soaked man in cowboy boots staggering towards her in a parking garage, her life begins to fall apart.

The police can find no evidence that any such man was in the garage, and they advise Monk to give Sharona some time off to relax. Unfortunately, things get worse, rather than better, for Sharona. Meredith Preminger, her creative writing professor, claims Sharona never turned in the short story that Monk's assistant was sure she submitted. Then Sharona sees the bloody man again while she's filling her car with gas.

Desperate for answers, Sharona pays a visit to Monk's psychiatrist, Dr. Kroger. But after she finishes her session, she sees the blood-soaked man once again, hanging from a hook in the ceiling of the lady's room. She runs to get Monk, but by the time she returns, he's gone, with no trace he was ever there.

Convinced that she can no longer care for Monk, Sharona asks her friend Varla to fill in while she takes some more time off. Varla's boisterous personality and her intolerance of Monk's quirks give Monk plenty of motivation to find the truth behind Sharona's breakdown. When Varla, who's a nurse, mentions that no one starts hallucinating overnight and that Sharona's symptoms don't make sense, Monk realizes that someone's deliberately trying to make his friend think she's losing her mind.

Monk goes back to the parking garage,

hunting for something that will prove his theory. And he finds it: the silver tip from the toe of a cowboy boot. He traces the tip to a security guard who works at Sharona's school and rushes over to Sharona's with Varla in tow. Varla informs Sharona that Mrs. Preminger has cancelled class because of her husband's untimely death from a heart attack. By not-so-curious coincidence, Sharona's missing short story, the one Preminger said she never received, was about a woman who poisoned her husband's soup with something that made it look like he had a heart attack. Varla notes that Mrs. Preminger's husband died while he was eating soup.

Mrs. Preminger clearly had decided to use Sharona's story as a blueprint for murder, but she knew that Sharona would recognize the circumstances of Mr. Preminger's death when she heard about it. Therefore, Mrs. Preminger and her lover, the security guard, carefully laid the groundwork to make people doubt Sharona's sanity. They broke into Sharona's house to misplace things, and made her think she was seeing a dead man (played by the security guard) following her around. The pair might have gotten away with their clever scheme if it hadn't been for Monk's desire to get Sharona back and Varla's desire to get Sharona to take Monk off her hands! But with a handwritten copy of Sharona's original story in hand, Stottlemeyer has all he needs to arrest Mrs. Preminger and her boyfriend—and to restore Sharona's sanity.

More than any other episode, "Mr. Monk and the Girl Who Cried Wolf" showcases the considerable talents of Bitty Schram. The actress was asked to display a gamut of emotions that weren't part of Sharona's traditional behaviors: horror, despair, and even dread as she begins to wonder if she's developing the same kind of mental illness that had afflicted her father. Questioning her own sanity, she makes the heart-wrenching decision to relinquish Benjy to the care of his father Trevor. This is not easy stuff, yet Schram pulled it off with aplomb.

Of course, Sharona isn't the first fictional character to be faced with psychological torments of this kind, which put Schram in good company. Ingrid Bergman, one of the greatest actresses of all time, faced a similar scenario in the classic George Cukor film *Gaslight*. "We didn't even bother to pretend that we weren't ripping off *Gaslight*," David Breckman chuckles. "And Bitty was great in the episode."

The 1944 film was so popular that, ever since, the act of methodically driving people insane has been referred to as "gaslighting" them. In the original film (and the play that it was based on), the villain wants to drive his young wife mad so he can have free access to the valuables that are hidden in her home. But trust executive producer Andy Breckman to add a unique twist to that bit of malfeasance. "We wanted to find a way to 'gaslight' a person in advance," he says, "to make Sharona think she's going crazy because eventually she's *going* to witness something," something that someone would like her to ignore because she's convinced she's not in her right mind.

As for the crime at the center of the episode, it didn't come from *Gaslight* at all. "It was suggested by an episode of the sitcom *Doctor Doctor* that I had written," Joe Toplyn says. "In that show, the central character, played by Matt Frewer, helped out a mystery writer who asked him, 'What's the perfect way to kill somebody?' " Toplyn recalls. "So he supplied her with a perfect way of killing, and found out later that the woman's invalid husband had died by that method. I mentioned that story to the group," Toplyn shrugs, "and it led to our concept of Sharona being a writer."

For actor Stanley Kamel, who rarely gets to trade lines with anyone other than Tony Shalhoub, working with Schram presented an interesting change of pace, and he greatly admired her performance in the episode. "The scene where she came to my office and opened up her heart about her father was incredible work by Bitty," Kamel says. "It's on my list of favorite scenes. She adds great color to any painting."

Of course, Kamel can't help having a soft spot for Schram. "When I first read for the part of Dr. Kroger," he says, "it was just a basic interview. But Bitty was in the room at the time, with David Hoberman, and I heard later that when I left she turned to David and said, 'Well there's a no-brainer—that's the guy.' "

The Quotable _Monk_

"I want you to stay with her, because y'all are a perfect team: Sharona, Monk and _not me_."—Varla

The Weirdest Clue: Four dead bugs—in the shape of a trapezoid—on the windshield of Sharona's car prior to her first encounter with the walking dead guy, but afterward, they're gone.

Idiosyncrasy of the Week: Monk takes a passionate dislike to Dr. Kroger's regular Tuesday patient, Harold Krenshaw, whose OCD-like behavior causes him to arrange magazines differently than Monk.

The Clue that Breaks the Case: The silver tip from the toe of the dead guy's cowboy boot convinces Monk that Sharona isn't crazy, and leads him to the lover of Sharona's husband-killing writing teacher.

"Mr. Monk and the Employee of the Month"

Episode 3-07
Written by Ross Abrash
Directed by Scott Foley
Original Airdate: August 6, 2004

GUEST CAST

Joe Christie	Enrico Colantoni
Jennie Silverman	Alanna Ubach
Benjy Fleming	Kane Ritchotte
Edna Coruthers	Maree Cheatham
Morris	Michael Weston
Ronnie	Kyle Davis
Delores	Esther Scott
Mr. Donovan	Patrick Thomas O'Brien
and	
Dr. Kroger	Stanley Kamel

The sun rises above a suburban Mega-Mart, and Edna Coruthers, the retail store's best employee, arrives early for work, as usual. But it seems that someone's arrived ahead of her today; there's a note on her locker, asking her to come to the loading dock. When Edna gets there, a forklift roars to life and charges towards her. Edna tries to flee, but the forklift shoves a stack of TV sets onto her and she's crushed to death.

Although Stottlemeyer and Disher attribute the death to a routine industrial accident, Joe Christie, the store's security manager, suspects foul play and wants Monk to investigate. But

Monk refuses. Christie is his ex-partner, a cop who was kicked off the force years ago for allegedly stealing drugs from an evidence room. Christie tries to show Monk some evidence he found that's related to Edna's case, but Monk is uninterested.

A month later, however, Monk realizes something about that evidence: three letters of complaint about Edna, supposedly from three different customers. But the stamps on the letters all came from the same roll—which means they all came from the same person. Maybe Christie was right. Someone was out to get Edna.

Reluctantly, Monk returns to the store to help Christie pursue the case. The detective goes undercover as a Mega-Mart employee and observes Edna's coworkers. Soon he narrows his focus to Jennie Silverman, a former slacker who's now a model employee. In fact, she's on her way to becoming "employee of the month" for the second time, a title that brings its bearer free dinner at a nearby restaurant, use of the "employee of the month" coffee mug, and a special parking spot in front of the store. There are things about Jennie that strike Monk as suspicious. For one thing, she appears to be friends with a couple of thugs. For another, she's making plans to leave the country. And not long after Monk asks her a few probing questions, the investigator is knocked out and left alone in the store with a killer guard dog. Fortunately, he's rescued in the nick of time by Sharona and Joe Christie.

Grateful for Christie's assistance, Monk takes a closer look at the case against him and finds a clue that clears Christie of all involvement with the drug theft. With the rift over between the two ex-partners, they turn their attention back to Jennie. Noting that Edna had been the reigning

"employee of the month" until her untimely death, Monk wonders if Jennie could have killed the woman for the title. Did she covet dinner at the Lobster Barrel restaurant, or that special mug?

Suddenly it all comes together for Monk. She wanted *the special parking space,* conveniently located over a sewer grate that's in close proximity to a nearby bank. Jennie's two thuggish friends have been digging a tunnel into the bank from the sewer, using Jennie's van as cover for their activities and as a way to remove the dirt from the tunnel each evening. Monk and Christie manage to intercept the three of them as they attempt to make their getaway from the bank heist. Not long after, Stottlemeyer returns Christie's detective shield to him, and welcomes him back to the force. Monk can't help being a bit envious, but he takes comfort in Sharona's counsel: "You're next," she says.

One of the highlights of "Mr. Monk and the Employee of the Month" is the winning performance by Enrico Colantoni as Monk's dishonored partner Joe Christie. It wasn't the first time that Colantoni, whose face is familiar to fans of TV's *Veronica Mars* and *Just Shoot Me!,* had the opportunity to team with Tony Shalhoub. As the Thermian Commander Mathesar in the film *Galaxy Quest,* Colantoni hung on every suggestion made by Shalhoub's Fred Kwan/Tech Sergeant Chen—not too different from Christie's early relationship with Monk!

Christie's prominent storyline meant less screen time for Monk's usual partners-in-crime-fighting, Stottlemeyer and Disher, but they both had memorable scenes. Stottlemeyer's deepening friendship with Monk is conveyed in his good-natured willingness to help Monk perform his compulsive duty to pop *all* the bubbles in the bubble wrap sheet. And while Disher may not be instrumental in catching the bad guys this time around, he *finally* gets a girlfriend—even though no one believes him. It's all in a day's work to Jason Gray-Stanford.

"Some of the best stuff that I've done on the show are things that aren't part of the mystery," says Gray-Stanford. Those times, the actor says, "tell the story behind the story, and that's what makes our characters so interesting. The writers have infused them with real humanity, which, I think is what saves Disher from just being a buffoon."

The idea that Disher had a girlfriend who was a top "wallet model" came from Joe Toplyn. "It was based on a spec *Seinfeld* script that I wrote but they didn't buy," Toplyn explains. "Kramer came in with a picture of a woman who'd answered his personal ad, and someone said, 'Hey, Kramer, you idiot, she just sent you a wallet photo.' It was," Toplyn admits, "very complicated, as *Seinfeld* stories go."

The nugget for the episode's actual mystery—the murder of an "employee of the month"—originated with a trip that Andy Breckman and his wife took to a local store. "We saw an employee-of-the-month picture," he recalls, "and I began wondering if someone would kill for that honor." Once he conveyed the notion to the crew in the writer's room, he says, "we began to think of possible perks or possible motives, and it occurred to me that the parking space could be very important."

Breckman then married that comical idea with a more serious one, derived from an actual incident during World War II. "British soldiers in an internment camp practiced vaulting over a wooden exercise horse that they put out over

the same spot every day," he explains. "It turned out that they were digging a tunnel, and they had two diggers inside the horse. I've always loved that story."

The Quotable *Monk*

"She's one of the top five wallet models in the world."—Disher

The Weirdest Clue: Jigsaw puzzle pieces remind Monk of the stamps he'd seen on three envelopes a month earlier.

Idiosyncrasy of the Week: Monk takes time to straighten a shelf as he flees from a vicious guard dog.

The Clue that Breaks the Case: Jennie's dirt-loaded van scrapes the parking lot speed bump at the end of the day, but not at the beginning of the day.

"Mr. Monk and the Game Show"

Episode 3-08
Written by Daniel Dratch
Directed by Randy Zisk
Original Airdate: August 13, 2004

GUEST CAST

Roddy Lankman	John Michael Higgins
Trudy Monk	Melora Hardin
Kevin Dorfman	Jarrad Paul
Dwight Ellison	Bob Gunton
Marcia Ellison	Rosemary Forsyth
Val Birch	Larry Brandenburg
Lizzie Talvo	Lisa Sheridan

Lizzie Talvo has discovered that her boss, Roddy Lankman, host of the game show *Treasure Chest*, has rigged the show. When she confronts him about it, Roddy admits his culpability, claiming that his debts drove him to it. Lizzie wants to give the damning evidence to Dwight Ellison, the show's producer, but Roddy talks her out of it, promising to resign as host. By the next day, however, Lizzie realizes that Roddy has lied to her. She jumps into her car and speeds towards the studio. But Roddy has sabotaged her brakes; Lizzie loses control of the car on a treacherous bit of road and smashes through the guardrail, plunging to her death.

Several weeks later, and a few hundred miles to the north, Monk is counting the days till Sharona returns from a trip out of town to care for her ailing mother. Sharona has asked Monk's annoying neighbor, Kevin Dorfman ("Mr. Monk and the Paperboy"), to look after the detective in her absence, but Kevin's incessant chattering is driving Monk crazy. When the doorbell rings, it's a welcome diversion, but Monk is shocked to find Dwight Ellison at his door. Dwight is Trudy's father, a TV executive who lives in Los Angeles. He's come to San Francisco to solicit Monk's help. Dwight is certain that a contestant on his game show, *Treasure Chest,* is cheating, and he'd like Monk to come to L.A. and help him figure out how. Monk is reluctant to travel—after all, Sharona isn't with him. But Kevin assures Monk that *he* can take Sharona's place. And before Monk knows it, they're in Hollywood.

Dwight takes Monk to the studio so he can watch a taping of *Treasure Chest*. Monk quickly realizes that Dwight is right; the contestant—Val Birch—*is* cheating, and Roddy Lankman is

helping him do it. But he's not sure *how* they're pulling it off.

That evening, Monk has dinner at the Ellisons' house—Trudy's childhood home. All of his memories of Trudy come flooding back, and he can't bring himself to enter her old bedroom. Trudy's mother Marcia sympathizes; it took her years to be able to open that door. At dinner, Dwight informs Monk that Roddy is going through a bad time. He's in dire financial straits, and he recently lost his personal assistant in a terrible car crash

The next day, Monk and Kevin check out the site of the assistant's accident and find evidence that Val Birch was at the scene. At Birch's house, they discover that the game show contestant ordered a very expensive car not long after Lizzie Talvo's death—but *before* he appeared on *Treasure Chest*.

Monk becomes a contestant on *Treasure Chest* so he can more closely observe both Birch and Roddy. From his new vantage point, Monk easily discerns how the men are cheating. Roddy has been manipulating the cards the questions are printed on to signal the correct answers to Birch. Monk also figures out *why* Roddy is doing it. Birch had witnessed Lizzie's alleged "accident" and recorded her dying testimony, which fingered Roddy Lankman as her killer. Birch then used that recording to blackmail Roddy, forcing the game show host to make him a big winner on *Treasure Chest*.

The case solved, Monk at last enters Trudy's old room and looks at the beloved possessions that played a role in her life, including a childhood diary. Leafing through it, he finds a passage in which Trudy mourns over the loss of her dog Ginger, proclaiming she will never be happy again. A few days later, however, she's happily looking forward to camp. Nine-year-old Trudy sagely observes that her father was right; nobody can stay sad forever. And as Monk studies a photo of Trudy and Ginger, he ponders her words.

During *Monk*'s third season, the writers and producers decided that the time had come to reveal more about Trudy Monk, the character at the tender heart of the show. But what kind of episode should it be? Building a standard police procedural around Trudy's background would bring up questions about the crime surrounding her death, and the writers didn't want to go in that direction. In fact, that would be one of the big mistakes that Andy Breckman takes pains to avoid. "That's almost what my job is, to not make big mistakes," says Breckman. "Letting Monk be reinstated in the Department would be a big mistake. And solving Trudy's murder would be another. In fact, that would be *the* big mistake."

In a bit of serendipity, an opportunity arose for the team to contrive an episode that didn't involve the police. Although it was the middle of the season, all of the series's principal actors (with the exception of Tony Shalhoub) were renegotiating their contracts. This created the window for a different kind of episode, one that took Monk out of his usual surroundings and focused—at least in part—on his relationship with Trudy. It still could be a mystery—but not one set in San Francisco, and it could even involve a murder—just not Trudy's murder.

And so it was that Sharona left town unexpectedly, and Monk found himself with a reason to go to Los Angeles, where he was re-united with Trudy's mom and dad, and the

show's viewers were introduced to a Trudy they'd never known—both figuratively (the young girl who fell in love with the brilliant detective) and literally (a new actress to play the role).

Canadian-born actress Stellina Rusich had been cast as Trudy during the series's pilot, when the deceased Mrs. Monk was thought of as a kind of silent partner for Monk. She appeared periodically, primarily in photographs and occasionally in short scenes. Now that the producers had plans for Trudy to join the repertory in a more substantial way, they reopened the casting process. "It was important that the new actress look similar to Stellina, because we didn't want the audience to think we had changed characters," Randy Zisk says. "We ultimately narrowed the search down to five women, and had them all come in to read with Tony. And Melora Hardin just knocked us out. She had an angelic quality without being too syrupy or heavy-handed. It's a softness that we liked, because Trudy would definitely have that quality."

Melora Hardin has been a professional actress since the day she read for—and got—her first commercial (for the now-defunct Peak Toothpaste). She was eight years old. She has acted ever since, appearing in dozens of productions, from classics like *Little House on the Prairie* to blockbusters like *CSI*.

"Trudy is like Monk's angel," Hardin says. "In 'Game Show' you could see how cute they were together and how excited she was by the mystery of what he does for a living. She was completely infatuated with him."

With the new Trudy in place, and a premise to lure Monk to Hollywood in hand, only one aspect remained to be dealt with: Monk needed a traveling partner. With Sharona temporarily out of the picture, the writers considered bringing back numerous characters, including Varla, the sassy nurse who'd briefly assisted Monk in "The Girl Who Cried Wolf." But they ultimately decided that the reappearance of Kevin Dorfman made the most sense. "We liked the idea of having seen Kevin exit from 'Mr. Monk and the Paperboy' as a rich guy," notes Hy Conrad, "and reappear in 'Game Show' having lost all his winnings," all cleverly encapsulated in one of Kevin's highly detailed monologues during dinner at the Ellison's home. "And since Jarrad Paul is very funny," adds Conrad, "we knew he could help carry the load and bring energy to what might have been a very sad episode."

The Quotable *Monk*

"I went to law school for three semesters. You can lean anywhere you want. It's in the Constitution." —Kevin Dorfman

The Weirdest Clue: The bite marks on the pencil found at Val Birch's house match the bite marks on the pencil Kevin stole from Roddy Lankman.

Idiosyncrasy of the Week: Monk obsessively adheres to the dictates of the studio's "Applause" sign.

The Clue that Breaks the Case: There are two crimes in this episode, hence two separate clues to solve those crimes: (1) Monk figures out how Roddy and Birch are cheating when he observes their interaction from close range. (2) When Monk notices a stagehand using a cell phone to leave a message for someone, he suddenly understands how Val Birch convinced Roddy to make him a wealthy man—and that Roddy Lankman killed his assistant.

"Mr. Monk Takes His Medicine"

Episode 3-09
Teleplay by Tom Scharpling; story by Tom Scharpling & Chuck Sklar
Directed by Randy Zisk
Original Airdate: August 20, 2004

GUEST CAST

Lester Highsmith	Ken Marino
Trudy	Melora Hardin
Dewey	Jeremy Roberts
Scat	Nate Mooney
Uniform Officer	Dwayne L. Barnes
Undercover Cop	James Intveld
Officer Hensley	Grant Garrison
Officer Salvatore	Nick Spano
Burger Girl	Meredith Roberts
and	
Dr. Kroger	Stanley Kamel

As Stottlemeyer and Disher arrive on the scene of a routine arrest, shots ring out and all hell breaks loose. The cops attempt to return fire, but no one is sure where the bullets are coming from. Confused, they call for backup, but seconds later, the firefight is over, as suddenly as it began. In its wake, two facts are painfully obvious: Dewey, the biker who was being arrested, has fled the scene; and Captain Stottlemeyer has taken a bullet in the shoulder.

With Stottlemeyer out of commission, Disher asks for Monk's help. They track down the biker—their only potential lead in the case—but thanks to one of Monk's many phobias, Dewey manages to get away.

Consumed with guilt, Monk decides to take some pills recommended by Dr. Kroger. The psychiatrist had told him that the medication might help his OCD symptoms.

By the following day, the pills have begun to

take effect. Monk has neglected to fasten the top button of his shirt, and he's eager to finish Stottlemeyer's lunch at the hospital, despite the fact that Stottlemeyer's already taken a bite out of it. Stottlemeyer tells the pair that Dewey's been apprehended, but it looks like he had nothing to do with the shooting. However, Disher has found something interesting. The gun used to shoot Stottlemeyer was registered to a woman who committed suicide shortly before the shooting. Monk and Sharona go to her residence, but the medicated Monk, who has loosened up to the point of obnoxiousness, can't

find a single clue. Sharona draws Monk's attention to a picture of the woman's ex-husband, Lester Highsmith, so Monk allows that it might be a good idea to check him out.

After buying a new red Mustang convertible, a garishly attired Monk—who now calls himself "The Monk"—joins Sharona, Stottlemeyer, and Disher at the ex's place of work, an armored truck company. The police are suspicious of Highsmith, but they have nothing concrete to go on. He was at work when his ex-wife Marlene jumped out of her apartment window. He left a few minutes later, in response to a voice mail message she'd left him, saying she was depressed and planning to kill herself. He headed for her apartment, he says, but he couldn't get there because of the police barriers surrounding the region where Stottlemeyer was shot.

The Monk's presence at the interview proves to be more of a hindrance than a help to Stottlemeyer and the others. When his friends attempt to do an "intervention" and take away his pills, The Monk zooms off in his new convertible.

He gets as far as a roadside motel just outside of San Francisco. After trying and failing to engage some college coeds in his own brand of poolside camaraderie, The Monk retires to his room, where the world begins to close in on him. The sight of Stottlemeyer on the TV, appealing to the public for some help on their unsolved case, adds to his feeling of isolation. But the worst moment by far is when he tries to summon up the image of Trudy in his mind— and fails. Apparently, even Trudy has abandoned the new, improved Monk.

The next day, a detoxed Adrian sheepishly meets Sharona at Marlene Highsmith's apartment. When he surveys the room this time, he notices everything he missed the first time around. The suicide note the police found was a fake, left by her ex-husband; Monk finds an impression, in a placemat, of the *real* suicide note. In it, Marlene reveals a robbery that her ex is about to commit. Apparently Lester was telling the truth about his ex-wife's last call to him. What he didn't reveal was that she mentioned her suicide note during the call. Lester knew that if the police found it, he'd end up in jail. When he got to Marlene's building, the police were already outside, but they hadn't gone upstairs. So Lester did the only thing he could think of to draw them away: he drove a few blocks and shot the first cop he saw— Stottlemeyer. Then he went back to the apartment and destroyed the original note, leaving a new one that he himself composed.

Monk and Sharona intercept Highsmith before he can complete an armored car heist, and Stottlemeyer and Disher haul him away. That night, alone in his apartment, Monk is able to close his eyes and envision Trudy lying next to him. He may have all his OCD symptoms back, but he's no longer alone, and from Monk's point of view, that's all that matters.

" 'Mr. Monk Takes His Medicine' was my pitch," says Tony Shalhoub. The actor had been studying Tourette's syndrome, a neurological disorder characterized by involuntary movements and vocalizations, when an idea struck him. "Jazz musicians with Tourette's find that taking their medication inhibits their ability to improvise," the actor explains. "So I wanted Monk to be at that crossroad, of making a decision to feel good or to detect well. Of course, I didn't come up with 'The Monk' and all of that. And," he adds, "it was Andy's brilliant idea to sprinkle in the complication that Monk could no longer conjure up Trudy after he took the medication."

Adrian's alter ego, "The Monk," is the flip side of the phobic character audiences have come to know and love, with an appetite for all the things he usually avoids. "The characterization started with the writers," Shalhoub notes. "And then I got help from Ileane Meltzer, our costume designer, and Randy Zisk, the director. We all had an image of what Monk would have thought was cool back when he was still capable of registering what was cool. It's a mesh of the fifties, sixties, and seventies cool detectives, from the guys on *77 Sunset Strip* through Mannix, Rockford, and Magnum."

The touching scene in which Trudy appears to Monk after he smells her pillow is the same scene that actress Melora Hardin had read with Tony Shalhoub while trying out for the role. Only days later, she found herself saying the lines again, on camera. (Although "Mr. Monk Takes His Medicine" aired after "Mr. Monk and the Game Show," it actually was filmed first.) "Adrian was trying to make a decision, and in his imagination Trudy appears to discuss it with him," Hardin says. "What matters most in his life right now is what she represents to him, something beautiful and grounded and pure. Because he has created her—she's not the Trudy that she was while she was alive, she's Adrian's idealized version of Trudy. She's really more about his memory of her than about what really happened."

As that memory of Trudy appears to Monk, the lighting in his room softens, thanks to some careful planning by director of photography Tony Palmieri and director Randy Zisk. "We give all the scenes with Trudy a sort of glow, to make them feel a little out of this world, a little like fantasy," Zisk explains. "Normally we shoot the show very straight, so that whatever the eye sees, we see. But in this case, we warmed it up with brown and orange lights. We did the same thing in 'Game Show' when we went back to Trudy's house in the seventies, although then we went with cyan, orange and yellow."

Lighting isn't the only trick the director used while shooting "Medicine." The script called for Zisk to shoot a high-speed marathon across San Francisco in Monk's red Mustang convertible—without leaving Los Angeles. "It was cost-prohibitive to go to San Francisico for only one day. We would have had to close the streets and hire the police and rent the trolley cars and all the things that we wanted," Zisk says. Instead, he reveals, "We went to Universal Studios back lot, mapped out a course where we passed four different street openings, and put green screens over each of those openings. Then in postproduction we inserted mattes of San Francisco. Now, you see the Golden Gate Bridge in one and things like the coastline of San Francisco in the others."

And as for that trolley car: "We rented the only one in L.A.," Zisk admits. "Unfortunately, it sits on rubber wheels, so we had to build skirts over the wheels. If you look closely, you can still tell that the bottom half of the trolley is on wheels, but we tried to frame each shot so that the lens was just a little bit above them.

"That's the biggest cheat we've ever done on *Monk*," Zisk says.

All of that work paid off, of course. The show is nearly everyone's favorite. It has heart and humor and scope, *and* it earned Randy Zisk an Emmy nomination. "The Emmy nod was a total shock," he laughs. "When the call came at six o'clock in the morning to let me know, I was sleeping!"

The Quotable *Monk*

"You're bringing The Monk down, man."
—The Monk

The Weirdest Clue: Marlene Highsmith's fake suicide note, written with a red pen that isn't in her apartment.

Idiosyncrasy of the Week: Monk can summon up the image of Trudy by smelling the pillow that she used to sleep on.

"Mr. Monk and the Red Herring"

Episode 3-10
Written by Andy Breckman
Directed by Randy Zisk
Original Airdate: January 21, 2005

GUEST CAST

Mr. Franklin	Anthony Armatrading
Lyle Peck	David Purdham
Mrs. Bowen	Amy Aquino
Julie Teeger	Emmy Clarke
Pet Store Clerk	Adam Wylie
Clemm	Raymond O'Connor
and	
Dr. Kroger	Stanley Kamel

Single mom Natalie Teeger hears a noise in the middle of the night. After checking to make sure her daughter Julie is all right, she grabs a baseball bat and heads downstairs. Suddenly an intruder lunges out of the darkness and grabs her. A vicious struggle ensues, with Natalie fighting for her life. With the intruder's hands around her throat, Natalie reaches out for something to stop him. Her fingers reach a sharp pair of scissors—and she plunges them into her attacker, killing him.

When Stottlemeyer and Disher arrive to investigate, Natalie reveals that this intruder is actually the *second* one to enter her house in a week. The first man posed as a water meter reader—one who never went near the meter. He seemed more interested in her living room, but when Natalie caught him poking around, he ran off. Stottlemeyer is puzzled; Natalie doesn't seem to have anything of value. He suggests she might be able to figure out what the crooks were after if she contacts Adrian Monk.

Monk, however, is in no condition to take on new clients. It's been three months since Sharona moved back to New Jersey to remarry her ex-husband—and Monk is still feeling traumatized. However, Natalie is truly frightened, for both her own life and that of her daughter. She's not ashamed to beg for Monk's help, and Monk finds he can't resist her entreaty.

At Natalie's house, Monk finds a fish net that the intruder brought with him. Was he after something in Julie's fish tank? It can't be the fish—it's a common pet shop variety. Disher reports there was a note in the dead man's pocket. It reads only "2:30 Sea of Tranquility." Natalie notes that the science museum has an exhibit by that name; Julie went there on a field trip a week ago.

Monk and Natalie head to the museum, where Natalie recognizes a tour guide as the fake meter reader. But why would he have tried to break into Natalie's house? Suddenly, Monk notices the stack of Aquarium Fun Kits in the museum gift shop. Something clicks in his mind, and sure enough, when he and Natalie talk to Julie, they learn that she bought one of the kits when she visited the museum. Could the tour guide have stashed something in the box before she bought it? Monk wants to take the whole tank to the lab for analysis, but he'll have to wait till after the science fair at Julie's school. The aquarium is Julie's project.

That afternoon, Monk has two epiphanies. First, he realizes that Natalie might make a good replacement for Sharona and offers her a job.

Then, while reading the local newspaper, he sees a photo of the moon rock that's on exhibit at the Sea of Tranquility exhibit, and recognizes the shape. It's one of the rocks in Julie's aquarium and it's worth millions of dollars! Summoning Stottlemeyer to the science fair, Monk explains what happened. The tour guide stole the moon rock—but he couldn't sneak it past the guards. Instead, he hid it in one of the Aquarium Fun Kits, and told his accomplice to purchase the kit. Unfortunately, Julie got there slightly ahead of the accomplice and purchased

the kit with the moon rock. The two thieves got her address off a mailing list she'd signed.

But even as Monk is explaining all this, the tour guide enters the room, creates a distraction, and scoops out both the moon rock and Julie's fish from her aquarium. Monk gives chase, but when the thief drops both the rock and the helpless fish, Monk opts to save the life of Julie's pet, while Stottlemeyer captures the tour guide—and retrieve the precious rock.

That evening, as Natalie reflects on the decision Monk made, she decides to quit her job

as a bartender and take Monk up on his offer of employment.

The defective detective has a new assistant.

" 'Red Herring' isn't about the mystery," Andy Breckman says. "It was a way to say good-bye to Sharona and to introduce Natalie Teeger as eloquently and as quickly as possible. By the following week I wanted to be in a groove and back on track."

While there *is* a dead body, there isn't a murder. It's pure self-defense. "The fight was

inspired by Grace Kelly's fight with the intruder in *Dial M For Murder*," Breckman admits with a smile. That bit of homage—and the sight of Natalie bravely defending herself against an intruder—seemed like a dynamic way to introduce her to viewers, not to mention a good way to bring her into contact with the police—and with Monk.

As for the rest of the story, as Tom Scharpling notes, "The mystery with the moon rock was small enough that it stayed out of the way of the character stuff. The tough part was that we had to finish the script before we knew who'd be cast in the role," Scharpling adds. "So Natalie wasn't written for Traylor Howard. But Traylor put the new character out there with a bang."

"It was really smart of Andy and the writers to introduce Natalie as a woman who's defending her family and her home, and then to intercut that with Monk interviewing nurses, so that when she comes to hire him he thinks she's a nurse," director Randy Zisk says. "The case and the character introduction just blended together."

But would the characters of Monk and Natalie blend as smoothly? "At the top of Act Four, Natalie is trying to get her paycheck," Tom Scharpling points out. "Monk's all agitated and bouncing from chair to chair, so she just comes over and gently sets him down. That's a real moment of compassion, where you see her understanding what he needs, and taking charge. It's a key moment."

However, it's not how the scene had been written. "Asking Monk to sit down seemed like a simple request, but then Natalie sees how difficult it is for him to choose a seat," Zisk says. "The first few times we shot the scene, Natalie got upset and just angrily shoved him down."

"It was written that I manhandle him," Traylor Howard says. "But it just didn't feel right that she'd be so mean to him. As we worked it out, the action sort of softened, until having me gently guide him down just evolved all by itself."

That may have been the moment that Monk bonded with Natalie; certainly he decided at that point that he trusted her enough to offer her the assistant job. But the scene also provided something of a template for the writers. According to Breckman, " 'Red Herring' was the one episode that season that hadn't originally been thought out as a Sharona episode." So although they were forced to drop Natalie into Sharona scenes for a number of episodes, the writers tried to keep in mind how well that scene in "Red Herring" worked after Howard softened her performance. "We started actively seeking ways to make Natalie more sympathetic towards Monk," Hy Conrad says, "and for her to give him more pats on the shoulder."

"Unlike Sharona, who cared deeply about Monk but was abrasive, Natalie is warmer to him," David Breckman says. "She calls him 'Mr. Monk,' and not 'Adrian,' and in some respects she's a bit like a doting daughter."

Despite the switch from Sharona to Natalie, the ratings remained high for the rest of the season, showing that viewers accepted and embraced the change. "We'd had no margin of error," Andy Breckman says. "We had given ourselves one hour to say good-bye to Sharona and to meet her replacement. If it hadn't worked, there'd have been no series. And since this series is my baby, it was very, very important to get this one right. It was," he stresses, "as important as the pilot."

The Quotable *Monk*

"Are you Monk? Adrian Monk? The detective? The famous, admired, respected detective?"—Natalie

The Weirdest Clue: The intruder left a fish net in Natalie's living room.

Idiosyncrasy of the Week: "The Miracle of Birth" is near the top of Monk's list of phobias.

The Clue that Breaks the Case: A newspaper photo of the moon rock.

"Mr. Monk vs. the Cobra"

Episode 3-11
Written by Joe Toplyn
Directed by Anthony R. Palmieri
Original Airdate: January 28, 2005

GUEST CAST

Master Zee	Mako
Trudy Monk	Melora Hardin
John Ricca	Harry Groener
Eddie	Patrick Fischler
Chris Downey	Mark Sheppard
Talk Show Host	Arthel Neville
First Disciple	Sung Kang

Author John Ricca knew his unflattering biography of martial arts superstar Sonny Chow was controversial, but he hardly expected Chow to rise up from the grave and kill him for it. Yet that seems to have happened. The police find Ricca dead in his apartment, killed with nunchucks, a classic martial arts weapon. Scrawled in blood next to the victim's body is the name "Chow," and clutched in his hand are hairs, apparently from his assailant's head. A DNA analysis establishes that they belong to Sonny Chow.

Stottlemeyer asks Monk to look into the case, hoping that he won't have to tell the public that his prime suspect is a man who's been dead for years. Because there are many rumors surrounding Chow's death—or *alleged* death, according to his fans—Monk and Natalie pay a visit to Chow's mentor, Master Zee. Zee tells them that he was with Chow when the star died. But the DNA evidence means that Stottlemeyer will have to dig up Chow's grave anyway, just to verify who's buried there.

At the cemetery, Stottlemeyer recognizes Chris Downey, a recent parolee that the captain once put away for assault and armed robbery. The jewelry Downey stole was never found, and Downey still claims that he never had it. He's back working as a gravedigger, the job he held before he went to jail.

Once Chow's casket is exhumed, the medical examiner concludes that the body within is undoubtedly Sonny Chow. Someone tried to frame a dead man. But why?

Monk and Natalie head for the Sonny Chow museum, where much of the star's paraphernalia is on display. The curator shows off a hairbrush that contains some of Sonny's hair. Monk quickly determines that the brush is a fake, concluding that the real one was stolen by whoever wanted to implicate Chow in Ricca's murder. As Monk studies the museum's unique hand stamp, he remembers that he's seen that stamp on the back of someone's hand.

Hustling back to the cemetery, Monk tries to explain his theory to Natalie. However, Natalie doesn't want to hear it. She's been arguing with Monk for days. The salary he pays her is fine, but she refuses to continue absorbing the expenses accrued during each case. Between cell phone bills, gasoline, and wipes, she's going broke. She knows Monk pays $600 a month for rent on an empty office downtown. Why can't he close the office and use that money to cover her expenses? But Monk won't hear of it. That was Trudy's office, and he refuses to let go of it.

With no alternative, Natalie takes a stand and abandons Monk at the cemetery. Seconds later, Monk is knocked out by Ricca's real murderer, Chris Downey, whose hand still bears the incriminating hand stamp from the museum.

When Monk comes to, he realizes that Downey has placed him inside a coffin and buried him alive! Unable to deal with that terrible reality, Monk escapes to an idyllic fantasy. Trudy is with him, and he tells her all about the case: how Downey hid the stolen jewels in Chow's coffin, and returned to the cemetery after doing his time in jail, only to find that a heavy monument had been placed over Chow's grave. He couldn't move it alone, so he killed a man and made everyone think the murder had been committed by Chow. He knew the police would exhume the grave for him—and after that, he could get at the jewels.

When Natalie returns to the cemetery to apologize to Monk, she finds him missing and calls Stottlemeyer. Stottlemeyer gets Downey to admit that he's buried Monk, but he dies of a heart attack before he can say where. A detail of cops conducts a frantic search of the graveyard, looking for the burial site. At last they find it, just as an image of Trudy asks Monk to close her office and pay Natalie what she deserves. When Monk recovers from his ordeal, he makes good on his promise, saying good-bye to one remnant of Trudy's life, but knowing that he's fulfilled her wishes.

For obvious reasons, family estates are careful with the reputations of their loved ones. Requests to use the image or even the name of a deceased celebrity are rejected more often than approved. But that didn't stop Monk's writing staff from making not one but *three* separate attempts at achieving their impossible dream.

And who can blame them? Who could resist watching an episode called "Mr. Monk Meets The Grateful Dead"?

It all started with a simple enough premise, posed by David Breckman: a map is hidden in the tooth of a dead gangster, and a dentist wants to get someone to dig up the body for him. But the suggestion didn't quite fly. "Andy liked the idea of forcing the authorities to disinter a body," David Breckman says, "but he felt that the *body* was almost irrelevant. So he suggested, 'What if the body was someone famous?' "

Suddenly a long list of celebrities buried in California was on the table—everyone from Richard Nixon to Jerry Garcia. Garcia made the most sense, because he was from San Francisco. So the writers worked out a plot that essentially hit the same story beats as the ones eventually played out in "Cobra," but that were centered around the famous guitarist. "I wrote an entire script," Joe Toplyn says. "But then we couldn't get permission to use his name."

Okay, if at first you don't succeed. . . . They went to the next name on the list: Audrey Hepburn, which led to "Mr. Monk Meets My Fair Lady." Andy Breckman chuckles at the memory. "I *loved* the idea that Audrey Hepburn was suspected of killing people," he says. "That was my favorite."

The staff modified their Garcia story to fit Hepburn, and Toplyn wrote a script—which was submitted to and, not surprisingly, rejected by the late actress's estate. Then Toplyn had an inspiration. "I'm a Bruce Lee fan," he says. "He's buried in Seattle, but that's close enough for me. And the story lent itself to him perfectly."

Toplyn completed yet another script, titled, "Mr. Monk vs. the Dragon," and after a period of discussion, the family of the legendary martial artist declined the offer.

Still, the group knew this version of the script had potential. So Toplyn "fictionalized" it.

"We were forced into a compromise," David Breckman explains. "Initially we were disappointed, but the episode turned out well."

Perhaps the most memorable scene in "Cobra"—which is directed by *Monk*'s director

of photography Tony Palmieri—takes place in a coffin, where the late Mrs. Monk helps her husband hang onto his sanity while in a very disturbing situation. Is she really a ghost, or, as Trudy herself says, just "a defense mechanism" conjured up by Monk's own subconscious to get him through his psychotic break? It's hard to say. "Trudy is extremely present, strangely enough, for being an apparition," says actress Melora Hardin. "And she's totally resigned about what happened to her." In the end, the only thing that matters is what her presence means to Monk. "I just love the sweetness between her and Adrian," Hardin says.

But if Monk had Trudy's presence to keep him company in the coffin, Tony Shalhoub didn't have that advantage. "In the scene where the cops find me and pull me out, the crew had to put the lid on the coffin for a few seconds," Shalhoub says. "So when they opened the lid, it was like I was like witnessing my own burial. I was in a cemetery, it was dusk and it was cold. I looked up, and standing around the grave were all these people, all these familiar faces, looking down at me in my coffin. It was nightmarish."

"Cobra" was a great success for all concerned, and yet the writers can't help thinking about what might have been. "When the script was about Audrey Hepburn," Hy Conrad recalls, "after they exhumed her body and looked at her, Disher's first line was 'She still has those cheekbones.' It was very, very funny."

The Quotable *Monk*

"Here's the thing: *I* am not Sharona."—Natalie

The Weirdest Clue: Although the killer was wearing a hood, the victim had some of the killer's hair in his hand.

Idiosyncrasy of the Week: When Stottlemeyer pays Monk a visit, he finds the detective polishing his light bulbs.

The Clue that Breaks the Case: The museum stamp on the back of the gravedigger's hand.

"Mr. Monk Gets Cabin Fever"

Episode 3-12
Written by Hy Conrad
Directed by Jerry Levine
Original Airdate: February 4, 2005

GUEST CAST

Agent Grooms	Josh Stamberg
Kathy Willowby	Faith Prince
Hayley	Moon Bloodgood
Martin Willowby	Glenn Morshower
Deputy Coby	Dylan Kussman
Mr. Handy	Paul Rae

Monk witnesses a Chinese gang murder, so he becomes a federal witness under the protective custody of his old pal Agent Grooms ("Mr. Monk and the Sleeping Suspect"). Grooms takes Monk, along with Stottlemeyer and Natalie, to a remote FBI cabin in the woods, where they're to remain until Monk's deposition the following week.

While they're picking up supplies at a local store, the group encounters Martin and Kathy Willowby, who live across the lake from the FBI cabin. The couple doesn't get along very well; she thinks his passion for fishing lures is stupid and he can't abide her fondness for country music. That night, as Monk struggles to fall asleep, he thinks he hears a man screaming in agony. The sound is coming from the Willowby cabin.

By the next morning, Monk suspects that foul play is afoot across the lake. When he sees Kathy Willowby carrying bag after bag of ice into the cabin, he's even more certain. And when he hears Kathy turn on some loud country music, he is convinced that she killed her husband the night before. However, Grooms refuses to let the investigator become involved.

In the meantime, back in San Francisco, Randy Disher has finally gotten lucky. He's met a beautiful Asian woman named Hayley, and she really seems to like him. Frequenting Hayley's favorite Chinese restaurant together, they end their meal with fortune cookies. To Randy's surprise, his fortune comes true in a matter of minutes! Although he initially thinks that's just an odd coincidence, it happens again when they get carry-out food from the restaurant.

At the cabin, Monk can't stop thinking about the situation across the lake. Knowing that Monk's hunches are never wrong, Stottlemeyer agrees to go with Monk to check out the Willowby home. After locking Grooms in the bathroom, Monk, Natalie, and Stottlemeyer take the car and drive towards the other cabin. However, the car becomes mired in mud when they get caught in a downpour. Come morning, they venture from the car and try to find their way on foot.

In San Francisco, Randy gets an alarming new fortune: "An old friend is in danger. Only you can save him." Surely this means that Monk

and the Captain are in trouble! Randy hastily takes off for the FBI cabin, unaware that members of the Chinese mob are tailing him. Hayley has set him up, and now he's leading the gang directly to Monk.

Monk, Natalie, and Stottlemeyer finally come across the Willowby cabin just in time to see the local police pulling Martin Willowby's dead body out of his fishing boat. The police have accepted Kathy's explanation for Martin's demise: he was struck by lightning while fishing during the storm. But Monk asks why Martin would have gone to fish without his brand new fishing lure. Before Kathy can think of an answer to that, and several other questions the trio poses, Randy Disher arrives on the scene— and right behind him, the Chinese gunmen, who begin firing on the Willowby cabin.

While they try to avoid being riddled with bullets, Monk provides his summation about how Mrs. Willowby electrocuted her husband, then kept his body on ice until the next night's thunderstorm, when she placed his body into his boat and set it adrift. At the same time, Disher does his own summation on how Hayley deliberately initiated contact with him and cleverly manipulated him with fortune cookies.

Outside, Agent Grooms has finally gotten out of the bathroom and tracked his cabinmates to the Willowby place. He gets the drop on one of the assassins while Stottlemeyer shoots the other. All that's left to be done is for the local cops to take Kathy Willowby into custody—and for Randy to accept the fact that Hayley will probably break up with him after he arrests her.

"Cabin Fever" was a blend of two premises, each too minor to support an entire episode. The first, Hy Conrad says, had to do with "the great lengths that a person would take to find someone. The second was about an odd fortune-telling machine. When we combined those two ideas, they seemed to work together."

Almost immediately, the fortune-telling machine premise shifted to a newspaper's horoscope column, as the writers contemplated a mystery about someone whose horoscope seems to be coming true. "Then that became, 'What would happen if *Monk's* horoscope seemed to be coming true?'" Breckman adds. "And then the horoscope idea morphed into fortune cookies." Evolution eventually led to a story in which Monk is hunted down by a gang that takes advantage of *Disher's* belief in the predictions inside fortune cookies.

The episode makes good use of the delicate friendship between Monk and Captain Stottlemeyer. While it's not likely that a real police captain, charged with the responsibilities of an entire precinct, would take time to go into hiding with a pretrial witness, viewers have come to expect this kind of behavior from Stottlemeyer, who is increasingly protective of the man who once annoyed the hell out of him. And the two actors who inhabit the characters make the most out of their scenes together. That's true whether they're sharing quiet moments—as when Stottlemeyer gives Monk permission to throw a pan of dirt into a trashcan rather than toss it into the rest of the dirt surrounding the patio—or the outright slapstick of scenes like Stottlemeyer's literally hamstrung exit from his bunk bed. "That's one of many Monk and Stottlemeyer scenes where I just throw myself into it," Ted Levine says. "After all these years, we know who these guys are and what their actions will be. The things we do together happen organically, and we just enjoy it."

"Ted is as funny as Tony in a completely

different way," observes Tom Scharpling. "He underplays things so perfectly, like the ultimate straight man, and it's just hilarious."

However, plans for one scene involving the two men—and Natalie, too—were scrapped when the producers realized that a special "guest" wouldn't perform under inclement conditions. "When the three of them are lost in the woods in the rain," Hy Conrad reveals, "we included a scene with a bear clawing at the car window. Monk goes into a dissociated fugue and thinks the bear is Dr. Kroger. Stottlemeyer and Natalie have to stop him from opening the window to say hello."

Unfortunately, mechanical difficulties eliminated the bear. "We found an automatronic bear," Randy Zisk says, "but we couldn't use it in the rain." And since the rain—artificially produced, of course—was essential to other aspects of the plot, the bear had to go.

One aspect of the episode no one particularly liked was, as David Breckman puts it, "the 'Ma and Pa Kettle' aspect of the show. We're in Marin County, for God's sake. I don't know what those Ozark Mountain hillbillies were doing up there."

While Andy Breckman admits that writing, casting, and costumes all may have contributed to that "bit of misjudgment," Randy Zisk takes it in stride. "Whenever we go five miles outside of San Francisco, we *always* meet the quirkiest and the oddest people," Zisk laughs. "It becomes like the movie *Fargo*."

Still, one person was downright inspired by the "down home" feel of the setting. "'Cabin Fever' had a kind of *Deliverance* palette to it," Composer Jeff Beal says. "So I used some dobro and slide guitar sounds. Just a little bit."

And speaking of *Deliverance*, perhaps the most entertaining part of the episode was the "dueling summations," in which Monk and Disher simultaneously recap their semi-related versions of the day's events. "We always try to challenge ourselves when it comes to writing the summations," Andy Breckman says. "After the third or fourth episode in Season One, straight summations got kind of boring, so we started doing variations. Now making the summations a fun ride is part of the game plan."

The Quotable *Monk*

"Every man's bent antenna diminishes me."—Monk

The Weirdest Clue: "Lightning" struck Willowby's boat rather than his metal fishing pole, which would have acted like a lightning rod.

Idiosyncrasy of the Week: Monk can't bear to throw the swept-up dirt into the dirt.

The Clue(s) that Breaks the Case: For Monk, it's the fried electrical outlet in the Willowby cabin, proving that Mrs. Willowby electrocuted her husband; for Disher, it's the handmade nature of the fortunes from his cookies.

"Mr. Monk Gets Stuck in Traffic"

Episode 3-13
Written by Tom Scharpling & Joe Toplyn
Directed by Jerry Levine
Original Airdate: February 11, 2005

GUEST CAST

Galardi	Jay Acovone
Sgt. Parnell	Steven Williams
Steve Marriot	Matt Champagne
Krystal	Diane Delano
Julie Teeger	Emmy Clarke
Traffic Cop	Keith Robinson
and	
Garrett Price	Larry Miller

At a remote construction site, Ray Galardi awaits Steve Marriot, the environmental activist who's thrown a wrench into Galardi's plans to develop the area. When Marriot arrives, Galardi tries to convince him to drop the lawsuit that's stymied construction plans. But when his words fail to budge Marriot, Galardi resorts to more physical means, smashing Marriot in the head with a pipe and killing him.

Later that day, Natalie is driving Monk and Julie home from one of Julie's field hockey games. Julie needs to use a restroom but there isn't one close by, so Natalie attempts to distract her with a game: getting the passing truckers to honk their horns. But the next trucker who passes the car—a dump truck driver—ignores Natalie's attempts at roadway socializing and speeds ahead.

Inside the truck's cab, Ray Galardi concentrates on his next step. He's loaded Marriot's Volkswagen—with the deceased activist inside—into the back of the dump truck, and now he's looking for a place to stage a fake accident. Reaching an isolated stretch of the highway, he dumps the Volkswagen, which flips over, blocking several lanes. As traffic converges on the site, vehicles slam into each other, triggering a huge multicar pileup. Natalie screeches to a halt just in time, but her wrist is injured.

With traffic at a standstill, Monk leaves the car to see what's happened. The state highway patrol concludes that the driver of the VW was going too fast and lost control of the car. But

Monk disagrees. He's sure the VW never passed Natalie's car, so where did it come from? Monk notices several other things that don't jibe with the state troopers' analysis, and concludes that the crash was no accident.

Miles up the road, Galardi discovers that he's inadvertently swapped his cell phone with Marriot's identical model. Realizing that the police will soon find *his* cell phone on the victim, Galardi heads back to the site of the accident. Since the troopers are keeping unauthorized personnel away from the VW, Galardi murders a paramedic and steals his uniform. But before he can get to Marriot's body, he's waylaid, and sent over to look at Natalie's wrist.

As Galardi is pretending to examine the injury, his cell phone—actually Marriot's—rings. He ignores the call, but Monk observes the initials "E.G.G." on the phone's caller ID window. He also notes that this so-called paramedic is wearing construction boots—and the boots have mud on them that matches the mud on the tires of the VW.

Although Monk is suspicious of the paramedic, Natalie insists that he has a more urgent responsibility: find a bathroom for Julie. Monk and Julie approach a tour bus snared in the traffic jam and ask the rock band Korn if Julie can use their bathroom. While Monk waits for Julie, he mentions that a man named Steve Marriot was killed in the accident. The band recognizes the name; Marriot was a member of the "Environmental Guerilla Group." Monk thinks about the name. Could that be what E.G.G. stands for?

Now Monk is certain that there's something fishy about that paramedic. He accuses Galardi of being an imposter and a murderer, but gets sidetracked when he sees that the wrecked VW is about to be towed away. Monk tries to convince the troopers that the VW is part of a crime scene and shouldn't be moved, but when they refuse to listen, Monk takes desperate action, trying to grab the ignition keys from the tow truck. In response, the troopers handcuff Monk and put him in a patrol car.

When Natalie finds Monk, he fills her in on his conclusions and she sneaks into the back of Galardi's dump truck, hoping to find some evidence. Just as she finds an E.G.G. flag from Marriot's VW, Galardi climbs into his cab and takes off—with Natalie inside!

Finally the police find the dead body of the real paramedic. They realize Monk was right, and allow him to lead them on a pursuit of the dump truck. When they catch up, Monk sees that Galardi is trying to dump Natalie onto the highway. Borrowing the trooper's gun, Monk shoots out the truck's hydraulics system, saving Natalie's life. Then the trooper cuts off the truck and places Galardi under arrest.

Natalie's impressed; Monk came through for her when the chips were down, risking his own life to do it. There's hope for him yet.

Andy Breckman thought that "Mr. Monk Gets Stuck in Traffic" would be the cheapest episode of *Monk* ever shot. "It had only one location, a deserted highway that we wouldn't have to move from, and a bunch of cars," Breckman explains.

Au contraire. "It turned out to be the biggest, most expensive show we've ever done," laughs Randy Zisk. "Just that pileup on the freeway took a tremendous amount of cars and extras. And the toughest problem was that it all took place outside during the day—and we were shooting during short winter hours! A typical day for us is twelve to fifteen hours, but it didn't get light enough to shoot until 8:00 A.M. and it was dark by 5:00 P.M."

"That shows how naïve I am and how much I have to learn about show business," Breckman shrugs.

Joe Toplyn came up with the concept for the episode, not so surprisingly, while driving to work one day. "I was behind a dump truck," he says, "and it occurred to me that a truck like that could dump a car with a dead body in it onto the road at sixty miles an hour. When I got to the office, I dumped that idea into the writers' room."

The group initially had begun toying with the idea while Sharona still was Monk's assistant. But after Natalie became a part of the series, it presented the writers with a golden opportunity: a chance to bring Natalie and Monk closer. "We wanted the emotional heart of the episode to be that Natalie could count on Monk," Breckman says. "So we included a stunt where Natalie jumps from the back of a moving truck onto a moving police car where Monk catches her. That stunt was the inspiration for most of the script. We wrote it backwards from that point. Of course, when we got to the location, we realized that the stunt was too involved and too dangerous to shoot," he adds.

So the stunt was changed to something a bit less risky. Stunt coordinator Charlie Brewer found a safe, albeit expensive, way for Howard to appear to dangle over the moving highway: a green screen placed across the back of the dump truck so that a visual effects shot of the moving road could be inserted during post-production.

"Even though I was hanging in front of a stationary green screen," Traylor Howard says, "it was tough, because I was strapped in and

they were throwing mud at me and blowing wind from a big fan. I kept slipping in the mud and I got covered in it. And then after we'd finished the shots in the truck, we still had to shoot the tag, and they realized I was really muddy." With the hours of daylight running short, there wasn't time for Howard to change into less muddy clothing. "That's why there's a big towel wrapped around me in the final shots," she says.

The episode was filmed on the Templin Highway, a lightly used four-lane road located north of Los Angeles. In order to make it look like a freeway, the crew trucked in hundreds of long cinderblocks and lined them up as a center divider. And the show got an inspired injection of humor from actor Larry Miller as accident chasing attorney Garrett Price. "Larry just took the role and ran with it, improvising all the way," Breckman says. "Just like with Garry Marshall in 'Mr. Monk and the Airplane,' some of the best lines came right from him."

The Quotable *Monk*

"You know, Mr. Monk, there'd be no crime in all of San Francisco if you never left your house."
—Natalie

The Weirdest Clue: The murderer and his victim both have the exact same model of cell phone.

Idiosyncrasy of the Week: Monk pays Julie $10 not to pee.

The Clue that Breaks the Case: Monk learns from Korn that the letters "E.G.G" stand for "Environmental Guerrilla Group."

The Doctor Is In—Analyzing the Scenes

"An odd thing happened to me a couple of years ago," actor Stanley Kamel recalls. "Unfortunately, my mother passed away. That can be one of the biggest emotional traumas of a person's life, so I went to a therapist to talk about it. I had already started on *Monk*, and the therapist didn't know me, and during one of our first sessions, he kind of paused and said, 'You're not coming to me to do research are you?'" Kamel laughs at the memory. "I said, 'My mother passes away—and you think I'm here for *research?*'"

That incident demonstrates how effectively the scenes with Dr. Kroger serve the show. "Several psychiatrists since have told me, 'Oh, you're spot-on,'" Kamel says. "Yes, we're doing a comedy, but the humor comes from playing it for total truth. As Monk and Kroger do a dance, Tony and I do a dance, and we dance with each other very well.

"Dr. Kroger usually serves a purpose in the story," Kamel says, ticking off some of his favorite scenes. "Like when he gives Monk a bottle of pills in 'Mr. Monk Takes His Medicine.' Or in 'The Kid,' when Kroger tells Monk that in his heart of hearts he knows he isn't ready to adopt the boy. But there are other times when it's pure comedy," Kamel continues, "like in 'TV Star' when he tells Monk that he went to a sixth-grade party that Monk wasn't invited to. Either way, it's always delicate, charming, and funny.

"The show is called *Monk,* and Tony is the star, but when we're in that office, it's *my* office," the actor says. "When we go in there, I'm there to support Monk, as his doctor, and Tony, as his supporting actor. But trust me, there's a reason they've never asked me to help out in editing, because all of a sudden they'd hear things like, 'Don't you think we should hold on Dr. Kroger a little longer?' After all," Kamel smiles, "Andy Breckman once told me that without Dr. Kroger, it's just *Columbo.*"

"Mr. Monk Goes to Vegas"

Episode 3-14
Teleplay by Daniel Dratch & Joe Toplyn; story by Tom
    Scharpling & David Breckman
Directed by Randy Zisk
Original Airdate: February 18, 2005

GUEST CAST

Daniel Thorn . . . . James Brolin
Sheryl Thorn . . . . Challen Cates
Lewis . . . . Maury Sterling
Teresa Telenko . . . . Krista Allen

Las Vegas casino owner Daniel Thorn and his beautiful wife Sheryl are about to leave for a fund-raising benefit when Sheryl announces she doesn't have their tickets. As she steps back into their private elevator to return to the penthouse suite, her trademark scarf gets caught in the doors. Before Thorn or any of the startled onlookers can do anything, Sheryl is strangled by the scarf. The authorities classify her death an accident.

A few days later, Monk is awakened by a phone call at 3:00 A.M. It's Stottlemeyer calling from Vegas, where he and Randy Disher have gone for a bachelor party. Stottlemeyer is drunk, but he tells Monk he has proof that Daniel Thorn murdered his wife and made it look like an accident. He wants Monk to join him in Vegas right away.

When Monk and Natalie arrive, however, Stottlemeyer is too hung over to remember much about the night before. He's especially fuzzy on whatever incriminating evidence he had discovered about Thorn. Nevertheless, since Monk is already there, he begins investigating Mrs. Thorn's death.

At the scene of the accident, Monk spots some clues that seem to support Stottlemeyer's theory. And after he discovers that the billionaire had the missing tickets in his coat pocket all along, Monk is convinced that Sheryl Thorn was, indeed, murdered—by her husband.

Using her feminine wiles, Natalie discovers that Thorn was having an affair with a showgirl named Teresa—who just happened to be absent from work the night Sheryl Thorn died. Monk suspects that Teresa conspired with Thorn to get rid of Sheryl.

Returning to the elevator, Monk and Natalie attempt to recreate Sheryl's death—but the recreation proves to be all too realistic when Monk is nearly strangled by a scarf. The close call does establish one important fact for Monk, however. The witnesses to Sheryl's death heard her cries of help coming from inside the elevator. But Monk now knows that if she were choking at that point, she wouldn't have been able to make a sound.

Monk is getting close to an answer, but he suddenly finds himself pulled in another direction. Randy Disher has been hooked by the allure of winning big at the blackjack table and he's lost $35,000. Stottlemeyer wants Monk to

help him perform an intervention on the lieutenant. Monk does better than that. After watching the game for a while, Monk figures out how it works, and his photographic memory actually allows him to remember all the cards he sees. Although Natalie—a former gambler herself—is against it, Stottlemeyer talks Monk into playing blackjack for Randy's money. Pretty soon Monk begins winning money hand after hand.

Monk's success draws the attention of Daniel Thorn. Thorn warns Monk that if he's cheating, he'll know it soon enough, because he has "friends in the ceiling"—security cameras, that is. But as Monk thinks about the phrase, he suddenly figures out how Thorn pulled off his wife's murder.

On the night of the fundraiser, Thorn and Sheryl entered the elevator together, but she never exited. Once the doors had closed, Thorn strangled his wife, and Teresa—Thorn's "friend in the ceiling"—that is, the person hiding on top of the elevator car—lowered a winch that she and Thorn used to hoist Sheryl up through the ceiling access panel. Then Teresa, who was dressed to look just like Sheryl, hopped down and stepped into the lobby with Thorn. They went through their charade of being unable to find the tickets, and then Teresa stepped back into the elevator and began shouting as if the caught scarf were choking her. At the same time, she lowered Sheryl's body down again, wrapped the scarf around Sheryl's neck, and escaped through the access panel in the ceiling. When the elevator opened again, the only occupant was Sheryl, apparently strangled by her own scarf.

Unfortunately, without something more tangible than Monk's brilliant deduction, the police won't be able to get a court order to

search the elevator shaft for incriminating evidence. But at last Stottlemeyer remembers what made him call Monk in the first place. He shows Monk, Natalie, and Disher his copy of a local tabloid, which features two pictures of Mrs. Thorn. One is of Teresa impersonating Mrs. Thorn, standing with Thorn outside the elevators seconds before reentering the elevator. The other is a photo of the real Mrs. Thorn—lying dead on the floor of the elevator. The two Mrs. Thorns look the same . . . *except* for their earrings, which clearly are different.

The two photos are enough to get a search warrant—and they find what they need to arrest Thorn. Monk compliments Stottlemeyer on his insight—but the Captain isn't entirely sure that he's proud of the fact that he can be just as smart as Monk *if* he's completely plastered!

After the less-than-positive results of taking Monk out of his environment in "Mr. Monk Takes Manhattan," the producers knew they'd need to approach "Mr. Monk Goes to Vegas" very carefully. "We learned from our mistakes," Andy Breckman acknowledges. "This time we didn't let the location drive the bus." So rather than set Monk loose in quintessentially wild and garish cityscape of "Sin City," they kept Monk confined to a single garish casino floor. And rather than have him beset with troubles brought on by the location, they assigned that fate to Lt. Randy Disher, gamble-holic.

But it's Stottlemeyer's vice that initially sets the stage for bringing Monk into the mystery. "I loved that Stottlemeyer had already solved the case, but couldn't remember," Breckman says. "That was kind of inspired by a 1947 Preston Sturges movie called *Mad Wednesday*. Harold

Lloyd wakes up, can't remember anything that happened the night before, and it turns out he bought a circus!"

Stottlemeyer's drunken antics didn't go quite that far, but it did provide a comical opportunity for him to sing, a touch that went over so well that Ted Levine would be asked to warble again a year later in "Mr. Monk and the Secret Santa."

Besides providing good moments for Disher and Stottlemeyer, the episode also offered some solid character development for Natalie. Viewers learn that her past includes two years spent in Vegas as a blackjack dealer, and, more darkly, the fact that Natalie once had a gambling problem of her own, one that she surmounted with her husband's help. And, at the end, Monk acknowledges that he was able to walk away from the tables because he had Natalie, a nice way of showing that the team is truly bonding, both on camera and off. "Tony and Traylor really gelled in 'Vegas,'" says Tom Scharpling (who named dancer Teresa Telenko after his wife). "There wasn't a lot of distracting character baggage in this episode, like Natalie running for election or something. It's just a mystery, so you get to see the two of them playing off each other unencumbered."

Getting along with the character of Monk has become a pleasure for Traylor Howard. "Tony is so good at what he does," Howard says. "When we were in the elevator with that really long scarf, he became obsessed with making the scarf the proper length to match a take we'd done earlier. It took fifteen minutes, and," she says, holding her thumb and forefinger a half inch apart, "I swear it was only *this* much, but matching it made Tony feel better."

The scene in the elevator is one of Breckman's favorites, with Monk and Natalie bickering about who's going to play the victim. "That kind of scene, when it works, can seem like an Abbott and Costello routine," Breckman interjects. "Larry David and Jerry Seinfeld also were inspired by Abbott and Costello. That's one of the reasons I've always said that *Monk* is Sherlock Holmes meets *Columbo* meets *Seinfeld*. And that scene in the elevator could have been a *Seinfeld* moment."

While Monk's outing to Manhattan took the entire production company to the Big Apple, the sojourn to Las Vegas only took them to a location across town. "We used the sets for the NBC show *Las Vegas*," Randy Zisk says. "They allowed us to shoot there on the weekend, and since it turned out they were at a different location the Friday before, we pushed most of our shooting schedule into just three days. The *Las Vegas* producers were really nice to us. I don't know how else we could have done the show."

Still, if things had worked out differently, they might have been able to borrow an Atlantic City casino location from a hoped-for guest star. The role of Daniel Thorn originally was written with Donald Trump in mind, and the producers actually offered the role to the Donald, but he turned it down.

The Quotable *Monk*

"There's an old saying: 'Don't change anything . . . ever.' "—Monk

The Weirdest Clue: The victim's thumbprint on the elevator button is upside down.

Idiosyncrasy of the Week: Monk can't look at the Vegas showgirls because they're "naked-ish."

The Clue that Breaks the Case: When Thorn says, "I've got friends hiding in the ceiling," Monk relates the comment to the elevator escape hatch.

"Mr. Monk and the Election"

Episode 3-15
Written by Nell Scovell
Directed by Allison Liddi-Brown
Original Airdate: February 25, 2005

GUEST CAST

Harold Krenshaw	Tim Bagley
Jack Whitman	Nick Offerman
Local Reporter	Sue Cremin
First Attendant	Neil Giuntoli
Julie Teeger	Emmy Clarke
Second Attendant	Christopher May
and	
Dr. Kroger	Stanley Kamel

Natalie has decided to run for an opening on the local school board. She's set up a storefront office, and has a crew of volunteers helping her with signs, mailings, and phone calls. Now, if only she could get the used office equipment that she purchased at a police auction to work, she'd be all set. But as Natalie and a repairman try to open the jammed copy machine, a rooftop sniper riddles the office with bullets. Fortunately, everyone within hits the floor and no one is hurt.

Monk joins Stottlemeyer and Disher on the nearby rooftop, where they find a spent shell from the weapon, which they identify as a Russian make. They also find a curiously folded note that demands Natalie's withdrawal from the election. Monk notices that the sniper spelled Natalie's last name wrong, dropping the final "R" from Teeger.

Who would benefit if Natalie withdrew from the race? The most obvious person is her opponent, Harold Jay Krenshaw, whom Monk recalls is a patient of Dr. Kroger's ("Mr. Monk and the Girl Who Cried Wolf"). But while Krenshaw's personality quirks drive Monk crazy, the detective explains that Krenshaw couldn't be the guy they're looking for; someone *that* obsessive would spell his victim's name correctly.

When Natalie refuses to quit the race, Stottlemeyer assigns Disher to be her bodyguard. As Monk is stuffing fliers at campaign headquarters, he finds a cutout letter "R" and realizes that it fell off of a campaign poster made by Julie. Monk notes that without that R, the spelling on the poster is the same as that in the sniper's note. Obviously, the sniper didn't really know Natalie's name; he read it on the poster. The shooting wasn't about the election—that was just a diversion.

Later that day, a grenade smashes through a window at Natalie's house. Monk snatches it up and sticks it in the refrigerator. The appliance contains the explosion so no one is hurt, but the kitchen is a wreck. Monk observes that, like the sniper's ammo, the grenade was made in the former Soviet Union. The would-be assassin, who apparently has a stash of Soviet arms, is stepping up his efforts to scare them—but why?

Again, Natalie refuses to quit. She explains to Monk that her late husband, Mitch, whom Julie believes to be a hero, is rumored to have panicked behind enemy lines when his plane was shot down over Kosovo. The Navy can't prove he was a coward—but his reported behavior is in an official file. Julie doesn't know about that report, but she might someday, so it's important to Natalie that Julie not feel that *both* her parents were cowards.

At Natalie's debate with her opponent, one of her campaign volunteers, Jack Whitman, hands Monk a new flyer he's designed. Monk notices that it's folded in the same distinctive way as the sniper's note. Is Whitman the sniper? Stottlemeyer runs a check and learns that Whitman's an ex-con. The Feds busted him because they suspected him of being an arms dealer. But with no tangible proof, they only put him away for a few months on tax evasion.

When Monk spots a box that Whitman had used to bring some food from his home to campaign headquarters, all the pieces fall into place. The box is labeled with the name of a defunct copy machine company—in fact, it's the same brand as the inoperative copy machine in Natalie's headquarters. The copy machine belonged to Whitman before his arrest, and he's desperate to get it back. He found out that Natalie bought it at a police auction and tracked her down, shooting up the machine so she'd get rid of it. When she didn't, he tried to get her to drop out of the campaign.

The police catch Whitman at the campaign office, pulling a crumpled document out of the old machine, and Stottlemeyer realizes it's just the proof the Feds wanted: a client list of Whitman's arms customers. It's been jammed in the machine ever since his bust six months ago.

Although Natalie loses the election to Krenshaw, Monk is more upset about it than she is. She didn't quit, which is all that counts to her.

*   *   *

" 'Mr. Monk and the Election' was one of the leftover Sharona stories," Tom Scharpling says. "It was caught in the flux, and it suffers a bit for that."

Indeed, running for the local school board is something that Sharona might have done, but with Natalie just having taken on a new job, it seems a less likely choice for her. "We kind of shoehorned Natalie into the story," David Breckman admits.

"We were all flying by the seat of our pants at that point," adds Andy Breckman.

Freelance writer Nell Scovell, who has a long television career, from *Late Night with David Letterman* and *Newhart*, to the live-action series *Sabrina, the Teenage Witch* (which she also created for television), accepted the task of writing "Election's" script. "Nell did a great job," Scharpling says, "even though she was at a complete disadvantage."

It may seem odd to viewers that Natalie lost the election, since all the attention the shooting must have brought her, she'd likely have been a shoo-in. In fact, the original plan had been for Sharona to win, and Scovell's script for Natalie hewed to that outcome. But then something unexpected happened. "Traylor called from the set while they were shooting, and pleaded with us to have Natalie lose," Andy Breckman says.

"I just thought it didn't play as well," explains Traylor Howard. "I called Andy from the set about five times and told him that just because she doesn't win doesn't mean that she's a loser. Finally I said that losing can make you stronger and she would still be strong for her daughter. And Andy said, 'You just won the argument.' "

"Traylor was right," Breckman says. "Natalie's not always a winner. She doesn't have the Midas touch. She struggles too, which explains why she's empathetic with her boss, who is struggling all the time."

One of Monk's struggles is with Harold Krenshaw, Natalie's opponent in the election, and, on a more personal level, Monk's opponent—or rather, his competition for Dr. Kroger's attention. "That says more about Monk than it does about Kroger," Tom Scharpling laughs. "Because as annoying as Krenshaw is, he's apparently gotten past a line that Kroger will not let Monk cross to get into his life."

But does that mean Kroger's relationship with Krenshaw will be a thorn in Monk's psyche from this point forward? Andy Breckman doesn't think so. "The Zucker brothers, who did the *Airplane* movies, often have visual jokes that they don't call attention to at all," he says. "They have a term for that kind of joke: 'It never happened.' It's a rule that we sometimes play by, too. The next time I write a Kroger scene, I don't have to think about the time he got onstage with that *other* patient. It never happened."

Regardless, adding Krenshaw to the mix is one of two things the writers feel saved the episode from being a mere casualty of the casting change. "Bringing Krenshaw in as Natalie's opponent got the episode over the hump," Scharpling says. The other thing that made the episode stand out was the scene where Natalie confides in Monk that her husband Mitch may have been a coward. "That scene was the key to making everything work," Scharpling points out. "Otherwise, having her decide to stay in an election where she's being shot at would have just played like a death wish."

"Mr. Monk and the Kid"

Episode 3-16
Written by Tom Scharpling
Directed by Andrei Belgrader
Original Airdate: March 4, 2005

GUEST CAST

Abigail Carlyle .... Brooke Adams
Janet Novak .... Nicole Sullivan
Jacob Carlyle .... Michael Goorjian
Theresa Crane .... Mary Mara
911 Operator .... Cleo King
Diner Waitress .... Liesl Ehardt
Julie Teeger .... Emmy Clarke
Raymond Novak .... Daniel Quinn
Tommy .... Preston Shores
Tommy .... Trevor Shores
and
Dr. Kroger .... Stanley Kamel

Frazzled foster mother Janet Novak has five young wards to look after, and it's a busy day at the local park. As Janet's attention flits from one child to the next, she realizes that one of them—two-year-old Tommy—is missing. The police join the search, and before long they find Tommy, safe and sound, holding a little surprise in his hand—a human finger!

The police lock down the park and look for a body, to no avail. Stottlemeyer calls in Monk, who attempts to question the boy—but how much can a two-year-old say? Surprisingly, though, Monk and the little boy bond immediately.

An analysis of the finger provides only a few clues: it belongs to a young Caucasian adult male who plays the violin professionally. Monk and Natalie visit the homes of several violinists, including the residence of Daniel Carlyle. When none of the visits pan out, Monk suggests they go back to talk to Tommy again. They arrive to find Tommy's caseworker removing the boy from the Novak home—standard procedure given the circumstances, she explains. When Monk learns that the family with whom the caseworker wants to place Tommy won't be able to take him for two weeks, he volunteers to take the child.

After a brief period of adjustment, Monk eases into his new role and becomes a doting dad. As he plays some classical music for the boy, he recalls his trip to the home of Daniel Carlyle. Something there wasn't right. The man introduced to him as Daniel had said he'd been rehearsing—and yet his bowstring was loose. He also said he had a concert that night—but no concert was scheduled. Suspicious, Monk and Natalie tail "Daniel" and his mother as they go out, and quickly learn the truth. The Carlyles are being blackmailed. Daniel has been kidnapped. The man who pretended to be Daniel is his brother, Jacob.

When Monk returns to the Carlyle home,

The Lost Episode: "Mr. Monk at Sea"

Hundreds of Monk nuggets have been jotted down on three-by-five cards and pinned to the wall in the writers' room, alongside hundreds of delightful clues that may or may not be used in future scripts. And dozens of plotlines have been discussed and expanded before being rejected or put on hold for later consideration. But only one idea actually has been approved, developed, scripted, and put into production before running aground: "Mr. Monk at Sea."

"It takes place on a cruise ship," explains Dan Dratch, who wrote the script, "and everybody thought it was going to be great—until we started getting bad news from the cruise lines."

While looking for a shooting location, the producers approached a number of cruise lines which, understandably, expressed concerns about their images. "We had lots of back and forth negotiations," Dratch says. "They'd say things like, 'Can you not have Monk make fun of the buffet?' so we'd change that. Eventually we'd changed every element except the mystery, and then it finally came down to, 'Can you do it without having a murder on the ship?'"

Since a murder on the ship is the basis of the episode, the location search seems to have reached an impasse. None of the staff, however, has become discouraged, and "At Sea" still is on the production's agenda. "It might become an episode in Season Five or Six," Dratch comments hopefully. "If we ever get a ship."

Mrs. Carlyle admits everything. The kidnappers made her promise to say nothing to the police. They cut off Daniel's little finger to prove they were serious. The Carlyles were supposed to find the finger at the park—but somehow, Tommy got to it first. Now the kidnappers have asked for $500,000, which Jacob is to deliver. But Daniel's brother is afraid he'll screw things up. Monk agrees to deliver the money in his place, but ironically, after receiving a report from Julie that Tommy is beginning to act just like Monk, *Monk* gets rattled and inadvertently gives the money to the wrong person.

Fortunately, Stottlemeyer recovers the cash, and the kidnappers agree to give the Carlyles another opportunity to hand over the ransom. In the meantime, Monk pays a visit to Dr. Kroger. Kroger can see how fond Monk has become of Tommy, but he feels obliged to tell him that he doesn't think Monk is ready for the full-time responsibility of raising a child.

That night, as Monk prepares to read Tommy a bedtime story, he discovers that Tommy has taken a lipstick from Natalie's purse. Suddenly, Monk knows exactly how Tommy found the finger—and who the kidnappers are. After placing a call to Stottlemeyer to fill him in, Monk makes up a story for Tommy, conveying all the details of the case in fairy tale form. Prince Tommy's wicked foster parents kidnapped the violinist and cut off his finger, Monk explains. But before they could get the digit to the Carlyles, clever Prince Tommy found the finger in his foster mother's purse and ran off with it.

By the time Monk finishes the summation, and Tommy is asleep, Monk concludes the tale for himself, confessing that he knows the little boy will never live "happily ever after" if he remains in the home of a man who can barely take care of himself—so they'll have to say good-bye.

Not long after, Stottlemeyer, Disher, and a heavily armed SWAT team rescue Daniel Carlyle and arrest the Novaks. And a few days later, Monk gives Tommy to his new parents, advising them to let him get dirty, because "kids should get dirty." And then Monk sadly watches the little prince go off to his wonderful new life.

Many *Monk* episodes track a mystery straight through from beginning to end, while others will tackle two parallel stories, with the A-story, generally the mystery, holding the more prominent position, and a smaller B-story providing a thematically related counterpoint. The A and B stories in "Mr. Monk and the Kid," are related by a family theme: a mother worries about her kidnapped son but gets him back at the end, while a surrogate father learns to love a temporary "son" but loses him at the end. But somehow, the B story about Monk's relationship with Tommy slowly took over, and relegated the mystery to a lesser position. In fact, Monk doesn't even accompany Stottlemeyer and Disher to the scene when the SWAT teams come in to bust the Novaks and rescue Daniel Carlyle.

While this kind of shift in emphasis isn't unprecedented in story development, it's likely to be frowned upon in a traditional screenwriting class. But when the results are as touching as "Mr. Monk and the Kid," it's clearly best to let nature take its course.

"We had a nugget about a kid finding a finger," Andy Breckman recalls. "And at some point, we realized that Monk could adopt the kid and spend time with him. *That's* what made the script take off."

What made the episode itself take off, however, may have been the casting of an adorable two-year-old boy—or, to be precise, *two* adorable two-year-old boys, named Preston and Trevor Shores. "We used a set of twins," Randy Zisk says, "and we found that one of them was better at performing, so we tried to use him more. He fell asleep in Tony's lap, and he delivered his lines to Tony at the exact right time."

"We didn't ask them to say much, but when they had to talk, like 'Monk, Monk, Monk,' they could do it," Tony Shalhoub recalls. "The director, Andrei Belgrader, took a risk by using really young kids that didn't know they were acting. Sometimes they did things that were not in the script, like wagging the hot dog in the restaurant. We ended up making the scenes kind of free-form."

The kids were real pros, although they didn't know it. Even when they reacted to things the camera wasn't supposed to pick up, they were in character. One of the boys, for example, was infatuated with the boom mike used to record sound, an interest that viewers can detect as the boy reaches up during the restaurant scene. "He was *always* reaching for the boom mike," Randy Zisk laughs. "With kids you don't know what you're going to get, but even that was gold. And the whole relationship with Monk, especially when they were holding hands in the park, was really special."

"My favorite moment in the episode is when we cut to Monk and Tommy walking down the hill and hear Monk saying, 'She died in this car bomb and her name was Trudy . . .'" Tony Shalhoub chuckles. "I just loved that he was telling the kid his own story."

The second story that Monk tells Tommy lent itself to what very likely is the most memorable summation of the entire series—an animated children's book. "Doing the summation as a children's book just seemed natural," says Hy Conrad, who first suggested the idea. "There's violence in fairy tales, so I thought that having Monk tell the kid a fairy tale while he's falling asleep, and covering this gruesome summation at the same time, would be very cool. But I didn't know that they were going to animate it."

The animation suggestion came from Andy Breckman. "We try to keep the show alive," he says. "I thought it would be fun."

Unfortunately, what sounds like fun on the page can be rather expensive to put on-screen, and initially, the idea of using animation was vetoed. "It's cost-prohibitive," Zisk says. "But I called a good friend, Scott Greenberg, and told him what we had in mind."

Scott Greenberg is chief operating oofficer of DPS Film Roman, the company that, as their

brochure states, "puts the blue in Marge Simpson's hair [on *The Simpsons*] and keeps Hank Hill [of *King of the Hill*] supplied with propane." Greenberg told Zisk that he loved *Monk,* and a deal was struck. "We'd never done animation before, and we'll probably never do it again," Zisk says. "But the fairy tale summation was a great opportunity."

Not to mention a storybook ending for the series's third season.

The Quotable *Monk*

"Nature dirty."—Monk
"Nature dirty."—Tommy

The Weirdest Clue: Monk notices that the strings on the violin's bow are loose, meaning the man posing as the violinist hadn't been rehearsing as he said.

Idiosyncrasy of the Week: After just a few days in Monk's care, Tommy is separating his food, cleaning stains, and objecting to having unevenly pushed up pajama pant legs.

The Clue that Breaks the Case: When Tommy takes a lipstick tube from Natalie's purse, Monk realizes that he lifted the finger from his foster mother's purse.

He's the Man

On July 8, 2005, USA Network launched an upscale marketing campaign with a memorable tagline: "Characters Welcome." The slogan "truly embraces everything that we do," announced Bonnie Hammer, president, USA Network and SciFi Channel. "Whether it's an obsessive compulsive detective like Monk, the tormented returnees of *The 4400*, or a real-life action hero from the WWE, it's the compelling, sometimes complicated, often funny characters that make USA Network what it is."

The campaign was responsible for a highly amusing series of short *Monk* promos that ran during commercial breaks on the network. Each played like a scene from an actual *Monk* episode: Adrian Monk cheerfully inspecting his now-pristine doorknobs as he removes them from the dishwasher; Monk rolling a cartload of groceries up to a startled supermarket check-out woman—not to purchase them, but to get her to dispose of them because all of the items had passed their expiration date; Monk separating newspaper sections for recycling by *topic*. A fourth ad gave viewers a tantalizing glimpse at what a crossover between two of USA's most popular shows might deliver: Adrian Monk and *The Dead Zone*'s Johnny Smith meeting amicably, but both noticeably reluctant to shake hands, the clairvoyant Smith for fear of learning something dark about Monk, and Monk for fear of germs. It was a subtle and hilarious depiction of each character's personal hell.

All of these spots perfectly illustrated USA's new tagline "Characters Welcome," a notation that fit *Monk* to a tee. "The most successful TV shows are about the characters," *Monk* producer Anthony Santa Croce says. "Whether it's *CSI* or *NYPD Blue,* the crime can be striking or boring, but you actually believe that the characters are there to follow the puzzle and see justice served. With *Monk,* it's probably less procedural and more eccentricity, but we love to see what lengths the characters will go to solve that crime."

It's no coincidence that the day USA launched its new branding initiative also was the launch day of *Monk*'s fourth season. And unlike the somewhat disappointing start of the series' third year, this time around viewers responded with a great deal of enthusiasm to the show's return. "Mr. Monk and the Other Detective," featuring guest star Jason Alexander, drew *Monk*'s highest premiere ratings yet, with 6.4 million total viewers, and managed to top all basic cable original series programming in the 25–54 demographic. That represented a 15 percent increase over the show's third season premiere ratings for total viewers.

The series improved its showing overseas as well, particularly in Gemany, where a number of U.S. shows were becoming primetime hits, an honor usually reserved for local product. During August 2005, *Monk* ranked as the second most popular U.S. import on German television, just behind *CSI: Miami.*

While no one could have predicted that *Monk*'s quirky concept could have such universal appeal, Andy Breckman is very grateful that it does. "I'm very proud of the fact that *Monk* does well around the world," he says. "I think that, in part, it's because of the kind of comedy we do. It's very physical, very simple, very universal." Since some of Monk's funniest moments highlight the character's movements during a nonverbal sequence, that's easy to understand. There's no idiomatic language barrier to surmount.

Fourth season is a turning point for many television shows. A premise that showed unlimited promise in the beginning can start to wear thin. Many TV shows try to disguise this by adding a new character. "They'll bring in, say, a child, in their fourth year," notes Randy Zisk. But *Monk* had no need for a new character just to beef up the novelty of the show. Half a season earlier, they'd filled an unexpected opening, and they did it without a lot of fanfare, without altering the show to accommodate the change. Everything happened organically, which suited the writers and producers fine.

"As we were coming out of Season Three, we all hoped that the changes in the show were behind us," Tom Scharpling says. "The one thing everyone wanted was a really good Season Four. That was the order of the day. And I think by the middle of Season Four we were having the best stretch we'd ever had."

But good stretch or not, Andy Breckman knows that he will need to face some changes somewhere down the line, just to let the show mature. "We'll be entering Season Five soon," Breckman says. "There are phases of a series, just as there are phases of a man's life. *Monk* is entering middle age, so we've got to think of how to tie up the loose ends."

Perhaps only three loose ends really matter to Adrian Monk—and to his fans: Monk's reinstatement to the police force; the possibility that his father may return; and the ever-present puzzle of Trudy's unsolved murder. For now, the only story thread on the near horizon is the return of Monk and Ambrose's dad. "He will arrive," Breckman confirms. "It'll happen next season."

As for Trudy's murder, Breckman will only say that he's been thinking about it. "I have some ideas," he says with a smile.

The question for fans of *Monk* is: When will we find out? Season Six? Or Seven? Or beyond? The good news *and* the bad news, is that quality television series tend to age gracefully, continually entertaining us with a radiant, silver-screened glow.

It's a gift.

"Mr. Monk and the Other Detective"

Episode 4-01
Written by Hy Conrad
Directed by Eric Laneuville
Original Airdate: July 8, 2005

GUEST CAST

Marty Eels	Jason Alexander
Mrs. Eels	Dana Ivey
Vic Blanchard	Rossif Sutherland
Harold Gumbal	Alan Wilder
Julie Teeger	Emmy Clarke
Eddie Dial	Rey Gallegos
and	
Dr. Kroger	Stanley Kamel

Jewelry shop manager Harold Gumbal shows up early one morning, surprising the mall's security guard. Gumbal isn't happy to see him; he's about to rob his own store. After shoving a

fortune in gems into a bag, Gumbal steps into the parking lot and hands the bag to one of the two occupants of a waiting car. In return, Gumbal is handed something far more precious to him: his kidnapped pooch, Peggy. When the suspicious guard returns and draws his weapon on the men in the car, one of them shoots him. Then he turns the weapon on Gumbal, leaving Peggy the only witness to two murders.

Stottlemeyer calls in Monk to investigate the scene of the crime, but before he can begin, another detective arrives. It's Marty Eels, a third-rate local P.I. who wants to lend a hand. To everyone's surprise, Marty quickly analyzes what happened in the parking lot and accurately predicts where the thieves will dump their getaway vehicle. Later, Marty somehow discerns the name of one of the thieves, allowing the police to make an arrest and recover the purloined jewelry. Although Monk is convinced that Marty is somehow cheating, Stottlemeyer decides to let Marty finish working the case, rather than Monk.

Discouraged, Monk considers giving up detecting for a teaching position at Fulton Community College. Natalie thinks that's a terrible idea and refuses to drive him to a job interview, so Monk decides to rent a car. While he's on hold with the rental company, he debates with Natalie about whether or not he'll need to cross a bridge to get to the school. Suddenly the two of them hear the voice of the rental company's quality control operator, offering advice on the route. Apparently, the operators can listen in on the conversations of callers, even when the callers are on hold.

Recalling that Marty said his mother was an airline quality control operator, Monk and Natalie confront the usurper. Monk guesses the

truth. The two thieves had called for airline reservations to flee the country. While on hold, they freely discussed their recent criminal activities while Marty's mother monitored the conversation. Afterwards, she opted to give her son all the details, rather than the police, so that Marty could "solve" the crime and dispel his reputation as a hack.

Marty admits the theory is accurate, but points out that there's no way Monk can prove his accusations. Stymied, Monk and Natalie leave . . . only to receive a frantic summons

from Marty a few minutes later. He's just received a phone call from the partner of the arrested robber. If Marty doesn't hand over the stolen jewels by 8:20 P.M., the thief says, his mother will be dead.

Marty pleads with Monk to help him rescue his mom. The police are now in possession of the jewelry. What can he do? It's easy for Monk to have Stottlemeyer and Disher stake out the drop for the jewels and catch the crook—but not so easy to figure out where Mrs. Eels is being held. After Monk forces Marty to remember details of the threatening phone call, the trio rushes to an arcade located near a pier. Beneath the pier is a dilapidated shed. Monk realizes that the shed will be completely flooded at high tide—8:20 P.M. Mrs. Eels must be trapped inside.

As Monk supervises from dry land, Marty and Natalie leap into the rising water and free Mrs. Eels just in time. But despite her son's heroism, Mrs. Eels expresses disappointment in Marty. He blew his one opportunity for fame. Suddenly feeling sympathy for his rival, Monk tells Mrs. Eels that *Marty* was the one who figured out where she was. Later, Monk and Natalie allow Marty to take credit for cracking the case, which ultimately pays off for Monk. Marty's newfound fame nets him a job teaching criminal investigative techniques at Fulton Community College—once again leaving the San Francisco crime scene to Monk.

It's always nice to start a season with a bang, and "Mr. Monk and the Other Detective" certainly drew in the viewers, with its amusing premise and crowd-pleasing casting.

The episode wasn't the first to go into production for Season Four—in fact, it was the fourth episode to be filmed. "But once we got Jason Alexander aboard as Marty Eels, it moved up to the premiere slot," Hy Conrad notes.

The writers didn't have Alexander in mind when they created Monk's rival. "Our concept of him was of someone tall, young, and full of bravado, like Jason Biggs from *American Pie*," explains Conrad. "But then we heard that Jason Alexander might be available and we modified it for him."

Randy Zisk had met Alexander at an event in Hollywood, and asked the actor if he'd be interested in working on *Monk*. "Jason told me

that he *loves* Tony Shalhoub, *loves* the show and would *love* to do it," Zisk says. "So we sent him the next script coming up—'Other Detective.'"

The role of Marty Eels seemed like a perfect fit for Alexander. "Marty is from another world," Andy Breckman says. "He's the 'Bizzaro World' Monk, and we'd written him to be funny because he had some of Monk's qualities." And who would know more about that Bizzaro world than the man who played George Costanza on *Seinfeld*?

"We all expected Marty be exactly like George Costanza," Dan Dratch says. "But instead, Jason came in with this whole other voice."

In fact, Alexander's portrayal of Marty wound up far more interesting than the one the writers had posed. "Jason found comic business that we didn't know was there," reports David Breckman. "He's a very inventive actor."

The episode's nugget, inspired by an article that appeared in *The New York Times,* was brought to Andy Breckman's attention by his sister Risa Breckman, a clinical instructor in Gerontological Social Work at the Weill Medical College of Cornell University. The article, about telephone quality assurance workers, alerted readers to the fact that although a caller may be listening to Muzak while he's on hold, someone else could be listening to *him*. "They do warn you," Hy Conrad points out. "When you first get on, a recording says, 'Your call may be monitored.'" But not many people realize that the warning includes the period prior to being connected to a customer service rep.

Principle production on the episode included one minor catastrophe. For the nighttime rescue scene, shot at the Santa Monica Pier, the construction crew had built a small shack under the pier at the water line. It looked great, but unfortunately, no one had briefed the scene's primary special effect—the tide—about the crew's shooting schedule. "The water level rose faster than we thought it would," Randy Zisk recalls, "and the waves came in much harder. We couldn't even go near the shack because a pole in the middle of it had broken loose and it became a ramrod, smashing the structure apart from the inside. All we could do was stand and watch as the whole thing dismantled."

The shack was rebuilt, but not until several of the shots were redesigned.

The Quotable *Monk*

"I love that thing you do with your hands. Very old-school."—Marty Eels

The Weirdest Clue: When Stottlemeyer talks to Mrs. Eels on the phone, he mentions hearing intermittent "beeps" on the line, leading Marty to reveal that his mom is a quality control operator at Pacific Global Airlines—and, ultimately, Monk to figure out how Marty manages to unravel the mystery so quickly.

Idiosyncrasy of the Week: The presence of doggy doo interferes with Monk's ability to concentrate.

The Clue that Breaks the Case: *Thud—Clang—Thud—Clang* . . . Monk figures out the location where Mrs. Eels is being held after Marty repeats the sounds he heard during her captor's call.

"Mr. Monk Goes Home Again"

Episode 4-02
Written by Tom Scharpling
Directed by Randy Zisk
Original Airdate: July 15, 2005

GUEST CAST

Ambrose Monk	John Turturro
Julie Teeger	Emmy Clarke
Paul Gilstrap	David Weisenberg
Store Manager	Brent Hinkley
Paramedic	David Batiste

An armored car driver is shot to death outside of a grocery store on Halloween. The case is rather odd. The driver was shot five times—with his own gun—but since there was no money in the car, the assailant's motive is unclear.

As Monk begins looking for clues, he receives a phone call from his brother Ambrose ("Mr. Monk and the Three Pies"). Ambrose reports that their long-lost father has called; he's in town on business and plans to stop by the ancestral Monk home that evening at 8 P.M. Having always believed their father would return, Ambrose is excited. Although Monk is skeptical, he agrees to come to Ambrose's house, accompanied by Natalie and Julie, and await the arrival of their prodigal papa.

There's a lot of activity in Monk's old neighborhood. The streets are alive with children in costumes, traipsing door to door in search of sweets. Ambrose has calculated exactly how much candy he should need for the occasion and ordered the requisite number of candy bars from the local store. When a trick-or-treater dressed as Frankenstein's monster tries to take more than his share, Ambrose attempts to stop him and gets clouted over the head with a pumpkin. As Monk and

Natalie come to Ambrose's aid, the monster runs away.

Later, when Julie goes out trick-or-treating with some friends, the monster reappears and tries to steal their candy. Monk realizes that the monster only accosted kids who had stopped at Ambrose's house. Could there be something special about his brother's candy?

Julie is miffed. She hasn't had much of an opportunity to collect her treats. But with a "monster" on the loose, Natalie won't let her go back out without an adult escort. Seizing on a chance to be alone with the very attractive Natalie, Ambrose drafts Monk for the task. The girl and the detective soon find themselves at the "Gilstrap" house. When Monk turns down Mrs. Gilstrap's offer of treats, she comments that

she can't resist having a chocolate Neptune bar every single night. Monk doesn't think about the comment for very long; his attention has been drawn to a dead pigeon on a nearby front lawn.

Monk recognizes the pigeon as the bird that had been nibbling on something on the ground near the dead driver earlier that day. Thinking it may have been poisoned, Monk summons Stottlemeyer and Disher to the scene and asks them to do an autopsy on the pigeon.

Monk and Julie return to Ambrose's home. It's after 8 P.M. and their father has yet to arrive. When Monk tells his brother that they're better off without the visit, Ambrose is furious. He grabs the big candy bowl and starts gobbling sweets like a petulant child. A few moments later, Stottlemeyer calls. Monk was right: the bird

was poisoned. What's more, the armored car driver was poisoned too, both with a highly toxic substance called Tetrachlorodrine. The poison, Stottlemeyer notes, came from a local lab. A plant manager caught a worker named Gilstrap *returning* some to the shelves this very day!

Gilstrap? Monk has a horrible thought. He tells Ambrose not to eat any Neptune bars. But it's too late. Ambrose just finished a Neptune bar, and there's no antidote for the poison. He's doomed.

As Monk rushes his brother to the hospital, he explains what happened. Gilstrap wanted to kill his wife. He took the Tetrachlorodine from the lab so he could dose her nightly Neptune bar. At the same time, he planted several other toxic bars, so that Mrs. Gilstrap's death would be attributed to a random killer. But when the manager at his lab caught Gilstrap returning the Tetrachlorodine bottle, Gilstrap knew his plan was ruined. If *anyone* died from Tetrachlorodine poisoning, he'd be blamed.

He went to the store to purchase all the Neptune bars he'd spiked, recovering all but two. One was eaten by the driver, who already was dying from the effects of the candy when Gilstrap found him in the parking lot. Figuring that no one would look for poison in a man who'd been shot five times, Gilstrap killed the man with his own gun. The other bar was part of Ambrose's candy order from the store, and Gilstrap—disguised as Frankenstein's monster— had been trying to steal it all night.

Suddenly Monk notices that there's yet *another* Neptune bar in the evidence bag they're bringing to the hospital. This unopened bar is the poisoned one. Ambrose isn't dying—he just has a tummyache from eating an old candy bar that's passed its expiration date.

When the two brothers return home, they find a note taped to the door. It's from their father, who stopped by after they left for the hospital. Monk doesn't quite know what to think, but Ambrose does. Their father will come back someday. He's sure of it.

Monk's producers had wanted to do a second episode with the reclusive Ambrose Monk ("Mr. Monk and the Three Pies") during the series's third season, but somehow it didn't work out. John Turturro simply wasn't available. "He was directing a movie right down to the wire, and he couldn't do both projects," Tom Scharpling explains.

Confident that an opening would appear in Turturro's schedule eventually, the writers prepared a script for him. At first glance, the concept that evolved into "Mr. Monk Goes Home Again" seemed an unlikely choice. For one thing, the story had been developed during Season One, before the writers had conceived of Ambrose. Back then, when it was referred to as "Mr. Monk and Halloween," the story concerned a villain who was following Monk and Sharona because Monk had purchased a box of "Munch 'n' Crunch" candy.

Then there was the fact that *Monk* doesn't air during the Halloween season. Normally, Tom Scharpling notes, seasonally themed television episodes "match the weather outside. And this," he admits, "would have to be an 'off-season' Halloween story." So the story was shelved— temporarily. However, by the fourth season, the Halloween story came back into play when the writers realized that it would make an excellent vehicle for Ambrose. After all, comments Scharpling, "There are only so many options when you're dealing with Ambrose. He's stuck in his house. But trick-or-treating is a great reason for people to come *to him*."

And so it was that the Halloween script was revised, and scheduled for airing during the beginning of Season Four—in the very un-autumnal month of July.

As in "The Three Pies," Ambrose enters the story via a telephone call, but this time Natalie answers the phone, rather than Sharona. And when he meets her in person, Ambrose is smitten. "He stares at her for the whole first scene," Director Randy Zisk points out. "But because he's initially a little tough on Julie, Natalie isn't inclined to like him very much."

"At first we all thought that she'd be cool to Ambrose," Traylor Howard says of her character. "But John Turturro is so likeable, and he made Ambrose so wonderful, that *I* started to soften. I started to act as though she might go out with him, and by the end of the episode the director agreed with me." A few last-minute changes were made in the script, and the rest, as they say, was history.

Zisk used a subtle camera angle to express the attraction between the unlikely pair. "The clock in Ambrose's living room is a key story element," the director notes. "I didn't want to just shoot it as an insert, so I shot the clock over their backs as they sit together, which was a nice, gentle way to play the scene. Their body language said a lot about who they were. He definitely won her over."

Julie may not have enjoyed her time around Ambrose's house, but actress Emmy Clarke certainly did. Usually, she explains, there's no one on the set that's her own age. "But in the Halloween episode," she says enthusiastically, "I got to work with all these other kids, and we

became really close friends. My favorite scene that I've ever done was when we all had to run away from the Frankenstein monster. Each time they stopped filming, we all were just cracking up, so we wanted them to shoot as many takes as possible!"

The episode also introduced another Monk family member—sort of. Initially the episode's tag had a taxi stopping in front of the house, and the camera following a man up to the door, only to find that no one was at home. The man was, of course, Ambrose and Adrian's father. "But we decided that we needed the time to resolve all the stuff that had gone down with Ambrose almost dying," Scharpling says. "So we had their dad arrive off-camera, and we showed Monk and Ambrose's reaction to his having been there. That's what you want to see."

As for the elder Monk—"He will arrive," Andy Breckman comments. "It'll happen."

The Quotable *Monk*

"Ambrose, I'm proud of you for getting out of the house."—Dad (Mr. Monk)

The Weirdest Clue: Monk knows that the dead pigeon is the same one that ate the remains of the driver's candy bar because it has five little brown spots on its back that resemble the constellation Cassiopeia.

Idiosyncrasy of the Week: Monk claims to be "allergic to food that's been sitting in a bowl all night that other people have been touching."

The Clue that Breaks the Case: The poison in the pigeon (and the driver), which leads the police to Mr. Gilstrap.

"Mr. Monk Stays in Bed"

Episode 4-03
Written by Hy Conrad
Directed by Phillip Casnoff
Original Airdate: July 22, 2005

GUEST CAST

Reggie Dennison . . . . David Valcin
John DeLancy . . . . Lennie Loftin
Julie Teeger . . . . Emmy Clarke
Mr. Gorman . . . . Jimmy Palumbo
Marv Chastwick . . . . Frank Novak

When a pizza deliveryman inadvertently gives Natalie a fifty-dollar bill as part of her change, she decides to return it right away. Driving off after him, she eventually finds the deliveryman's car parked on a dark street—and the driver within, beaten to death.

Stottlemeyer, Disher, and Monk arrive to assess the situation, but before they can cover much ground, the cops are called away to investigate the disappearance of a Supreme Court judge and Monk is waylaid by a case of the flu. When Natalie follows up with the police the next day, she discovers that the dead deliveryman—identified as Julio Alverez—is *not* the man who brought the pizza to her door. What's going on? With the Mayor putting pressure on Stottlemeyer to find Judge Jillian Garr, no one at the station has time to listen to Natalie. So she takes it upon herself to get to the bottom of things.

Natalie gets the previous night's order slips from the pizzeria where Alverez worked. Reconstructing his delivery route, she comes to the home of Reggie Dennison. But before she can ask Dennison if he received a pizza the

night before, she notices that his thumbnail is badly bruised, just like the thumbnail of the man who delivered her pizza. Because that deliveryman was wearing sunglasses and a cap, Natalie doesn't recognize Dennison's face, but she has a strong feeling it's the same man.

Natalie contacts Disher, but he's too busy to follow up. Stottlemeyer, too, is occupied, going over leads regarding the missing judge with Monk, who's convalescing at home. Alone, Natalie stakes out Dennison's house, and come nightfall, she sees Dennison stuff something the size of a human body into his trunk. Then he drives away, leaving Natalie with an opportunity to sneak into his house.

Once inside, Natalie calls Monk on her cell phone. The detective is still under the weather, but when Natalie conveys details of her discoveries, he realizes there's a connection to Stottlemeyer's case. In the fireplace, there's a partially burned photo of Dennison and a woman in front of the Oakley Inn, a place that Monk knows the judge visited with an unidentified lover. And in the bathroom, despite its spic and span appearance, is one bloody fingerprint.

As Monk pulls together his thoughts, Natalie hears Dennison's car return. She hides, but in the process, drops her cell phone. Drawn by the sound of Monk's coughing on the other end of the line, Dennison finds Natalie's cell. He puts it to his ear just in time for Monk to present his hypothesis about the murders of Judge Garr and Julio Alverez—both committed by Dennison. Monk says Dennison was spending an evening at home with his lover Garr when they presumably got into a fight. He killed her just as deliveryman Alverez arrived on the scene. An inconvenient witness, Alverez was killed as well. But because the pizzeria knew Alverez's

route, Dennison realized that the police would probably show up at his door and begin asking uncomfortable questions. He needed someone *else* to be the last person to see Alverez alive, so he disguised himself and delivered the final pizza to Natalie.

Because Dennison's fingerprints are all over that pizza box, Monk figures it will be easy to convict him. Of course, first the police will need to get the box back from the recycling dump.

By now, Dennison has captured Natalie, and Monk has realized that he's been talking to the murderer. Guessing that Dennison will take Natalie with him to help find the pizza box, Monk jumps in a cab and meets them at the dump. He manages to fend the killer off until Stottlemeyer arrives with backup. With Dennison in custody and Natalie safe, there's only one remaining bit of business: find the pizza box amidst a sea of recycled goods. Amazingly, Monk does just that, thanks to the musical chip in an annoying Get Well card that Julie gave him—which Monk had put in with the week's recycling.

The story for "Mr. Monk Stays in Bed" is a blend of two ideas that had been pinned to the writers' board for a long time. "We always wanted to see if Monk could solve a case from his bed," Andy Breckman says. "Kind of like the protagonist in the movie *Rear Window*. And we also liked the idea that if a delivery boy were murdered, his killer would have to continue with the delivery guy's route because the police would focus on the guy's last stop. It amused us that the killer would be forced to deliver pizzas."

As one might expect, illness doesn't bring out the best in Monk, who requires both a humidifier and a *de*humidifier, and insists that each used tissue be double-bagged and taken directly to the trash. But when the chips are down, Monk lives up to the high standard that Mitch Teeger's widow expects of a hero: the great ones play hurt. Monk puts aside his concerns over his own health and does the right thing—not only coming to Natalie's rescue, but actually tackling the killer. "It's good to remind the audience that Monk once was a cop and hopes to be one again," Breckman explains. "So it's healthy for us to see him fighting occasionally, or actually running down a suspect."

Of course, since this is *Monk*, even a fight with a killer tends to incorporate humor, especially if there's a big pile of recycled paper in the vicinity. Shooting in it, for Tony Shalhoub, was a joy. "There was a *mountain* of paper," the actor says with a laugh. "We could jump, fall, roll, and attack each other in it. It was *so* much fun."

Credit the wardrobe department for Monk's resemblance to the abominable snowman as he emerged from the shredded mess. "They sprayed my clothes all over with adhesive, so when I rolled around, the paper stuck to me," Shalhoub reveals.

Composer Jeff Beal joined in the fun by punctuating the score for that sequence with an appropriate blend of heroism and humor. "The music has to support both qualities," he explains. "So I suggested a bit of seventies music in there, just a touch of *Mannix* and *Hawaii Five-0*."

However, it was another piece of music that dominated the episode, "That musical get well card," sighs Joe Toplyn. "We wanted it to play 'You Are My Sunshine,' but . . ."

But since that song, cowritten by former Louisiana state governor Jimmie Davis and Charles Mitchell, is an official song for that Gulf Coast state, the writers suspected it wouldn't be heard in the final cut of the episode. "Whenever we suggest a particular piece of music be in the plot," Toplyn says, "by the time the episode airs, it'll have changed into a song by somebody like Stephen Foster, because it'll have to be a public domain piece. The show can use those for free."

"Yeah, that's true," admits Breckman. "But it *was* fun that we got to make Tony say 'Polly Wolly Doodle.' "

The Quotable *Monk*

"That's the worst part, you know—getting used to it. It's something you never really get used to."—Disher

The Weirdest Clue: Natalie finds blood on the killer's bathroom light switch when she pushes the toggle to the "on" position. (But wouldn't that mean that Dennison cleaned the room in the dark?)

Idiosyncrasy of the Week: Monk tries to consume his alphabet soup in alphabetical order.

The Clue that Breaks the Case: The photo of Dennison with the victim at the Oakley Inn, where Monk knows the missing judge had vacationed.

"Mr. Monk Goes to the Office"

Episode 4-04
Written by Nell Scovell
Directed by Jerry Levine
Original Airdate: July 29, 2005

GUEST CAST

Warren Kemp . . . . Eddie McClintock
Abby . . . . Jennifer Hall
Chilton Handy . . . . Christopher Neiman

The Killer . . . . Brett Rickaby
Angela . . . . Meredith Scott Lynn
Greg . . . . Fred Stoller
Frances . . . . Nicole Randall Johnson

A mysterious assailant has killed a parking garage attendant and broken the right hand of stock analyst Warren Kemp, who entered the garage a moment after the murder. Because the assailant addressed Kemp by name, it seems the unlucky attendant was collateral damage in a preplanned attack on Kemp. Could the attacker be someone Kemp knows? The injured analyst wants Monk to find out. Much to Natalie's surprise, the detective offers to go undercover and pose as an office worker. Monk is tantalized by the idea of people performing the same mundane tasks every single day, like drones. It sounds like heaven.

Occupying one of the anonymous cubicles in Kemp's office proves to be everything Monk had hoped for, and more. He reorganizes the file room, straightens other people's desks, and retypes his coworkers' messy reports. For the first time in his life, his obsessive organizational skills are appreciated *and* he's considered one of the gang.

When Monk stands Natalie up for a lunch they had arranged, Kemp invites her to share lunch in his office, and she accepts. As she flirts with him, she notices that the office has a nice view of the courtyard restaurant where Monk and his coworkers are dining. It's clear that her boss is having a good time.

After lunch, Monk is recruited for his gang's office bowling league. The finals are that very night. The best bowler on their team was Kemp, whose broken hand will prevent him from participating in the event. Monk wonders if that was the motive for the attack in the garage.

Strangely, the detective proves to be a quick study on the lanes. Soon his team is just three pins from victory, and Monk has become incredibly popular with his teammates. But all that ends when the opposing team notices that Monk is wearing street shoes. If he doesn't put on a pair of rented bowling shoes, they say, his team will forfeit the game. Monk is horrified. Wear shoes that have been *on someone else's feet?* It would be the ultimate sacrifice, and sadly, he just can't make it. In an instant, Monk loses the game *and* all of his new friends.

Not long after, the company's interior designer is murdered. As Natalie and Monk share lunch the next day, she ponders a connection with the earlier violence, while Monk studies her soup. "Is that a hair?" he asks.

When Natalie checks her soup, Monk is astonished to note that an apparently deaf man sitting across the room by the window checks his soup as well. And in that instant, Monk breaks the case. The man at the window is a lip-reader, the detective reveals, taking care not to move his lips as he talks. That's why he checked his soup when Natalie did. The guy can see Kemp's window from where he's sitting, and he's been reading the analyst's lips to get valuable inside financial information. But after the interior decorator changed Kemp's furniture around, the lip-reader no longer had a clear view of Kemp's mouth; his right hand blocked his lips while he was on the phone. That's why the lip-reader broke Kemp's right hand—so he'd be forced to hold the phone in his *left*. Realizing that the decorator was about to make more changes— *curtains!*—the lip-reader killed her.

Unfortunately, although Monk has hidden his own lips, the killer has been watching Natalie's verbal responses in a mirror. He comes over to their table and shows them a gun, then tells them to accompany him outside. Thinking fast, Natalie screams in the man's hearing aid and incapacitates him, allowing Monk to grab the gun.

The case solved, Monk cleans out his cubicle and departs, taking one last look at paradise lost.

"Mr. Monk Goes to the Office" almost could be subtitled: "A Week in the Lives of the Writing Staff." It started one day at lunch—which is actually where a lot of *Monk* episodes are born (see "Mr. Monk Gets Jury Duty").

"We were in a restaurant together and we saw a guy sitting next to the window in an office across the street," Andy Breckman recalls. "We started wondering if he could read our lips. And we began to play with that idea." After a while, they had tweaked the concept to: What if a guy sitting in a diner was reading the lips of someone in an office across the street—say, a stockbroker?

A few days later, with the story a bit more developed, the writers realized that they needed to do some research. "So we went *bowling,*" Joe Toplyn says. "I was terrible. I embarrassed myself. But it really helped us to create jokes. The high point for me," he adds in a conspiratorial tone, "was that we got to write it off to expenses."

Later that week, another research opportunity presented itself. "Andy had a business meeting at USA's corporate office in New York," Dan Dratch says. And so, rather than making the usual commute to their New Jersey office, the writing team decided to join their boss in Manhattan. That way, they'd be able to spend a maximum amount of working hours together once Breckman became free. "We all met in one of the USA conference rooms," Dratch explains. "It was behind a glass partition, so we could see the interaction between the office workers in that little world. We were just observing," he laughs, "but we wound up deciding to use *their* names (conveniently provided by the nameplates outside the offices and cubicles) as our character's names."

Not that they patterned their characters' odd behaviors after those of the USA employees (at least, no one has copped to who might have inspired the man who Xeroxed his "white Caucasian buttocks"). They had other, more famous role models to work from. For example, Abby—played by Jennifer Hall—was styled after Janeane Garofalo, notes Hy Conrad, "although the actress ended up playing her a bit broader than Janeane. We do that sort of thing a lot. For instance, in 'Mr. Monk Goes to Jail,' our template for Monk's cellmate was Mickey Rourke."

So does this staff have too much fun to call their daily work "routine"? Andy Breckman shrugs. "That's how our stories get done," he says. "Every week, it's a little miracle."

The Quotable *Monk*

"I have a gang. I'm in the gang. They're waiting for me. They like me. Nobody's laughing at me."—Monk

The Weirdest Clue: The tire iron used by the killer is metric, so it doesn't match any of the American-made cars in the parking garage.

Idiosyncrasy of the Week: Monk would have preferred that Kemp's hand injury involved *ten* broken bones, rather than nine, because ten is a nice round number.

"Mr. Monk Gets Drunk"

Episode 4-05
Written by Daniel Dratch
Directed by Andrei Belgrader
Original Airdate: August 5, 2005

GUEST CAST

Al Nicoletto	Paul Ben-Victor
Larry Zwibell	Daniel Roebuck
Dr. Sobin	Richard Libertini
Mrs. Willis	Peggy Miley
Pierre Lecoste	Maurice Godin
Heidi Gefsky	Felicia Day
Cal Gefsky	Chris D'Elia
Rudy	Larry Clarke
Ricardo	Assaf Cohen
Wine Expert	Bianca Chiminello

Rudy Schick is in trouble. He and his partner Ben Gruber stole $3.1 million from the mob, and now hitman Al Nicoletto has come to collect. Rudy doesn't have the money. He's supposed to meet Gruber to get his split, but Gruber hasn't told him where. All he knows is that Gruber is somewhere in California. Nicoletto believes Rudy—which means he no longer needs him. He shoots Rudy and sets out to track down his partner.

Meanwhile, in California's beautiful wine country, Monk and Natalie arrive at the lovely bed-and-breakfast where Monk and Trudy honeymooned. Monk explains to Natalie that he's fulfilling his promise to Trudy that he would visit the place once a year.

That evening, after Natalie retires, Monk celebrates a private tradition. Sitting at his and Trudy's table, he toasts his wife with a sip of her favorite wine. But the ritual is interrupted when a new guest seats himself at Monk's table. The loquacious man, who reeks of Aqua Velva aftershave, introduces himself as Larry Zwibell and chatters at Monk for a while. Noticing that Monk seems a little tipsy (the detective doesn't normally drink), Zwibell offers to share a hangover cure with him in the morning. Then he excuses himself to join the other guests in a game of poker.

The next morning, Monk seeks out Zwibell for the hangover cure—only to find that no one at the inn has any recollection of the man. In fact, there's no sign that he ever checked in. When Monk persists, one of the guests suggests that the detective merely imagined Zwibell.

Disturbed by what has transpired, Monk and Natalie are about to leave the inn when Al Gruber arrives. He shows them a photo of his missing brother, Ben Gruber, whom Monk immediately identifies as Larry Zwibell. Al explains that Ben stole some money from a bank and fled; the authorities have promised to go easy on him if he returns the money. Al wants to find Ben and let him know.

Monk is ecstatic to find that he hasn't been imagining things. But why won't the other guests at the inn admit that they saw Ben Gruber? As the detective tries to puzzle it out, details surface that suggest that "Al Gruber" is *not* the brother of the man Monk met. Why, then, is he so interested in finding Ben Gruber?

Monk decides to get Al drunk. Perhaps when he's loosened up, he'll spill the beans. To keep Al from getting suspicious, Monk also drinks some wine. But although he's told the bartender to serve him a nonalcoholic vintage, he receives the real thing and unexpectedly gets totally inebriated.

Meanwhile, Natalie breaks into Al's car and discovers his real name is Al Nicoletto. When she calls Stottlemeyer, she learns Nicoletto is a contract killer for the mob! She hustles back to warn Monk, who's in an alcoholic haze. But by the time he comprehends, Nicoletto has drawn a gun on the pair. Natalie fends him off, and during the struggle, Monk manages to hit Nicoletto over the head with a bottle—knocking him out.

When Stottlemeyer arrives to secure the scene, Monk offers an intoxicated summation of what transpired at the inn. Gruber, posing as Larry Zwibell, did check in and participate in the poker game. After a while he went to his room to get more money, but he never returned. When the innkeeper and the guests went to check on him, they discovered he'd died of a heart attack. They also discovered he had over $3 million in cash, so they decided to split the cash and hide the body.

But where's that body? By now, Monk has passed out, so he can't tell them. But Natalie figures it out when she realizes that the wine she's been sipping smells like Aqua Velva. Gruber is in a vat at the winery next door! The case solved, Natalie apologizes to her sleeping boss for doubting him, and drives him home.

Two scenes in "Mr. Monk Gets Drunk" stand out for Traylor Howard: one she loved that *didn't* make it into the final cut, and one she didn't love that *did*. "Tony and I made up some lines for the scene where Monk goes to find the hangover cure," Howard recalls. "I said, 'A little hair of the dog,' and since Monk had no idea what that is, he says, 'Hairy dog?' And I say, 'What?' And he looks at me and says, 'What?' It was a really fun moment, but it didn't make it into the show."

The scene that *did* survive called for Howard to sing about "the kissing fern." "I'm the worst singer," she admits. "My attempts to sing were a big joke when I was a kid. So when we were rehearsing and they were trying to get me to sing it right, I was thinking, 'If only my family could see me now.'"

The initial idea for the episode came from a card on the writers' board that said, simply, "Class Reunion." "The original idea was that one of Monk's classmates at the reunion goes missing," Tom Scharpling says, "but we had to scale it back, because that concept meant a hundred people would be lying about where the guy went. You could drive a truck through the cracks in that kind of a grand conspiracy."

Scaling it back led to talk of a disappearance at a bed-and-breakfast, which prompted writer Dan Dratch to suggest that if the B&B were a winery, they could hide the body in a wine cask. And where there was wine, there were the comic possibilities of Monk sampling a bit of the grape. "We didn't immediately think, 'Wouldn't it be great to get Monk drunk?'" Dratch says. "We were focused on the conspiracy. It's always, mystery first, comedy second."

"Getting Monk drunk was a challenge," Andy Breckman notes, "but we *had* to do it, because I realized he could do a drunken summation."

The phrase "California wine country" generally brings to mind regions north of San Francisco, such as the Napa Valley. But there is also a burgeoning vineyard community in the state's beautiful Central Coast area. So the production hit the road for a four-day shoot—its longest overnight stay since "Mr. Monk Takes Manhattan"—at Firestone Vineyards in Los Olivos. And yes, it's one of the wineries featured prominently in the 2004 film *Sideways*. "We shot all our exteriors at Firestone," Randy Zisk reports, "as well as the interior of the barrel room."

For the interiors, they chose "a very old, eccentric house north of Pasadena," Joe Toplyn says. "It was crammed with most of the stuff you saw on the show."

"By coincidence," Andy Breckman says, "Tony Shalhoub came to visit us in New Jersey while we were working on the 'drunk' scene. He comes out only once or twice a year, but he was in the room for this one, and he steered us in certain ways. The script reads like any other script of course," Breckman says, "but when Tony performed the scene, he made it all his own."

The Quotable *Monk*

"It's *foot* wine! I can taste it. I can taste the feet now. And the toes. And what's *between* the toes."—Monk

The Weirdest Clue: The missing victim refers to soft drinks as "pop," but his alleged brother calls them "soda," a regional difference that indicates to Monk that they *aren't* brothers.

Idiosyncrasy of the Week: Monk gets a buzz (and a next-day hangover) from a single sip of wine.

The Clue that Breaks the Case: A two-parter: When Natalie utters the words "heart attack," Monk realizes what happened to Zwibell/Gruber; and when Stottlemeyer tells Natalie that the wine smells like Aqua Velva, she realizes the dead man's body is hidden in a wine vat.

"Mr. Monk and Mrs. Monk"

Episode 4-06
Written by David Breckman
Directed by Randy Zisk
Original Airdate: August 12, 2005

GUEST CAST

Trudy/Cameron	Melora Hardin
Zach Ellinghouse	Harve Presnell
Jim Bollinger	Kevin Kilner
Sorenson	GregAlan Williams
Receptionist	Frankie Ingrassia
and	
Dr. Kroger	Stanley Kamel

While reading an old poem of Trudy's, Monk has an epiphany. He feels that his dead wife wants him to know that there's a reason he's here in this world without her. Trudy wants him to let go, he tells Dr. Kroger.

The psychiatrist is pleased. Monk seems to have taken the difficult first step on the road to recovery. He may even be ready to return to active duty on the police force.

Monk is still basking in his new feeling of contentment when he goes home. But Natalie is strangely quiet. She can't bring herself to tell Monk what she saw while Monk was in his session with Kroger.

She'd gone into a diner after running some errands for Monk. Suddenly, into the restaurant walked a woman who looked exactly like Trudy. Shocked, Natalie eavesdropped on the woman's conversation with a man named Zach Ellinghouse. She heard "Trudy" tell him that she'd faked her own death to protect her family from an extremist group that she was writing about. She'd come out of hiding, she said, because she'd heard that Zach's daughter Janice had passed away—and she needed a key that belonged to

took the film from Natalie's camera, and warned her not to let Monk know she was alive.

But circumstances soon force Natalie to do just that. Monk accompanies Stottlemeyer and Disher to a crime scene where an elderly man has died. It looks like an accident, but there are signs of a struggle. Monk is surprised that the victim is Zach Ellinghouse, an old friend of Trudy's. Curiously, Disher reports that a neighbor heard Ellinghouse cry out Trudy's name during the altercation.

Natalie can't keep her secret any longer. She tells Monk about seeing Trudy, and Trudy's meetings with Ellinghouse. Unable to process what Natalie is saying, Monk bolts outside—only to spot Trudy standing across the street. But before he can get to her, a car picks her up and speeds away.

Traumatized, Monk falls into a kind of stupor. If Trudy is alive, he tells Kroger, then nothing he thought was true is true. When Kroger suggests that Trudy might be in trouble, Monk rallies, determined to get to the bottom of the mystery. He heads for Trudy's grave, and there he comes to the sad but reassuring realization that his beloved is still dead. The woman who looks like her is an imposter.

His mind clear, Monk goes to see Trudy's old boss at the newspaper. He shows Monk an article that Trudy wrote with Janice Ellinghouse about corruption in the dockworkers' union. The article relied heavily on a confidential source whose identity was never revealed. As a result of the article, the head of the union was thrown in jail. After studying Janice's desk at the paper, Monk deduces that Trudy's co-worker had been renting a locker at a local storage facility, and that the key "Trudy" wanted was for that locker.

Janice. Although Zach seemed reluctant to part with it, he agreed to bring it to her the next day.

When the pair next met, Natalie hid nearby. Zach hadn't brought the key; he wanted money first. Trudy agreed to bring it to him, then, as she was about to leave, she spotted Natalie, taking pictures of them. Apprehending her, she

Monk and Natalie get to the locker shortly before the fake Trudy shows up with Jack Bollinger, a union official. Monk realizes that Bollinger must have been Trudy's confidential source. He wants to get into the locker because he's afraid that Janice and Trudy's notes on the old story are in there. If anyone sees them, they'll know he ratted out his boss years ago. He hired someone to get the key from Ellinghouse by impersonating Trudy.

Natalie calls Stottlemeyer, but Monk can't wait. He's transfixed by Trudy's doppleganger, an actress named Cameron. As Bollinger pours gasoline on the contents of the garage, Monk approaches Cameron. Seeing the pain in Monk's eyes, Cameron can't help feeling sorry for her role in the charade. She didn't mean to hurt him—and Ellinghouse's death was an accident. But Bollinger is terrified that Monk's presence means his secret is about to become public knowledge. As Stottlemeyer arrives, Bollinger pulls out a gun and fires wildly, inadvertently hitting the actress. Stottlemeyer returns fire and Bollinger goes down. Monk rushes to help Cameron, but she's been mortally wounded. As he cradles her in his arms, she promises to tell Trudy how much he loves her . . . and she dies.

The incident causes Monk to lose some ground in his path to recovery, and the department decides not to reinstate him. But Monk is surprisingly at peace. Trudy is where she's supposed to be, safely stored within his memories, and the things that were true, are still true.

"From the beginning of the series, we wanted Monk to be haunted by something, so Trudy was a crucial part of the show's conception,"

Andy Breckman says. "We put each episode together like a witch's brew, with certain ingredients that go into the mix: some mystery, some comedy, and some emotional character material."

"On the surface, *Monk* seems to be the most conventional show," USA Network's Jeff Wachtel says. "And yet it's less predictable than almost anything on cable. You don't know from one moment to the next if it will make you laugh or bring tears to your eyes."

No other episode demonstrates Wachtel's point more clearly than "Mr. Monk and Mrs. Monk." At the beginning of the show, viewers are as buoyed by Monk's apparent progress as Dr. Kroger is. But when "Trudy" appears on the scene, they find themselves cast into the same horrible feeling of apprehension as Natalie. How will Monk respond when he finds out his dear departed wife is alive?

"Andy and his team of writers handled it so incredibly," director Randy Zisk says. "In the beginning they really built up the idea that Monk had gotten over losing Trudy. So when Natalie tells him, 'I saw your wife,' he goes from the biggest high to the biggest low. And when he sees the woman across the street, it's all over for him."

Zisk and director of photography Tony Palmieri worked out ways to visually express Monk's emotional crash-landing with some poignant camera moves. "After Monk sees 'Trudy,' he grabs hold of a lamppost on the corner, and we raised the camera up on a crane, to give the audience a sense of what he's feeling," explains Zisk. The vertical pull-back gives viewers the sense that, for Monk, gravity has come unhinged. He's completely devastated.

Zisk and Palmieri orchestrated another

affecting crane shot when Monk goes to the cemetery. "We wrapped the camera move around him as he's staring at Trudy's grave," Zisk says, "and put the viewer in the same place that he is." In this sequence, the camera's point-of-view floats from the treetops to the ground, encompassing Monk, and connecting him with Trudy's final resting place. It's a visual foreshadowing of what Monk will explain to Natalie at the end of the episode: that the wondrous connection he has to Trudy is still there—it still hurts—so he knows she's still in her grave, just as she should be.

The nugget for the episode had been floating around the writers' office for a long time. "We'd always had a note that said, 'What if someone's actually dead, but someone else engineers a sighting of that person,'" Hy Conrad recalls. "The idea never took off because we couldn't figure out how to get Monk into that story. Then I said, 'What if it's Trudy?' and everybody said, 'Whoa!' I thought that might be too off the wall, but they kept with it and the plot sprang from that moment."

Given the traumatic circumstances, it wasn't easy to incorporate the requisite humor into the story. "It's one of the heaviest stories we've done," Tom Scharpling says. "We came up with the 'You're the man,' runner [with Disher and Stottlemeyer], but even that had to flow around outside the mystery. Too many jokes would have been a disservice to the story."

"It is one of our less comedic episodes," David Breckman agrees, "but the material demanded that. A dishonest, almost desperate woman tries to hoodwink an old man. She's not angelic like Trudy. I think Melora was just wonderful in the role."

"Cameron was not a bad person," Melora Hardin says of her character. "She was just a young actress who needed money to pay her rent. This guy came along and offered her a fantastic job that was a little out of the ordinary."

Playing someone who looks like her character but *isn't* her character was a bit of a challenge. "They wanted Cameron to be similar to but different from Trudy," she says. "I wound up trying to play her trying to play Trudy from what she'd heard about her. It was weird."

Portraying a character's death before the cameras is a performance moment that actors understandably enjoy. So while Cameron's death was tearfully dramatic for the audience, it was all in a day's work for Hardin. "I got shot through the head in the Clint Eastwood movie *Absolute Power*," she says with a smile. "That was pretty dramatic too."

The Quotable *Monk*

"I got her back. For an hour and a half, I thought she might be alive. I had hope. Isn't hope the worst?"
—Monk

The Weirdest Clue: Monk knew that Cameron was an imposter because being near Trudy's grave "still hurt," meaning his beloved wife was still dead.

Idiosyncrasy of the Week: Before Monk hears about Trudy, he almost seems normal. He doesn't try to straighten a crooked picture, put a glass back on a coaster, or try to make some cut-up pieces of potato perfectly even—all pretty idiosyncratic behavior for the poster child for OCD.

The Clue that Breaks the Case: When Monk recognizes Jim Bollinger at the storage locker, he realizes what the "Trudy" charade was all about.

"Mr. Monk Goes to a Wedding"

Episode 4-07
Written by Liz Sagal
Directed by Anthony R. Palmieri
Original Airdate: August 19, 2005

GUEST CAST

Theresa Scott . . . . Ashley Williams
Jonathan Davenport . . . . Rob Benedict
Bobby Davenport . . . . Michael Cavanaugh
Lt. Bristo . . . . Mik Scriba
Emmy Clarke . . . . Julie Teeger
Photographer . . . . Ryan Bollman
and
Peggy Davenport . . . . Holland Taylor

Natalie needs a last-minute date to her brother Jonathan's wedding, so she reluctantly accepts Randy Disher's offer to accompany her. She needs someone to act as a buffer between her and her wealthy, overbearing family, from whom she's been estranged for years. The Davenports never approved of Natalie's late husband, Mitch; however, they *do* approve of Jonathan's fiancée, Theresa, even though the lovebirds have known one another only for a short time.

The wedding is being held at a posh hotel in Pebble Beach. After Natalie introduces Randy to her parents, he goes to check in. But he doesn't make it to the front desk; as he's crossing the hotel's parking lot, a car deliberately runs him down. The driver, wearing sunglasses and a baseball cap, flees from the scene, leaving the car behind.

Stottlemeyer and Monk arrive to investigate, and quickly deduce that the assailant was a member of the wedding party. But why would one of Natalie's relatives want to kill Disher? To find out, Stottlemeyer goes undercover as a wedding photographer—replacing the real one who has mysteriously disappeared—and Monk becomes Natalie's date for the event. The detective soon becomes suspicious of the bride-to-be, who makes several significant verbal slips in Monk's presence. Monk and Stottlemeyer ask Randy, who's laid up in his hotel room with a broken arm, a broken leg, and several broken ribs, if the driver who hit him might have been a woman. As Randy admits the possibility, the phone rings. A body has been found in one of the mud baths at the hotel spa—it's the missing photographer!

Stottlemeyer accompanies the local police to the dead photographer's studio and joins in a search of the man's belongings. Two items are of interest: a wedding portrait of a woman who looks very much like Theresa, and an old newspaper clipping about a police investigation of a woman suspected of murdering her new husband. The investigator on the case was Randy Disher. Stottlemeyer rushes back to the hotel to fill in Monk: Theresa is a "Black Widow"—a woman who marries for money and then kills her spouse. She killed the photographer because he was blackmailing her, and she obviously tried to kill Randy because he might remember her face.

But the wedding ceremony has already concluded and Theresa is pushing her groom to leave the reception for their honeymoon. Stottlemeyer can't bust her because there's no hard proof of Theresa's real identity. But there will be if Randy can get out of bed and make a positive ID. So while Stottlemeyer struggles to bring the convalescing Disher downstairs, Monk attempts to stall Theresa and Jonathan's departure. When Disher finally arrives, he fingers his murder suspect from years before. However, a defiant Theresa grabs the large cake knife, holds it to her new husband's throat, and demands transportation out of town. Without thinking twice, Natalie knocks Theresa to the ground and disarms her. In the process, she saves her brother's life and, at long last, wins the respect of her haughty mother, who makes amends for her treatment of Mitch by moving his photo to a place of honor on the family piano.

"When I started the show, they were still writing for Sharona," Traylor Howard says. "They had to learn how to write for Natalie, and I think by the time we did 'Mr. Monk Goes to a Wedding,' you could see that Natalie was becoming more alive to everyone."

It's clear that something had gelled in Natalie's characterization by "Wedding." In fact, in some areas the lines between Natalie and Traylor actually seemed to blur. "My manager started joking with me about a strange rumor going around that my family is loaded—in real life!" chuckles Howard. "It's odd how rumors get started."

Of course, the rumor may have had something to do with the fact that Natalie's parents are named "Peggy" and "Bobby"—and so are Traylor Howard's. "Andy called me while they were writing it," Howard laughs. "It cracks me up that they gave my parents' names to Natalie's parents."

Howard also adored the actors that were cast as Natalie's parents, particularly Holland Taylor (*Two and a Half Men, The L Word, The Practice, Bosom Buddies*), whose face is familiar to generations of TV audiences. "Holland was perfect, because she has so much energy," enthuses Howard. "She reminds me of my mom, while I was growing up. When we

were bickering in our fight scenes, I was just tickled."

The crew was just as taken with Taylor, who's known for playing catty sophisticates with a wicked sense of humor. Following one take of a scene in which Natalie called her mother "a bitch," director Tony Palmieri called out from across the set, "We pay her a lot of money to be a bitch—and she's great at it!"

Palmieri, Monk's regular director of photography, welcomed the opportunity to helm his second episode (see "Mr. Monk vs. the Cobra"). He's renowned for his high level of activity while working, constantly moving about the set, and literally *running* from his video monitor station to where the actors are standing, and back again. All the while, he flashes a sincere smile, which is accompanied by a de-vilish twinkle in his eyes and expansive hand movements.

But some scenes were enough to bring even Palmieri down. Case in point: the shot where Monk is hit by the bride's garter. Try as he may, actor Rob Benedict couldn't make the floppy garter stay within the camera's frame as he threw it over his head. Finally, from the side of the set, producer Anthony Santa Croce called out, "Give it to the boom mike man; he knows how to get it in the frame!" It's a show-biz joke, and the kind of friendly repartee that the *Monk* set is known for. That repartee extended even to the group of one hundred extras who could be heard joking, "Traylor Howard, Holland Taylor— say *that* fast three times."

If it was easy to come up with the given names of Natalie's parents, their surname was more of a challenge. "We wanted a name that people would think they knew, like 'Kellogg.' But we couldn't use a trademarked name, so we had to make something up," Joe Toplyn recalls. "We went through a lot names before we settled on Davenport."

Ironically, it wasn't the last name that almost got the writers in trouble. People generally are flattered to hear their names used on television, yet when Traylor Howard told her father that the toothpaste magnates would be named for him and his wife, she says, "He was like, 'Well, are we *jerks? I* don't want us to be *jerks.*' And I told him, 'Dad, it's not *real!* '"

The Quotable *Monk*

"Not *like* the toothpaste. We *are* the toothpaste."
—Natalie

The Weirdest Clue: After taking into account the amount of condensation left on the ground by the car's air conditioner and the day's relative humidity, Monk establishes that the Volvo that hit Randy had idled in the parking lot for twenty minutes, lying in wait for its victim.

Idiosyncrasy of the Week: Monk uses correction fluid to amend his imperfect signature on Randy's cast.

The Clue that Breaks the Case: Stottlemeyer finds a newspaper clipping about Theresa's previous brush with the law in the dead photographer's studio.

"Mr. Monk and Little Monk"

Episode 4-08
Written by Joe Toplyn
Directed by Robert Singer
Original Airdate: August 26, 2005

GUEST CAST

James . . . . Brett Cullen
Michael Norfleet . . . . David Hunt
Sherry Judd . . . . Donna Bullock
Mrs. Ledsky . . . . Susan Ruttan
Young Sherry . . . . Katelyn Pippy
Leo . . . . Kevin G. Schmidt
Jimmy . . . . Shane Haboucha
Travis . . . . Brent King
George . . . . Michael Dunn
Mrs. Monk . . . . Rose Abdoo
Principal Thicket . . . . Karl T. Wright
and
Young Adrian Monk . . . . Grant Rosenmeyer

Monk is startled when Sherry Judd shows up at his front door. She's as pretty as she was when she attended junior high with Monk, over thirty years ago. Back then, Monk had helped her out of a jam. Now she's tracked him down to solicit his help once again. An intruder broke into her home, killing her housekeeper and defacing a cherished painting of Sherry's great-grandmother. Can Monk find the person who committed the crime? Seeing Sherry triggers a flood of old memories for Monk. Always a bit smitten with her, he agrees to help her out.

At the crime scene, Monk determines that there were *two* intruders, and that they came to the house to deface the painting, not to rob her. While Monk's there, Sherry's ex-husband Michael arrives, expressing concern. But Sherry isn't interested; she wants him to leave. Before he goes, Michael writes her a large alimony check, describing it as her monthly "pound of flesh."

Disturbed by her ex-husband's brief appearance, Sherry tells Monk she's glad he's there for her. Her vulnerability makes Monk flash back to the period thirty-three years ago when she got into trouble at school. At the student bake sale, he and Sherry were in charge of selling the goods and collecting the money. A bully named Leo stole a cupcake and refused to pay for it, so Sherry reported him to the principal, despite the boy's threat that he'd get even with her. Later, the principal found evidence that seemed to indicate Sherry had pilfered the money from the bake sale. Young Adrian was sure that Leo was the real culprit . . . but how to prove it?

Back in the present, Monk accompanies Sherry when she goes to the museum to see a restoration expert about her painting. They're surprised to discover that the restorer is James Duffy, another old classmate. Duffy promises to take good care of the painting, and as he chats with Sherry, it's clear to Monk that the two are kindling a relationship. Although Monk had considered asking Sherry on a date, he realizes that he's too late, just as he was in eighth grade, when James beat him in asking her to the Spring Fling.

It occurs to Monk that the odd fingerprints in Sherry's house were made by someone wearing biker's gloves. After checking a list of suspects, Monk and Natalie track two likely candidates to a biker's bar. During an altercation, one of the bikers drops his wallet, and inside, Monk finds a diagram of Sherry's house. Obviously, it was drawn by someone who had hired them to break in—and Monk suddenly realizes who that person is.

At the police station, Monk reveals his findings to all: Sherry's ex wanted her to remarry so he could stop paying alimony. When he realized that her junior high heartthrob worked at the museum, he tried to "play Cupid," and arranged for the bikers to deface the painting—hoping Sherry would go to the museum to get it restored. Unfortunately, the bikers inadvertently killed the housekeeper in the process—making Michael guilty of murder. Monk figured it out when he saw the diagram, in which the zero in the street address was written in a distinctive way, the same way Michael wrote a zero on Sherry's alimony check.

Ironically, a zero also led to young Adrian's break in the bake sale theft. He knew Sherry had a habit of setting her combination lock to zero when she closed it. But the day the principal found the money in the locker, Adrian noticed that the lock was *not* on zero, meaning someone else had been in her locker: Leo. After finding the cash on Leo—complete with the bill upon which the principal had written "Good Luck!"—Sherry was cleared.

Sherry is as impressed with Monk as she was decades earlier, but he resigns himself to the fact that their relationship will never grow deeper. It's just as well. For now, he has room in his heart for only one woman: Trudy.

"We wanted to create an 'origins' story," David Breckman explains, "a 'Young Monk Adventure' that would show Adrian solving his very first case. But, realistically, the only way we could do that would be to split up an episode and show him in 1972 solving a relatively minor case, and then intercut that with him as a grownup solving a related but much more serious case."

The "more serious case" they chose originally had been developed as "Mr. Monk Meets the Big Bird" before being put on the back burner. "Big Bird" was about a man who wanted to stop paying alimony payments, so he hired someone

The Cruelest Place

Alert viewers will notice that an inordinate number of the crimes Monk investigates take place on the same street— Vinton. "Vinton Street is a dangerous place to live," Randy Zisk says. "You've got to be careful if you move to Vinton Street, because it's the center of crime in San Francisco."

The Vinton Street crime spree first came to viewers attention in Season One with "Dale the Whale," continued in Season Three with "Panic Room," "Takes His Medicine" (although for undisclosed reasons it was identified as Vinton Avenue), and "The Kid," and again in Season Four in "The Other Detective," "Mrs. Monk," "Stays in Bed," "Little Monk," "Goes to the Dentist," and "Jury Duty." And counting.

For worried homeowners, tourists, and viewers in general, where exactly is Vinton Street? It's a street near Andy Breckman's home in New Jersey.

Oh. No problem then.

to poison his ex-wife's pet parakeet in hopes that she would reconnect with an old flame: San Francisco's most prominent exotic bird veterinarian. "Alimony is a great motive," Andy Breckman notes, "but we felt we'd already done too many animal stories."

"We'd had the chimpanzee and the goldfish and a couple of episodes with dogs, so that was enough," Hy Conrad agrees. "But then we revisited it, and when we took out the bird, we came up with the idea of defacing a painting. That morphed into making the guy's wife an old crush of Monk's." And suddenly they realized they had a story that would accommodate the "Young Monk Adventure."

Creating parallel scenes that would intercut smoothly turned out to be quite a challenge, but it paid off in the end. "It's one of the nicest things in the script," Conrad says. "We spent a fair amount of time juggling scenes to mirror each other so the edits would dovetail."

Being assigned writer on a script has its perks. This time it gave Joe Toplyn an opportunity to give Monk's childhood crush his wife's name, Sherry Judd. He also got to name their junior high, "Westover," after the street he grew up on. "My mom still lives on Westover," Toplyn says.

The casting department struck gold when they found New York actor Grant Rosenmeyer, a veteran of the TV series *Oliver Beene* and the film *The Royal Tenenbaums*. "We couldn't have gotten a better actor," states Randy Zisk. "Grant spent one day with Tony to learn Monk's mannerisms, and he had the character down perfectly."

"He already knew the show," Tony Shalhoub confirms. "Grant was very well versed, so there was very little that I had to do."

Shalhoub's favorite aspect of the episode was hearing where all of Monk's "Monkisms" came from. "Like when the lunch lady says, 'It's a gift. And a curse,' " he says. "And when his mother says, 'You'll thank me later.' That scene with his mother was really, really fun because she was just so *creepy*."

"Well, his mother *couldn't* have been normal for Monk to grow up to be the way he is," says Andy Breckman with a chuckle.

The Quotable *Monk*

"I only remember the date . . . and what everybody wore . . . and what everybody said . . . and what everybody did."—Monk

The Weirdest Clue: Leo leaves blue icing fingerprints at the scene of the crime.

Idiosyncrasy of the Week: Monk gives Sherry a whole new perspective on art when he explains that her favorite painting actually shows a woman about to poison her abusive husband.

The Clue that Breaks the Case: As Monk says, "It's all about the zeros." In the present, Sherry's ex writes his zeros in a very distinctive way; and in the past, Leo neglected to set young Sherry's combination lock back to zero when he replaced it.

"Mr. Monk and the Secret Santa"

Episode 4-09
Written by David Breckman
Directed by Jerry Levine
Original Airdate: December 2, 2005

GUEST CAST

Alice Westergren	Rachael Harris
Frank Prager	Gill Gayle
Julie Teeger	Emmy Clarke
Sister Heather	Clare Carey
Charlotte Prager	Michelle Azar
Dori Prager	Casey Longstreet

The annual Christmas party is in full swing at the police stationhouse when Sgt. Alice Westergren announces that it's time for everyone to play "Secret Santa." As each person prepares to deliver a gift to the person whose name he or she drew out of a hat, Stottlemeyer realizes that he can't find the one he bought for Detective Chasen. Alice suggests Stottlemeyer regift the bottle of port that he received that day. Since Stottlemeyer hates port anyway, it seems the perfect solution—at least until Chasen samples his gift, then collapses and dies. Apparently, he was the unlucky victim of a poisoned potable meant for Stottlemeyer. As Monk studies the evidence, which includes a Christmas card addressed to Stottlemeyer, Disher puts together a list of suspects who might have a grudge against the captain. But Stottlemeyer says the list is unnecessary; he's sure Frank Prager did it.

The captain had shot and killed Frank's brother Mike during an arrest. Not long after, Frank Prager came looking for revenge. Confronting Stottlemeyer outside of a bar, he fired five shots and ran off. Somehow, the bullets missed their target, plowing instead into the wall behind the captain. When Stottlemeyer takes Monk back to the scene of that encounter, the investigator expresses surprise that Prager missed at such close range. He notices that the bullet holes in the wall seem to form a pattern, but he doesn't immediately recognize it.

To help find Prager, Monk goes undercover, first as a Christmas caroler who snoops around the home of Prager's wife and young daughter, and then as a shopping mall Santa Claus. It's in the latter disguise that Monk learns of Prager's whereabouts and the police soon have Prager in custody.

It doesn't take long for both Monk and Stottlemeyer to realize that Prager isn't the poisoner. Yes, he blames the captain for his brother's death, and yes, he waited outside the bar with the intention of avenging Mike. But at the last minute, he decided to send the captain a message instead of killing him—so he fired five bullets into the wall, forming the letter M, for Mike. Stottlemeyer is frustrated. If Prager didn't poison the wine, who did?

On Christmas day, Monk celebrates at Natalie's house. As he picks up the Secret Santa gift he received from Alice Westergren, he notices that she folded the accompanying card because it was too big for the envelope. Suddenly he recalls that the card that was attached to the poisoned port was too *small* for its envelope. The same person must have handled both cards and mixed up their envelopes—which means Alice is the killer!

Monk, Stottlemeyer, Disher, and Natalie confront Alice, and she admits to the crime. Terry Chasen was her target, not Stottlemeyer. She'd been having an affair with Chasen, and when he broke it off to go back to his wife, she couldn't bear the thought of being without him. She poisoned the port, addressed it to the captain, and then hid the captain's gift for Chasen so that he'd have to substitute it with the port. It was a clever bit of misdirection, designed to draw attention away from her. Mixing up the envelopes was her only mistake.

When Monk, Natalie and Julie resume their celebration, it begins to snow outside—the first snow San Francisco has seen since the day Trudy died. It's a true Christmas miracle. And as Monk gazes up at the heavens in astonishment, he can't help feeling a little closer to his wife.

*　　*　　*

"Mr. Monk and the Secret Santa" stands out from the average *Monk* episode in several ways. First of all, the story is a traditional whodunit (wherein the killer is unknown, even to the viewer at home). Andy Breckman tends to favor less common structures, so most of Monk's cases are "howdunits," and, occasionally, "whydunits."

Another unique aspect of the episode is that it had an untraditional December airdate. Generally, the series takes a long unbroken winter hiatus, with no new episodes airing between August and January. "We don't do much original programming in the fourth quarter of the year, because the broadcast networks are so competitive," USA's Jeff Wachtel explains. "But when Andy told us he had a nugget for a Christmas episode, we decided it could be fun."

Breckman had come up with his "regifting" nugget a year earlier, for Christmas of Season Three. "It was intended as a Sharona and Benjy story, in which Benjy had never seen snow," writer David Breckman recalls. With the possibility of casting changes looming over the production, the younger Breckman wrote a draft substituting Stottlemeyer and his sons for Sharona and Benjy, but eventually, the idea was shelved for later production.

In the final version, Julie Teeger is the child who has never seen snow, but she's far from alone in that respect. Snow is a rarity in San Francisco. The city has experienced snowfall only eleven times in over two hundred years, and, in fact, the local weather service has discontinued measuring snowfall altogether. "We took enormous liberties with the snow," David Breckman laughs. "We wanted the final scene to be magical, so we didn't even research it."

Snow is equally as rare in Los Angeles,

where the final scene was shot, so the weather was turned over to Special Effects Coordinator Michael Gaspar and Foreman Phil Bartko. "We put two foam-making machines up on sixty-foot cranes and dispersed the foam with fans," Gaspar says. "Of course, Mother Nature was still involved, because once we scattered the foam, we were at the mercy of the prevailing winds."

And how much "snow" fell over the Teeger household? "About two gallons," Gaspar reports.

"It's always fun to shoot a Christmas episode in July," Randy Zisk comments. "We completely decorated an area of the Town Center Mall in Burbank." Since filming is common in that part of the city, known locally as "The Media Center," the shopping public presumably was not surprised by the out-of-season decorations, and the mall remained open. Which is why, Zisk adds, "We had to shoot at night, from 6:00 P.M. to 6:00 A.M."

In spite of the offbeat hours, Tony Shalhoub got a charge out of playing Santa. "One of the best things about casting is that you get to meet all these nice kids," Shalhoub says. The actor found it easy to identify with the group of very young actors. "I was only six when my sister first took me up on a stage," he smiles. "I didn't even know it was going to happen; she just did it."

As for the "regifting," nugget that led to the story—and the poisoned bottle of wine—"You have to put a lot of misdirection in a situation like that," Hy Conrad observes. "That's why we brought in an old enemy of Stottlemeyer's. And because we set it at Christmastime, we naturally incorporated the theme of forgiveness, with Stottlemeyer being able to experience it and share it with Frank Prager and his family."

The Quotable *Monk*

"We have some new rules here in Santa's workshop. Before anybody can sit on Santa's lap, you have to use these magic wipes and wipe your hands. Yeah—wiping is fun!"—Natalie

The Weirdest Clue: Prager's five shots in Stottlemeyer's direction formed the letter M (for "Mike") in the wall.

Idiosyncrasy of the Week: While decorating the Teeger Christmas tree, Monk carefully applies one piece of tinsel at a time, making sure each strand is straight and perfectly balanced.

The Clue that Breaks the Case: One card is too big for its envelope, and the other is too small, meaning the same person erroneously reversed them and sent both.

"Mr. Monk Goes to a Fashion Show"

Episode 4-10
Written by Jonathan Collier
Directed by Randy Zisk
Original Airdate: January 13, 2006

GUEST CAST

Julian Hodge	Malcolm McDowell
Natasia	Mini Anden
Gordo	Scott Adsit
Maria Ortiz	Anne Betancourt
Julie Teager	Emmy Clarke
Pablo Ortiz	Alejandro Chaban
Salesman	Brian Palermo
Security Guard	Joe Latimore

Monk is trying to buy a new shirt, one that's not only identical to all his other shirts, but also inspected by Number 8, Monk's favorite garment worker. The good news is that the clothing store has the exact shirt. The bad news is that Number 8 seems to be off her game. There's a small tear in the shirt and one of the sleeves is crooked.

Monk believes something is seriously wrong. Inspector Number 8 *never* lets anything get past her! The detective is so worried he can barely concentrate on Stottlemeyer's latest case (although he manages to solve it in minutes). At last Monk decides to go directly to the shirt factory and talk to Number 8.

As it turns out, something *is* wrong with Maria Ortiz, a.k.a. Number 8. Her heart is breaking because her son Pablo has just been sentenced to life in prison for the murder of Clea Vance, a fashion model. Maria swears Pablo is innocent, despite irrefutable DNA evidence and testimony by Clea's roommate that Pablo had been stalking the model. When Monk goes to see Pablo in jail, the detective learns something interesting: Pablo can't read English, and it seems that the killer—who carefully avoided using a clearly marked emergency exit that would have triggered an alarm—*could.*

Monk quizzes Howard Gordon, the forensic technician who presented the DNA evidence at the trial. Although Gordon tells Monk he's certain of his findings, Monk can't help wondering if the boy was framed.

When Monk and Natalie meet fashion designer Julian Hodge, they observe that Hodge is an arrogant perfectionist, nearly as obsessive about small details as Monk. He constantly fusses with the clothes on his models, adjusting and straightening. Monk accompanies Hodge to a fashion photo shoot at the beach so he can meet Clea's roommate Natasia Zorell, while Natalie arrives separately with Julie. Hodge spots Julie and offers her an opportunity to model in his upcoming show. Despite Natalie's reservations about allowing her thirteen-year-old daughter to model, she ultimately agrees.

Monk's interview with Natasia proves fruitless. She still claims Pablo was stalking Clea. That night, Natasia dies in her home. Howard Gordon pronounces the death a suicide, but Monk suspects she was murdered. Perhaps someone was afraid that Monk eventually would convince Natasia to reveal the truth about Clea's death.

At a dress rehearsal for the fashion show, Hodge scolds Julie for her appearance and tugs at her clothes. The incident makes Monk take a closer look at a photo of Clea's corpse. Although her body is sprawled and contorted, her clothes are lying perfectly, with collar and buttons lined up. Someone adjusted the clothes after he killed her—and there's only one person besides Monk who would have paid that much attention to detail: the fastidious Julian Hodge. Alarmed, Natalie pulls Julie out of the show.

The next day Stottlemeyer and Monk summon Howard Gordon to the scene of Clea's death. They tell him they've discovered new evidence—some hairs on a fly strip that was found after forensics had finished the investigation. Monk says they must belong to the real killer, Julian Hodge. Gordon promises to test the hairs immediately.

That evening, Natalie discovers that Julie has sneaked off to the fashion show on her own, and she and Monk rush to the event. Spotting Julie on the runway, Natalie climbs onstage and retrieves her daughter, regardless of the huge audience that is watching.

After the show ends, Stottlemeyer and Disher bring Howard Gordon to see Hodge, and ask the forensics expert to report on the new evidence. When Gordon announces that the new hairs, like the old ones, belong to Pablo Ortiz, Stottlemeyer charges Gordon with falsifying evidence and Hodge with the murders of both Clea and Natasia. Suddenly, Gordon realizes he's been "stung" by Monk and Stottlemeyer. Monk had wondered why all of the evidence kept pointing away from the most likely suspect. He ultimately came to the conclusion that Gordon had buried the evidence against Hodge for a significant amount of money. Gordon then had fingered innocent delivery boy Pablo Ortiz as the culprit, and Natasia had provided testimony to back up the faked DNA evidence. Gordon proved his guilt when he reported that the new hair samples—which actually came from Monk's head—were from Ortiz.

Maria is thrilled when Pablo is released from jail. When she asks Monk how she can repay him, Monk suggests that she go back to work and inspect some shirts—perhaps she'd like to work on Saturday?

"Mr. Monk Goes to a Fashion Show" was conceived because none of the writers wanted to carry out a menial office task—so menial in fact, that not one of them can remember just what it was. "We were trying to decide who would do *something*," Joe Toplyn attempts to explain. "So Dan Dratch mimed holding out his hand as if he was 'passing the hat,' and I mimed picking a number out of it. I said, 'I've got Extra Large,' as if I'd gotten that tag instead of one of the imaginary slips of paper. Then Andy reached over and said, 'I've got Inspector Number 8,' and he just started riffing on that," Toplyn laughs. "Then he said, 'What if something is *wrong* with the inspector?'"

That thought eventually attached itself to an idea Toplyn had pitched about a model being shot. Although the group had rejected that idea, "it gave us the fashion show venue," Hy Conrad says, "and the Inspector Number 8 joke gave us a great teaser."

While the story initially posited that Stottlemeyer had mistakenly sent an innocent boy to jail, Breckman worried that such a grim mistake would reflect badly on the captain's character. Thus, the writers shifted the blame to a department forensic technician, played by Scott Adsit, reprising the role that he'd played in "Mr. Monk Gets Fired."

Although the group considered connecting Natalie to the fashion world, they ultimately decided that was too similar to Sharona's brief history as a nude model in "Mr. Monk and the Playboy." But that didn't preclude shifting the fashion focus to Natalie's pretty daughter, Julie. "Young kids often are recruited into the fashion world," Conrad states. "We worked hard to get Natalie's 'mother' voice right. By the fourth act, she couldn't be 'pro' letting her daughter model because we'd have no tension. But when Monk suggests that Hodge is the killer, Natalie would want to prevent her daughter from being involved, and then we could have Julie be a bit defiant and run away."

That twist offered a spotlight to Emmy Clarke as Julie. "I've never really thought of modeling before," Clarke says enthusiastically, "so the episode was *so* much fun. I got a whole new perspective."

"And," laughs Kate Clarke, the young actress's mother, "Emmy had never worn high heels before. She *loved* that!"

"The episode required the biggest wardrobe we've ever had," comments Director Randy Zisk." The producers hoped to find a designer who would supply the dresses for the photo shoot and fashion show scenes, and thankfully, Zisk says, "Nicole Miller helped us out." Nicole Miller, one of America's most elite designers, supplied the finest selections from her 2005 line.

"We asked for seventeen dresses," Costume Designer Ileane Meltzer says. "I chose two for [actress] Mini Anden to wear at the photo shoot on the beach, and fit the rest to our runway models. I also wanted to put Julie in Nicole Miller dresses," Meltzer says, "so I bought two more dresses and cut them down to Emmy's size."

The producers also asked one of the models, Katie Savoy, to act as "technical advisor" for Clarke. "Katie spent a day teaching Emmy how to walk like a fashion model," Zisk says. "That was fun for all of us."

The producer's final concern, and the last to be settled, was who would play their murderous designer, Julian Hodge. "It was very late in the schedule when Ted Levine suggested his friend Malcolm McDowell," Zisk recalls. "We knew he'd be great, so Ted called him and Malcolm agreed."

"I'd seen a couple of episodes of *Monk*," McDowell says. "And I'm a great admirer of Tony Shalhoub. I knew *Monk* had very good writing, so when I read this script, I thought, 'You know what? I'm doing it.'"

As for the character he plays, McDowell says, "I *had* to be the bad guy, because Tony and Ted play the good guys. That's the way it works."

The Quotable *Monk*

"Inspector Number 8 is very important to me. No matter how bad things got, I knew I could always count on her. She's my soul mate."—Monk

The Weirdest Clue: The body of Natasia, who allegedly killed herself by overdosing on pills and alcohol, is found clutching an empty glass. But the glass has no lipstick prints on it—and she was wearing lipstick when she died.

Idiosyncrasy of the Week: Natasia has a mole on one shoulder, so Monk wants to draw a fake one on her other shoulder to balance her out.

The Clue that Breaks the Case: The photo of Clea's corpse suggests that Hodge is the likely killer. But since the DNA evidence doesn't support that theory, Monk realizes someone in the police department must have faked the evidence.

"Mr. Monk Bumps His Head"

Episode 4-11
Written by Andy Breckman
Directed by Steve Surjik
Original Airdate: January 20, 2006

GUEST CAST

Cora	Laurie Metcalf
Sheriff Bates	Charles Napier
Debbie	Bre Blair
Roger Zisk	Jim Parrack
Truck Driver	Gregg Daniel
Ned the Beekeeper	Michael Shalhoub
Kirby the Barber	Robert Bagnell
Informant	Robert Catrini
and	
Dr. Kroger	Stanley Kamel

Late at night, Monk and Natalie pull into a dark, isolated roadside rest area. Pocketing an envelope full of crisp new bills, Monk directs Natalie to keep out of sight. She's reluctant to leave his side, but Monk reminds her that the informant he's come to meet won't appear if she's hanging around.

Moments later, a man steps from the shadows and shows Monk a photo of a six-fingered man—the guy responsible for Trudy's death, he claims. He'll provide the killer's name for a price. But Monk notes that the photo's been doctored and refuses to hand over the money. The phony informant hits Monk over the head, grabs the cash, and takes his wallet. Then he stows Monk's body under a tarp on a flatbed truck and departs. Seconds later, the truck driver pulls out, unaware of his unconscious passenger.

The next day, Monk awakens in the desolate town of Purnell, Wyoming. He doesn't remember who he is, or what he's doing in Purnell. The startled truck driver offers him a five-dollar bill and tells him to buy himself a meal. Dazed, Monk wanders over to the local diner, attracting the attention of Cora Brundley, the lonely town eccentric.

After Monk eats, he discovers he doesn't have enough money to cover the bill. Debbie, the kind-hearted waitress, tells Monk he can owe her the balance. The amnesiac detective wanders over to the town's tiny sheriff's office and solicits Sheriff Bates's help in determining his identity. Suddenly, Cora Brundley appears in the doorway, claiming that Monk is her new husband Jerry, who she met on her recent cruise. Jerry's just confused because a paint can fell on his head, she says.

This doesn't ring any bells for Monk, but he takes Cora's word for it and allows her to take him home. Cora tells Monk he's a roofer, which surprises him since he seems to be afraid of heights. Cora insists he repair her roof all the same, and while he's up there, he observes the fancy BMW of Roger Zisk zipping down the road.

Zisk's car heads towards the home of Ned the beekeeper, and plows through the fence, destroying a number of Ned's hives. Ned watches in amazement as Zisk leaps from his car, pursued by hundreds of angry, stinging bees.

Back in San Francisco, Natalie enlists Stottlemeyer's help in finding Monk. They recover his stolen wallet and track Monk's crisp new bills to a man named Teddy Mulligan. After Mulligan confesses to hitting Monk and stowing him on a truck, Stottlemeyer sends out flyers describing the detective to truck stops all over the region.

When Monk returns to the diner to repay Debbie, he hears that she's abruptly left town, allegedly to follow a boyfriend to Denver. But as Monk studies the note she left behind, he grows suspicious. A smudge in the ink indicates that someone left-handed wrote the note, he says, but Debbie was right-handed. In Debbie's apartment, Monk finds a used pregnancy test strip and notices signs of a violent struggle. He concludes that the girl didn't leave town—she was murdered!

Monk seeks out Sheriff Bates to tell him his theory, and finds him at Ned's bee farm, investigating the chaos left behind by Roger Zisk's drunken rampage in his car. Monk tells Bates that he saw the BMW before the accident, and Zisk hadn't been driving erratically at the time. He doesn't think Zisk was drunk.

"Jerry's" observations lead Bates to wonder if Debbie's disappearance and Zisk's accident are

somehow connected. He offers Monk a job as his deputy, but Cora won't hear of it. She tries to distract Monk by getting him interested in a little romance, but Monk can't picture getting romantic with Cora, either in the bedroom, nor at the local lover's lane, Lookout Point. Besides, he's heard that Lookout Point is experiencing a hornet infestation. Everyone who goes there winds up getting badly stung—

Suddenly, Monk solves the case. He directs Bates to investigate the area around Lookout Point. Sure enough, state troopers, dressed in bee-proof protective gear, find the girl's body in a nearby gully. Monk explains his theory. Debbie was involved with Roger Zisk, and when she learned she was pregnant, she threatened to tell Zisk's wife. Zisk and Debbie got into a fight and he killed her, then took her body to the gully. While there, he got badly stung and realized he needed an alibi to explain his swollen appearance. So Zisk deliberately drove into Ned's bee farm, making sure that Ned saw him getting stung.

As Bates goes to arrest Zisk, Monk finds himself surrounded by old friends. Stottlemeyer, Natalie and Disher have managed to track him down! The sight of them triggers Monk's memories of his life in San Francisco and he happily bids Purnell—and the disappointed Cora—farewell.

When Dr. Kroger hears that Monk may have lost his memory, he speculates that the defective detective "could be out there meeting himself for the very first time." And that, according to Andy Breckman, is the nugget of "Mr. Monk Bumps His Head."

"We thought it would be fun if Monk didn't know who he was and kept annoying *himself.*

He'd keep wondering, 'Why am I *doing* this?'" Breckman says. Of course, half the fun would come from seeing how Tony Shalhoub chose to interpret his alter ego's predicament. "It's so much fun for us to throw him curveballs like that and see if he can hit them," Breckman observes.

"Well, that's the great thing about this show," Shalhoub responds. "With every episode, it's like I'm entering a different world. Each one is slightly different in tone, in comedic levels and in its own set of challenges. *Monk* has a lot of range."

In order to temporarily extricate the man from his memory, the writing staff resorted to amnesia, which, as Dr. Kroger notes, "is actually very rare." Of course, Kroger was referring to *real life* amnesia cases. Had he been talking about television, it would have been a different story. "Amnesia is a contrivance that's been used in *all* sorts of shows, successfully and not so successfully," Hy Conrad admits. "But we really liked the idea that Monk's phobias would remain with him, even though he'd have no idea of how those phobias came about."

Setting up a scenario to accommodate this nugget was more difficult than usual. "We had to find reasons for Monk to lose his wallet, to get separated from Natalie, and to end up in the middle of the country," says Breckman. "And then we added the subplot of Monk dealing with a woman who claims to be his wife. And, of course, it wouldn't be *Monk* if we didn't have a murder, so we had to weave the murder mystery throughout the story. All this in forty-one minutes."

The episode featured Laurie Metcalf (*Roseanne*) as Cora, the strange, lonely woman looking for love. "Laurie made the character all her own," Breckman states. "She found her own voice and hit the performance out of the park."

She also found her own unique appearance. "Laurie came in with a set of fake teeth," Randy Zisk says appreciatively. The cosmetic affectation, combined with an equally unflattering coiffure, rendered the daring actress's character decidedly less than attractive.

If fending off Cora's romantic urges was Monk's biggest challenge, the scene in which the detective is swarmed by bees was it for Tony Shalhoub. Although some of the bees in other scenes (such as when the BMW driver runs from his car) were added in postproduction by the visual effects department, the sequence where Monk gives his bee-covered summation required the real thing. "They put a beekeeper suit and headgear on me and let the bees swarm," Shalhoub chuckles. "I had to do it."

"Our bee wrangler put a queen bee in a tiny cage, and buried it in Tony's shirt," Zisk explains. "And all of the other bees clustered around the queen."

In spite of the danger and discomfort, Shalhoub doesn't feel that the producers are *really* out to get him. "I've made it this far, so I trust them," he notes good-naturedly. "They haven't killed me off yet, so I do it all."

Perhaps he felt secure because his brother, Michael Shalhoub, also was in the sequence, as Ned the beekeeper, making his second appearance in the series (see "Mr. Monk and the Missing Granny").

The Quotable *Monk*

"If you wanna look around, look around like a normal person. I gotta live in this town."—Cora

The Weirdest Clue: Monk knows the picture of the six-fingered man is a fake because there's no hair on the knuckle of the sixth finger.

Idiosyncrasy of the Week: Monk has all of his usual fears, of milk, of heights, of foods that touch each other—although he has no idea as to why.

The Clue that Breaks the Case: When Monk recalls that there's a hornet infestation at Lookout Point, he realizes where Debbie's body is, and why Roger Zisk drove into the beehives.

"Mr. Monk and the Captain's Marriage"

Episode 4-12
Written by Jack Bernstein
Directed by Phil Casnoff
Original Airdate: January 27, 2006

GUEST CAST

Sgt. Sharkey	. . . .	Nicky Katt
Gerald	. . . .	Robert Clendenin
Karpov	. . . .	Misha Collins
Dr. Bradley	. . . .	Kitty Swink
Peter	. . . .	Michael Ray Bower
and		
Karen Stottlemeyer	. . . .	Glenne Headly

In an automobile junkyard, a homeless man named Gerald shares breakfast with his pet mouse. But the tranquil meal ends when Gerald overhears two men arguing nearby. Suddenly, one man attacks the other with a stun gun. The second man defends himself vigorously, but eventually he succumbs to the weapon, and his opponent bludgeons him to death.

Gerald, the only witness, flees from the junkyard, the killer in hot pursuit. When he reaches the street, he flags down a patrol car and tells the cops that there's a killer in the junkyard. Then he hustles away, leaving the police to deal with whatever they find within.

A short time later, Monk and Natalie arrive on the scene. Stottlemeyer and Disher are already there. The victim is a small-time drug dealer known as Chicklet. He worked for a much bigger fish, Michael Karpov, who's about to go on trial for criminal conspiracy and money laundering. Chicklet was scheduled to testify against him, and Stottlemeyer is guessing that Karpov is behind his death.

Suddenly the captain's cell phone rings. It's his wife, Karen, and, as often is the case, their conversation quickly turns into an argument. As he snaps the phone shut, Sgt. Ryan Sharkey tells Stottlemeyer he should treat his wife better. The captain is startled by Sharkey's comment, and pushed to rage when the cop insinuates that he knows Karen intimately. Without thinking, Stottlemeyer punches Sharkey so hard that the cop's mouth begins to bleed. Disher quickly steps in to break up the fight, but it's too late—the crime scene has been contaminated.

Karen tells her husband that Sharkey is lying, but things remain tense between the couple. Stottlemeyer asks Monk and Natalie to follow Karen to see if she's really cheating. They reluctantly comply and discover that she *is* meeting a man, but they can't tell who it is. In the meantime, Stottlemeyer unsuccessfully attempts to get his volatile emotions under control at an anger management course.

With no proof that Karpov was responsible for Chicklet's death, the police search for Gerald. But Chicklet's killer finds the transient first, and throws him out of a window. Amazingly, Gerald survives the fall, and he agrees to view a police line-up of suspects. Although Disher anticipates that Gerald will pick Karpov, he fills out the line with several cops in plain clothes, including Sharkey. Unfortunately, before Gerald can finger the killer, the captain joins the lineup and goads Sharkey into an all-out brawl.

Just as it seems the killer will go free, Monk notices something odd about Sgt. Sharkey. He's eating an apple and chewing it on the left side of his mouth. Sharkey explains that it's because Stottlemeyer knocked out his tooth when he hit him. But Monk points out that Stottlemeyer actually hit him on the *left* side of his face, and Sharkey is favoring his *right*—the side that's missing a tooth. Monk deduces that the captain wasn't the first person to hit Sharkey that day. Chicklet must have knocked Sharkey's tooth out, right before Sharkey killed him. But Sharkey realized that his blood and his tooth would be found at the crime scene, so he goaded Stottlemeyer into taking a swing at him. That way, the crime investigators would think any evidence pointing to Sharkey came from the fight with Stottlemeyer.

It's clear that Sharkey is on Karpov's payroll. Sharkey tries to deny the charge, but once Gerald identifies him as the man in the junkyard, it's all over. Stottlemeyer is momentarily relieved. Karen *wasn't* cheating on him. Unfortunately, she *was* seeing another man: a divorce attorney. Karen feels their differences have become insurmountable and she wants to end their marriage. Crushed, Stottlemeyer packs his suitcases and moves out—his destination: a future without the woman he's loved for twenty years.

* * *

"You could argue that Ted Levine has the hardest job in the cast," Andy Breckman says. "His character's purpose is to 'ground' the series, and we asked a lot of him in 'Mr. Monk and the Captain's Marriage.' " Indeed, Levine was required to display an atypically broad range of emotions for the episode, expressing everything from jealous rage to profound regret, while still hitting the usual comedy beats. "When I saw Ted's performance in the episode," adds Breckman, "I couldn't help but think that it was a kind of balancing act, an amazing feat. And I applaud him for it."

Although the episode took Stottlemeyer out of his usual "comfort zone," Levine was prepared for it. "I've done so much homework on Stottlemeyer over the past three and a half years that I just know who the guy is," he says. "It's what we do as actors. We find a certain reality in the situation, and that's what happens."

Levine's character is a solid cop, trusted to be just as grounded as the actor who plays him, but when Stottlemeyer suddenly has doubts about his wife's fidelity, he loses control. "Stottlemeyer has his own vanities and things that make him jealous," Levine comments. The producers weren't reluctant to show this darker side of the captain, since, as Breckman says, "we'd already established that he has a temper."

They were much more reluctant to have one of the cops exposed as a bad guy on the take. "We don't like to show the police department in a bad light," Randy Zisk points out. "We really respect what they do, and they've always been a big help to us. And with this one exception, we always try to paint them in the good light we know they deserve."

The central premise of the episode demanded the exception. "It began with an interesting idea," Breckman says. "A cop picks a fight at a crime scene because he knows he's left his blood and DNA there, and that it's going to be discovered any minute. Once we had that, the rest just followed naturally."

Sadly, part of what followed was Karen Stottlemeyer's decision to leave her husband after twenty years together. That twist may limit actress Glenne Headly's appearances on the series in the future, but she takes it all in stride. "Karen is so much less forgiving in the episode than I would be," Headly says, "but I felt fine about the separation. I feel that whatever makes the show interesting is the right thing to do."

Breckman sees the separation as an opportunity. "For the first time, we have four characters that are single," he says with a cryptic smile.

Viewers who may wonder why Gerald, the homeless witness to the murder, is so incensed by the "degenerate" who tore out the last two pages of his *Diagnosis Murder* mystery book are hereby clued in to the fact that the line is a tip of the hat to Lee Goldberg, cowriter of the episodes "Mr. Monk Goes to Mexico" and "Mr. Monk Meets the Godfather." Goldberg recently had written the first *Monk* novel, *Mr. Monk Goes to the Firehouse*. Among Goldberg's other credits: four *Diagnosis Murder* novels.

The Quotable *Monk*

"When God closes a door, sometimes he breaks your heart."—Stottlemeyer

The Weirdest Clue: The memory in Chicklet's cell phone has been erased, so Monk deduces that he was attacked with a stun gun.

> **Idiosyncrasy of the Week:** Monk is appalled by all
> the junk in the junkyard, and suggests they should
> get rid of it and put it somewhere. Like a junkyard.
>
> **The Clue that Breaks the Case:** Sharkey is chewing
> on his left side because he lost a tooth on the right
> side—but Stottlemeyer, who's right-handed, hit him
> on the left side, not the right.

"Mr. Monk and the Big Reward"

Episode 4-13
Written by Tom Scharpling & Daniel Dratch
Directed by Randy Zisk
Original Airdate: February 3, 2006

GUEST CAST

Rufus . . . . DJ Qualls
Dirk . . . . Tyler Mane
Gladys . . . . Davenia McFadden
Warren . . . . Ryan Alosio
Jennie . . . . Jamie Brown
Museum Official . . . . Faran Tahir
Danny Chasen . . . . Daniel Browning Smith
with
Inspector St. Clare . . . . Darrick O'Connor
and
Dr. Kroger . . . . Stanley Kamel

The natural history museum has a new exhibit:
a private collection of European *objets d'art*.
The Alexander Diamond is the exhibit's star
attraction, so valuable that—after it's stolen—its
insurer offers $1 million to anyone who finds it.

When Natalie hears about the reward, she's
ecstatic. A recent drop in homicide cases may
be good for the city but it's lousy for her and
Monk's finances. They haven't had a new case

in weeks. But if Monk could solve the jewel
theft, she says, their worries would be over—or,
at least, *her's* would. Reluctantly, Monk agrees
to try.

But they're not alone in their quest. Three
other investigators are hungry for the big
reward: retired Scotland Yard Inspector St.
Clare; eager young private eye Rufus Fulcher;
and big, tough Dirk the bounty hunter. When the
three recognize Monk at the scene of the crime,
they realize they have serious competition.
Aware that he's a better super-sleuth than any of
them, they decide to let Monk do all the "heavy
lifting" and follow along in his wake.

Monk quickly determines the robbery was
an inside job; someone who worked at the
museum stole the jewel. Monk also concludes
that the thief had to be small—he hid inside a
rolltop desk until the museum closed, and
there he inadvertently left behind a distinctive
ivory necklace. As Monk and Natalie prepare
to leave with the clue, the three investigators
introduce themselves. Realizing that they're
rivals for the reward, Natalie and Monk hastily
depart.

After tracing the necklace to a large
meditation center in Monterey, they ask elderly
Master Kwan if he has a very short disciple.
Kwan is too caught up in a Tai Chi meditation
to respond, so Monk and Natalie proceed to
look around on their own. They eventually find
their quarry, one Denny Chasen, in his cabin,
dead. He's been poisoned. The diamond isn't on
him or in his cabin, so Monk assumes that
Chasen's partner—the insider who worked at
the museum—has the gem.

Back at police headquarters in San
Francisco, a bemused Disher reports that a
woman named Jenny Mandeville keeps coming
in and confessing to nonexistent crimes. Later

that day, when Monk has his regular session with Dr. Kroger, he mentions having been to the meditation center. Kroger is familiar with the place; he notes that it used to belong to a woman, now deceased, named Jenny Mandeville! As Kroger goes on to explain that there's a big plaque that features Jenny's name and likeness in the middle of the center, Monk announces that he's solved the case. He knows where the diamond is.

Unfortunately, Monk's three rivals have been tailing him and they now know that *he* knows where the diamond is. Natalie and Monk get to the station house just seconds ahead of their three pursuers. They find Stottlemeyer and Disher in the observation room outside of Interrogation Room B, and soon St. Clare, Rufus and Dirk are in there with them. Jamming the door's lock, Dirk announces that *nobody* is leaving the room until Monk reveals where the jewel is. So Monk explains what happened.

The woman who's been confessing to Disher isn't really Jenny Mandeville; she saw that name on the plaque at the meditation center when she went there to kill Denny Chasen for her boyfriend, the security guard at the museum. It seems her boyfriend didn't want to share the proceeds from the diamond with his partner-in-crime. Unfortunately, the security guard is now in jail. He'd been brought in for routine questioning right after the robbery, and Monk had tipped Disher that the guard's hands bore stains that indicated he was a producer of crystal meth. When the guard realized that Disher was about to bust him on the drug charge, he stuck the diamond, which was still in his pocket, underneath the interrogation room's table using a wad of used chewing gum. After he called "Jenny" to let her know, she

started coming to the station and confessing to bizarre crimes in the hope that they'd take her into Interrogation Room B, where she could recover the diamond. Unfortunately, they never did.

And now, with the diamond—and its reward—so close, the seven people stuck in the observation room watch in horror as Gladys the cleaning woman enters Room B—and finds the diamond as she cleans the room. After all that chasing around, Gladys will be the one to collect the big reward.

Still, Stottlemeyer is able to give Monk and Natalie some good news. The commissioner has agreed to give them a contract and put them on retainer. It appears that their financial woes are, for the moment, behind them.

"Mr. Monk and the Big Reward" is a flat-out romp, a 180-degree shift in mood from the episode that precedes it. And that, essentially, was the whole point.

"We had just finished writing 'Mr. Monk and the Captain's Marriage,' which was an emotionally heavy story," explains Andy Breckman. "We wanted to lighten up completely, and do an episode that didn't have a sentimental 'golden moment.' We called 'Big Reward' our *It's a Mad Mad Mad Mad World* episode."

The reference to the classic 1963 film about the madcap pursuit of a stash of stolen cash is certainly apt, and the subject matter was certainly familiar to Breckman, who penned the movie *Rat Race*, another zany comedy about human greed. "I guess I'm drawn to that kind of story," Breckman relates.

The light, playful tone of the script carried over into Tony Shalhoub's performance, which the actor dialed back to make Monk a bit less serious than usual. "The material dictated it," Shalhoub says. " 'Big Reward' is all about chasing money, which is not a high priority for Monk. But for Natalie, it's huge. She wants the money because they're both broke. Looking for money is not Monk's life work," Shalhoub adds with a chuckle. "He's just not a mercenary type."

The trio of investigators who compete with Natalie and Monk for the reward, however, are as mercenary as they come. "We started out with only one other guy chasing the reward, a *Dog the Bounty Hunter* type," Hy Conrad comments. "But pitting Monk against a single detective would have been too similar to our episode at the beginning of the season, 'Mr. Monk and the Other Detective,' so we opted for *three* detectives."

In addition to the reality-based bounty hunter, the writers came up with "a geeky kid with gadgets who we thought of as 'the Radio Shack detective,' and an older, Miss Marple-type woman," Breckman says.

But according to Conrad, they decided to axe the Miss Marple/Jessica Fletcher-type, because that type of detective exists only in fiction. "So we morphed that character into a retired Scotland Yard detective," notes Conrad. While that tweak made little difference to the story, it pleased the writers.

The writing of "Big Reward" coincided with the making of a featurette planned for inclusion in the fourth-season *Monk* DVD set. With Breckman's whole-hearted encouragement, his daughter Julie and nephew Jake Wolk documented the entire process on videotape. "I think the way that we [writers] approach these episodes is unique, and I wanted to document it

for our audience," Breckman says. "There were a lot less dirty jokes in the writers' room while my daughter was there," he admits, "but it should capture the experience of how an episode is hammered together."

One additional item was being hammered together at the time. "I was renegotiating my contract," Breckman reports, "and was about to sign for two more years." The writers injected that real-life activity into the episode, with Natalie pushing Stottlemeyer to put Monk on retainer with the police department. The deal that the captain finally makes with Monk— "Sixteen homicides a year, for the next two years"—is good news for Monk and Natalie— and for Breckman. "I don't think there's ever been *that* inside a joke on any show," Breckman observes. "It's an inside joke written almost solely for my own amusement."

The Quotable *Monk*

"It's like Sophie's choice—except it's soup."—Monk

The Weirdest Clue: St. Clare can tell which street Monk went down because the promotional flyers under the windshield wipers of the parked cars are all perfectly straight and aligned.

Idiosyncrasy of the Week: When Rufus slips a tiny tracking device into Monk's pocket, Monk immediately is aware of its presence because he's "not balanced."

The Clue that Breaks the Case: Kroger mentions that there's a plaque bearing the deceased Jenny Mandeville's name and likeness on the grounds of the meditation center.

"Mr. Monk and the Astronaut"

Episode 4-14
Written by David Breckman and Joe Toplyn
Directed by Randy Zisk
Original Airdate: March 3, 2006

GUEST CAST

Steve Wagner . . . . Jeffrey Donovan
Darrell Cain . . . . Eric Allan Kramer
Julie Teeger . . . . Emmy Clarke
Joanne Raphelson . . . . Brianna Brown
Benny Cain . . . . Michael Belcher
Donna Cain . . . . Ariel Winter
Nicole Wagner . . . . Natasha Pavlovich
and
Dr. Kroger . . . . Stanley Kamel

Steve Wagner is a national hero, a space shuttle captain. Yet he'll never be a hero to Joanne Raphelson, Steve's one-time mistress. Joanne has written a tell-all exposé about her many relationships, and Wagner has a juicy chapter in the book. That's why she's invited him to read it—so the astronaut, who hopes to become a senator, won't be caught by surprise. Wagner arrives on the eve of his next sojourn into space. Joanne finds him surprisingly gracious considering that the book reveals he once beat her so badly she had to be hospitalized. Wagner fixes her a "Space Walk," his own special cocktail recipe with some distinctive ingredients: an onion, an olive, a cherry . . . and some very potent barbiturates.

A week later, Joanne's housekeeper finds her with a noose around her neck and a tipped-over wooden stool near her dangling feet. Although Joanne's death appears to be suicide, Stottlemeyer senses it might be murder. The computer upon which she wrote her book is missing, and she was too short to reach the suspended noose by using the nearby eighteen-inch stool. As he looks around, Monk notes a martini glass containing a speared onion, olive, and cherry, and files the information in his head. Joanne's phone records reveal that the last call she made was to astronaut Steve Wagner.

When Monk, Stottlemeyer, Natalie and Disher arrive at Wagner's home, he's in the midst of a party celebrating his return from a recent trip to space. Wagner isn't surprised to hear of Joanne Raphelson's death; his former lover had been depressed for a long time, he says. He freely admits to the phone call he received from her, but, he points out, on the day Joanne died, he was in space. Nevertheless, when Monk notices that the astronaut's wife is drinking a martini that contains an onion, an olive, and a cherry, he becomes convinced Wagner is guilty.

The next day, Wagner agrees to speak at Julie's school. After his speech, Monk and the astronaut have a verbal confrontation in the school corridor. Monk accuses Wagner of killing Joanne to stop her from soiling his public image. Wagner doesn't deny it. Instead, he belittles Monk, telling the detective that he'll never be able to get him, because in a standoff, when the chips are down, Monk will flinch.

But Monk is nothing if not persistent. Returning to Joanne's house, he shows Natalie some holes that recently were drilled in a wall. As they try to figure out what might have caused the holes, he and Natalie spot Wagner out front, searching for something. Wagner explains he came to pick one of Joanne's roses— something to remind him of her.

While they're out front, Monk overhears

Joanne's neighbors, the Cains, arguing about their garage door. The father accuses his son of repeatedly leaving it open, but the boy denies it. Suddenly the Cains recognize the famous astronaut across the street and come over to meet him. Wagner seems uninterested until he spots the little girl's doll. Suddenly he becomes Mr. Congeniality as he invites the family to watch him perform a flight test. Suspicious of Wagner's motives, Monk and Natalie invite themselves along.

At the air force base, Wagner offers the girl and her brother a close-up look at a training simulator. While the children are gone, Monk hears an officer grill a young airman about a door that was left open in a nearby maintenance garage. Seconds later, the Cain children return and report that Wagner has stolen the girl's doll—and Monk is able to put all the clues together.

Wagner gave Joanne a heavy dose of barbiturates the night before his flight—heavy enough to keep her unconscious for days. Then he installed a new garage door opener in her front hallway—the location of the holes Monk found—and attached one end of a rope to the

opener's vertical track, and the other to Joanne's neck. He left, taking one of her dolls with him. Later, he taped down the activator button on the garage door opener's remote unit and slipped the unit into the doll. Then he packaged the doll up and sent it to Joanne's house via second-day delivery. When the deliveryman dropped it off on the porch, the activated remote triggered the device Wagner had set up to hang Joanne. After he returned from space, Wagner snuck back into the house, dismantled the device, and moved Joanne's body into the room where it was found. It was a perfect plan . . . except for the fact that Cain, the neighbor, stole the doll from Joanne's porch before Wagner could retrieve it. Now that Wagner finally has the doll, he plans to get rid of it by dropping it from the cockpit of his test plane!

Monk and Natalie find Wagner on the runway, preparing to depart. With no other option, Monk places himself in the path of the jet fighter. The only way Wagner will be able to take off is by taxiing through him. As Wagner considers doing just that, base security forces arrive and level their weapons on Monk. Still the detective refuses to move. For a moment it looks as if Monk is bound to die, one way or another. Then Stottlemeyer and Disher arrive on the tarmac, just like the calvalry, riding to the rescue. Word quickly spreads across the runway: "Stand down."

Wagner realizes the jig is up and lets the security forces lead him away. But before he goes, he glances back at Monk, and nods. The detective didn't flinch, and Wagner respects that. A few days later, Julie presents Monk with a homemade medal of valor, letting him know he's a hero in *her* book, too.

*　　　*　　　*

Within minutes of meeting Steve Wagner, Monk is *positive* that the astronaut killed his former mistress. There's just one little problem. He was orbiting the earth in a space shuttle when she died.

"It's the gold standard of alibis," Andy Breckman says gleefully.

According to Hy Conrad, Breckman has been dying to use that alibi for years. "He's always said, 'I really, really, really want Stottlemeyer to say, 'Monk, he couldn't have done it; he was up in space,' " Conrad recalls. When at last the opportunity presented itself in "Mr. Monk and the Astronaut," the crusty captain didn't let the writing staff down. Stottlemeyer even hammered the point home by inviting everyone in his office to "take a minute to see if we can think of a *better* alibi."

The alibi is so good, in fact, that it took the writers until Season Four to figure out exactly how an astronaut *could* kill someone while he was up in space. But once David Breckman came up with the insidiously complicated death-by-garage-door-opener solution, they were free to let their creative juices flow—within reason, that is.

Joe Toplyn, who shared the script writing chores with David Breckman, recognized that the final scenes should be accurate and respectful of the military. Accordingly, he contacted the public affairs office of Edwards Air Force Base near Los Angeles and wound up talking to Master Sergeant Larry Schneck. Schneck graciously answered Toplyn's plot-related questions and helped the producers secure permission to film on the base, including use of the Air Force's most modern aircraft, the F/A-22 Raptor. Toplyn later learned that the script he and Breckman wrote had gone to the Pentagon for approval.

"It's great that we were allowed to shoot at Edwards," director Randy Zisk says, "because we didn't have a fallback position. And we didn't know that we could use the Raptor until the last minute," he adds. "There was another airplane we could use, but it was small, and not intimidating at all."

On the other hand, the stealth design F/A-22 Raptor is impressive to the nth degree. With a length of 62'1", a wingspan of 44'6", a titanium alloy body, airspeed of 1,325 mph and a ceiling of 60,000 feet, it's the most advanced airplane in the world today. "We were in a hanger when we got a phone call saying, 'The Raptor is going to take off in five minutes, so if you want a shot of it taxiing down the runway, you can get it right now,'" recalls Zisk. "So Tony and I grabbed a camera and literally raced outside, because we knew the plane wasn't going to wait for us. We were still plugging the camera's batteries in when it came around the corner, and we pointed the lens over Tony's shoulder and shot it. That one take is the only time the Raptor was moving under its own power." For the rest of the scenes, the plane was pulled by a "tug." "If the engines had been running," Zisk laughs, "they would have blown Tony away."

"It had to look like it was running on its own, and I certainly had to run alongside of it on my own," Shalhoub says with a smile. "Then, when Monk stopped the airplane, we were trying to visually suggest that famous shot of the young man facing down the line of tanks in Tiananmen Square. It was quite a terrifying moment for Monk."

"When the idea of Monk facing down an airplane came up in the writers' room," Andy Breckman says, "I immediately saw the whole episode in my head, and we wrote it backwards from that point. The laser targeting marks from the guards' weapons echo the earlier moment in the script when the kids frighten Monk with their laser pens in the classroom. So facing down the plane gave us two things: a great theme of courage *and* a great ending."

The Quotable *Monk*

"I'm a mutant: half man, half wuss. I'm a *muss*."

—Monk

The Weirdest Clue: The noose was suspended 7'6" above the floor; the victim was 5'5"; the stool she ostensibly stood on was eighteen inches tall. Something doesn't add up.

Idiosyncrasy of the Week: Monk doesn't like being "touched" by the little red dots of light emitted by the students' laser pens.

The Clue that Breaks the Case: When a door at the base is triggered by the stolen doll, Monk realizes that there's a garage door opener hidden inside.

"Mr. Monk Goes to the Dentist"

Episode 4-15
Teleplay by David Breckman & Tom Scharpling; story by
    Daniel Dratch & Joe Toplyn
Directed by Jefery Levy
Original Airdate: March 10, 2006

GUEST CAST

Terri . . . . .Brooke Langton
Detective Peterson . . . . .Michael Dempsey
Neal Graham . . . . .David Shackelford
Aaron . . . . .Brian Kimmet
Brendan . . . . .Sven Holmberg
Chad . . . . .Joel Bryant
Hal . . . . .David Pressman
Marty . . . . .Rick Yudt
and
Dr. Bloom . . . . .Jon Favreau

On a dark, rainy night, an armored truck disappears from its route. Three days later, the police find the truck in an abandoned warehouse, its two drivers dead. Monk notices that there are no tire tracks leading to the truck's position in the warehouse, the side mirrors are pushed back, and the rear fender is dented. His conclusion: the armored truck was pushed into a larger vehicle and transported to the location. But Lt. Disher has a hard time focusing on the evidence. He's got a miserable toothache and Stottlemeyer is sick of hearing about it. He orders Disher to go to the dentist—*immediately*.

Disher goes to see Dr. Bloom, a cheerful man who informs him that the bad tooth has to go. Terri, the dental assistant, places an anesthetic mask over Disher's face, and he goes to sleep. Some time later, the lieutenant begins to come to. Although he's tremendously groggy, he realizes that there's another person in the room, a tough guy who seems very angry at Bloom. It sounds to Disher like they're fighting about Barry Bonds, and soon the argument escalates to an exchange of blows. Even the assistant gets into the fray. Then, just as it seems that Bloom and Terri have killed the intruder, Disher falls back into his druggy sleep.

When Disher awakens and asks about the fight, Terri and Bloom seem amused. The only fight they had, Bloom says, was with Randy's molar. Bewildered, Disher leaves the office.

The next day, Disher finds his team hard at work on the armored truck case, but he can't stop thinking about what he witnessed—or *thinks* he witnessed—at the dentist's office: Bloom and Terri killed a man who accused them of kidnapping Barry Bonds. Stottlemeyer assures Disher that everybody imagines strange things when they're under anesthesia.

Unconvinced, Disher asks Monk to help him check out Bloom's office. Despite Monk's tremendous phobia about dentists, he finally agrees to go. They find nothing—but Dr. Bloom seems pleased to be introduced to Adrian Monk.

Not long after, Stottlemeyer summons Monk and Natalie to a crime scene where they've found the body of a dead man—identified as Denny Jardeen—who may be connected to the armored truck heist. Disher excitedly claims the victim is the man his dentist killed, but no one believes him. When Stottlemeyer suggests he take some time off, Disher becomes infuriated. He's tired of no one believing him. And in the heat of the moment, he quits his job.

The next night, Stottlemeyer visits Disher and asks him to come back to the force. But Disher tells him it's too late. He's reunited his high school rock band and plans to make the band his life.

In another part of town, Monk receives a late night guest. It's Dr. Bloom's assistant. Terri is crying; she claims that Disher was right—Bloom *did* kill someone and she needs Monk's help. Monk starts to call Stottlemeyer, but Terri stops him by telling him there's something on his face. He allows her to wipe it off, but realizes too late that she's trying to chloroform him.

When Monk comes to, he finds himself bound to Bloom's examination chair. It's his worst nightmare come true! As he looks around the room, Monk puts all the random details together. Randy saw Bloom and Terri kill Denny Jardeen, who was indeed one of the men who hijacked the truck. Jardeen got hit in the mouth during the robbery and went to Bloom for dental work. While under anesthesia, Jardeen blabbed about the robbery, and where he'd hidden the truck's cache of bank certificates. Bloom and Terri recovered the loot, figuring Jardeen would never remember telling them about it. Unfortunately, he *did*. He came back to Bloom's office while Disher was there, and demanded to know where the bearer bonds were.

But why has Bloom kidnapped Monk? Bloom is happy to explain. He needs to sell those bonds, and he's found a "fence" in Chicago. But he needs Monk to tell him if the cops have that fence under surveillance. Monk says he doesn't know, but Bloom doesn't believe him. He prepares to perform some oral surgery—perhaps *that* will change Monk's mind.

In the meantime, Disher's cop instincts kick in when he sees a newspaper article about the truck heist. It mentions $13 million in bearer bonds. Suddenly, he realizes what he actually heard in the dentist's office. Not Barry Bonds—bearer bonds!

A short time later, Natalie, Stottlemeyer, and Disher burst into Bloom's office, rescuing Monk in the nick of time! With the dental team in custody and the truck heist case resolved, Stottlemeyer cheerfully welcomes Disher back to the force. It's a happy moment for everyone except Monk, who realizes that one of his teeth was loosened in the recent altercation. Natalie recommends that he see a professional—after all, what are the odds of *another* dentist torturing him?

People who work with classified material are prohibited from being put under with anesthesia, a tantalizing bit of trivia that inspired "Mr. Monk Goes to the Dentist." "It occurred to us that a dentist might be in a position to learn something and take advantage of it," Andy Breckman explains. A quick consultation with a dentist whose practice just happens to be located downstairs from the writers' New Jersey office confirmed that patients "talk all the time" while under anesthesia, and the stage was set. A criminal would blab about where he'd hidden his ill-begotten gains while sitting in the dentist's chair. And one of the show's main characters would witness that criminal's murder while occupying the same seat.

Given the variety of "insane theories" that Randy Disher has generated over the years, the writers concluded that he was their man. "No one would believe Randy if he says he saw a murder while in the dentist's chair," says Breckman.

In the end, of course, Disher would regain, and even enhance, his credibility by actually solving the case, a denouement that made Jason Gray-Stanford ecstatic. "That was history being made!" he proclaims. "Disher may occasionally come up with a crucial piece of evidence, even inadvertently help solve a case. But this—this was *history*."

But before that history was made, the writers had to figure out what Disher would do to occupy his time while unemployed. It was Dan Dratch who suggested the lieutenant reform his old band. "I'd been in a Boston band called the Cake Eaters," Dratch admits with a smile. "I wrote the scene with the band in the garage. That 'five, six, seven, eight' joke is one that I've wanted to use for a long time."

When early drafts of the script suggested Disher would sing a few lines of a song, the producers in Los Angeles jumped on the band wagon and asked that the lines be fleshed out to accommodate shooting an original music video. Script coordinator/New Jersey Salvatore Savo happened to be the one who fielded the request to Breckman, "And Andy said, 'Well, why don't you write the lyrics,'" Savo relates. His "song," titled "Don't Need a Badge," fit Disher's personality perfectly.

Postproduction coproducer Scott Collins quickly sent the lyrics, which include humorous jibes against Stottlemeyer, to his friend, songwriter Evan Brau. "I told Evan to make it sound like a band that hasn't played together for seventeen years," Collins says. "We were worried that it might end up sounding too good. But we knew the funny part would be having Jason sing it on a really cheesy video."

Gray-Stanford had never imagined being the star of his own music video. "I'm a campfire guitarist at best," he admits. "Nor am I a singer by trade. So I looked at it as a great acting challenge."

"The Randy Disher Project" video footage was shot against a green screen just outside the main *Monk* soundstage. Assistant editor Rick Rodono cut the footage together with silly and outdated graphics to make it appear as though Disher, using "the worst computer software of all time," had assembled it by himself, at home.

Meanwhile, Breckman was pleased that the scenes with Monk in the dentist's chair wound up looking exactly as he'd envisioned them. "Our first conversations about dentists led to discussions about the dental torture scene in the movie *Marathon Man*," Breckman explains, "and we decided to show Monk being the victim."

As an actor, Tony Shalhoub found the torture scenes to be rather freeing. "The obstacle of being restrained feeds you emotionally," he explains. "And with that huge prop in my mouth, I didn't have to try hard to sound as if I was trying hard. At least," he says with a grimace, "not for the first take."

The Quotable *Monk*

"I can't even *discuss* it. I can't even *think* about discussing it. I can't even *talk* about thinking about discussing it."—Monk

The Weirdest Clue: The bruises on Jardeen's body are ten inches apart—and so are the roots on the big plastic tooth in Dr. Bloom's office.

Idiosyncrasy of the Week: Monk describes his fear of dentists as a "super-mega-phobia," ranking wa-a-ay above his fears of germs, snakes, and everything else.

The Clue that Breaks the Case: Being kidnapped by a killer dentist is a pretty big giveaway.

"Mr Monk Gets Jury Duty"

Episode 4-16
Written by Peter Wolk
Directed by Andrei Belgrader
Original Airdate: March 17, 2006

GUEST CAST

Ex-Marine	Benito Martinez
Mr. Cobb	Wings Hauser
Escobar	Carlos Gomez
Pat	Emmanuelle Vaugier
Agent Lapides	Michael Weaver
Judge Rienzo	Clyde Kusatsu
Housewife Juror	Bonita Friedericy
Pierced Girl Juror	Kimi Reichenberg
Sneezing Juror	Bryan Coffee
Prosecutor	Aaron Lustig
Teacher Juror	Carlease Burke
Sweet Old Lady	Darlene Kardon
Patel	David Ackert
Sports Fan Juror	Kevin Berntson
Postal Worker Juror	Van Epperson
Baliff	Emilio Borelli

Monk is dismayed when he receives a summons to jury duty. It's not that he doesn't *believe* in the justice system; he just doesn't want to be a *part* of it. Despite his protestations to the judge, Monk is selected as a juror in a robbery/assault case. It looks like a slam-dunk "guilty" verdict to the other eleven jurors. The knife that injured the victim was found in the suspect's knapsack with the victim's blood still on the blade. And the victim identified the suspect in court. What sane person wouldn't declare him "guilty?"

Monk wouldn't. He wants to study the evidence and think for a while because he's not convinced the accused man is guilty. The other jurors will just have to wait him out.

Stottlemeyer, too, is entangled in the legal system. He and Disher have captured Miguel

Escobar, a major drug kingpin. But before Stottlemeyer has the opportunity to savor his achievement, Special Agent Dan Lapides appears in his office. Lapides says the Escobar matter is a federal case, and he's authorized to take the drug lord off Stottlemeyer's hands. The captain is to bring Escobar to the courthouse for an extradition hearing in a few days, then walk away from the case.

In the jury room, Monk proves to the others that the victim lied during his testimony. What's more, Monk suggests that the victim actually stabbed himself and blamed an innocent man. But just as the other jurors begin to come around to Monk's rationale, the detective becomes distracted by a dumpster located next to the courthouse, three stories down. Monk has noticed that a previously rolled-up tarp is now stretched across the top of the refuse in the dumpster, and that lime powder has been poured over the tarp. He comes to the conclusion that there's a dead body in the dumpster—and the other jurors come to the conclusion that he's nuts.

Spotting Natalie outside the courthouse, Monk shouts at her to get Stottlemeyer to investigate the dumpster. Sure enough, the cops find a dead body: an old woman with orthopedic shoes. Monk remembers having seen a juror who looked like that, but when his efforts to communicate with the police are noticed by the judge, the jury is sequestered. After a sleepless night at a cheap motel, the jurors return to the courthouse to hash out the case. Monk reveals yet another piece of evidence indicating the victim made up his story; now ten of the jurors agree that the accused man isn't guilty. But strangely, Juror Number 12, a young woman who had previously sided with Monk, changes her vote to guilty. When questioned by the other jurors, she refuses to

explain her rationale, and goes into the bathroom.

While she's gone, Monk notices traces of lime on her jacket. He suddenly recalls that he saw Number 12 talking to the lady in orthopedic shoes a few days earlier. Monk concludes that the young woman killed the old woman just to get on the jury, and now she's stalling so she can remain in the juror room a little longer. But why?

When Number 12 returns, the other jurors confront her—and suddenly she pulls a tiny handgun from her coffee thermos. After securing them all to their chairs, she tapes the jurors' mouths shut and lowers the window blinds. Now Monk knows what's going on. Number 12 is the girlfriend of Miguel Escobar. His hearing is today in the courthouse, and she plans to be there to help him escape!

As Natalie arrives at the courthouse with Monk's lunch, she glances up at the window for the jurors' room and notices that the blinds are askew. Realizing that something's wrong— Monk would never tolerate uneven blinds—she goes up to the room and breaks in. After releasing Monk, the pair race down the hall in pursuit of Number 12. But it looks like they're too late; Lapides and another agent are lying crumpled on the floor and neither Number 12 nor Escobar are anywhere in sight. Then Monk notices that the elevator is moving up to the roof. He grabs a cell phone and contacts Stottlemeyer.

Minutes later, when Escobar and his girlfriend slide down a debris chute from the roof to the dumpster below, they find Stottlemeyer and Disher waiting to greet them, thanks to Monk's tip. The detective may not *want* to be part of the justice system, but thanks to him, justice has been served once again.

*   *   *

"Don't Need a Badge"
The Randy Disher Project

(As heard in "Mr. Monk Goes to the Dentist")

Music by Evan Brau, Lyrics by Salvatore Savo

I'm tired of suckin' up, and workin' for The Man,
Keepin' people down, 'cause a Law Book says I can,
'Cuffin' my brothers and sisters, oh it's not the way to be,
But honey, those days are gone, 'cause baby, I am free!

CHORUS
I don't need a badge, to tell me wrong from right,
I don't need a badge, to tell me day from night,
I don't need a badge, 'cause my eyes can see!
I don't need a badge, 'cause baby, I am free!

It's been a long long time, cleanin' up the streets,
Now papa's got a new gig, he's got a brand new beat,
It's called Rock and Roll, and baby I hold the key,
This guitar here is my badge, and the music has set me
   free!

I'm feelin' real fed up, so you'd better be aware,
I'm done with all your rules, 'cause man I ain't no square!
Music is my savior, with that you must agree,
This guitar here is my badge, and the music has set me
   free!

CHORUS
I don't need a gun, to make me feel strong,
I don't need a Captain, to shoot me down all day long,
I don't need your mustache, don't you condescend to me,
I don't need nobody, cause baby I am free!

This guitar is my badge!
Rock and Roll set me free!
This guitar is my badge!
You better not try and take it from me!

CHORUS
I don't need a gun, to make me feel strong,
I don't need a Captain, to shoot me down all day long,
I don't need your mustache, don't you condescend to me,
I don't need nobody, 'cause baby I am free!
No, I don't need nobody, 'cause baby I am free!

Monday, August 15, 2005.

A card selected from the board on the previous Friday says, simply, "Monk on a jury." The writers have pondered this idea over the weekend and will attempt to "break" the story over the next five days. Stefanie Preston, whose title is Writers' Office Coordinator/NJ, arrives early, shortly after 10:30 A.M. At 10:45, Hy Conrad appears, along with his pair of peppy gray schnauzers, Charlie and Jake. The dogs quickly find comfortable spots on the carpet. Over the next hour, the rest of the group slips in, each settling into his individual office: Joe Toplyn, freelancer Pete Wolk, Tom Scharpling, Dan

Dratch, David Breckman, Production Assistant/NJ Daniel Gaeta, and Script Coordinator/NJ Salvatore Savo. The last to arrive—at 12:05 P.M.—is Andy Breckman. By 12:15, the writers have gathered around a conference table in the communal room, and the work begins.

"Let's break the story into beats by Wednesday so we can have two days to work on the comedy in the deliberation room," Breckman says. The "Jury" card has been up on the board for several years, and for the next twenty minutes they review ideas that they've touched upon whenever anyone mentioned it. Finally Breckman says, "We have three mysteries—the case of the trial Monk is on, Monk seeing the body outside, and the killer in the other case, along with the woman on our jury, trying to break out."

The killer in "the other case," which will bring Stottlemeyer and Disher into the episode, becomes the focus of the group's attention. "Maybe he's like Hannibal Lechter," Breckman says.

"Or Sideshow Bob, from *The Simpsons*," Hy Conrad contributes.

The discussion moves to a possible sequence that would feature Lt. Disher watching the killer. David Breckman has an idea: "Disher wants to watch TV, but he inadvertently picks up the remote unit that activates an electrical device the killer is wearing," he says. "Disher hits the button with his back to the guy and the guy screams. Disher says, 'If you're gonna keep screaming, I'm gonna have to make the TV louder,' and he keeps hitting the button. Meanwhile, the prisoner is on the floor, just vibrating and screaming."

The group laughs, then Andy Breckman says, "It's funny, but it's not us. That's not our show."

At 1:30 P.M., the executive producer picks up a notebook and everyone stands. Work will continue during lunch, and also during the walk to and from a favorite Mexican restaurant two blocks away. Breckman is thinking about the case Monk is supposed to deliberate on at the courthouse. "Why would Monk *not* want to do jury duty?" he asks, then instantly adds, "That's a dumb question."

"Yeah," brother David says, "but he'd go, 'It's a great system! Twelve guys. Civic duty. I just don't want to be a part of it.'" Passersby turn and stare as the group breaks into laughter.

While the writers enjoy their enchiladas, random questions and comments about all aspects of the story bounce around the table.

"Which reporter can we bring in from CNBC? Geraldo Rivera?"

"Monk should say, 'He's gotta be guilty—he's a nudist!'"

"Maybe we should look at *My Little Chickadee,* where Mae West reacts to the Gentleman Bandit."

"Is there a way we can have somebody stab himself?"

The writers are so comfortable with one another that they speak in shorthand, tossing out lines that make sense only within their cozy circle.

3:45 P.M. The group, still animated and discussing ideas, treks back up the street. In the writers' room, Andy Breckman slips a DVD of the 1957 courtroom drama *12 Angry Men* into the deck. They fast forward through the film, pausing at several key scenes. "Can we have one of our jurors not need to have a photo ID?" Breckman asks.

"No," answers Pete Wolk, the only law school graduate in the room, and he explains the facts. Obviously, courtroom rules are stringent, but the group refuses to be discouraged by reality.

"Didn't we rent a copy of Pauly Shore's *Jury Duty?*" Tom Sharpling asks, glancing around in vain for that DVD.

The conversation moves on, settling into intriguing ways to inflict a very slow death.

"Make him move close to power lines."

"Substitute his low-cal peaches with heavy syrup peaches."

"Take away his sixty SPF sunscreen and replace it with thirty SPF sunscreen."

Four forty-five P.M. Andy Breckman reads aloud, recapping the notes that he's typed into his ancient WordStar program, admittedly the only computer program he knows how to use. "Usually our teasers end with blood and a chainsaw," he says. "This one is just mail call."

"Tomorrow we eat Italian," Dan Dratch says emphatically as the seven men stand and reach for their belongings.

And the next day, Tuesday, August 16, they do it again, *a la Italiano*.

The Quotable *Monk*

"You know, I usually don't like shaking hands, but if I ever met the man who invented Tupperware, I would shake his hand."—Monk

The Weirdest Clue: Natalie knows that Monk's in trouble because the window blinds are crooked.

Idiosyncrasy of the Week: Monk panics at the thought of being drafted by the Army and forced to shower with naked people.

The Clue that Breaks the Case: The fact that the "victim" in the court trial seems to have prepared a towel to press against his wound *before* he was wounded cinches that case for eleven-twelfths of the jury.

Top, from left to right: Dan Gaeta, Tom Scharpling, Randy Zisk, Andy Breckman, David Breckman, Stefanie Preston, Daniel Dratch, Salvatore Savo. Bottom, from left to right: Tony Shalhoub, Joe Toplyn, Hy Conrad.

From left to right: Doug Herzog, former president of USA Network; Jackie de Crinis, senior vice president of original scripted series programming; Tony Shalhoub; Jeff Wachtel, executive vice president of original programming; David Goldhill, former president and chief operating officer of Universal Television.

"And In the End . . ."

In a December 2005 *Los Angeles Times* article about "the year in, and the state of, television," critic Robert Lloyd noted that in spite of there being five hundred channels, the big three broadcast networks continued to dominate the marketplace. And then, almost off-handedly, he added, "But *Monk* is as good as any network detective show."

At the time the article appeared, new episodes of *Monk* weren't being aired. The series was on hiatus during a period when the broadcast networks were bringing out their big guns. Most shows produce twenty-two or more new episodes per year, while *Monk* maintains an annual total of sixteen. The USA Network airs them in two batches: nine (usually) during a period that runs from just before the Fourth of July to just before Labor Day; and seven, beginning in January of the following year.

And yet find it they do. *Monk*'s viewers apparently are as intent on following the show as Monk is on following the clues. This kind of loyalty to a particular series isn't unique to *Monk*, yet marketing departments can't explain why it exists, and even *increases* over time, for series A, but never seems to percolate at all for series B. For the executives at the USA Network, the answer, this time at least, is easy.

"It's because of Tony and Andy," Jackie de Crinis says simply, quietly discounting the fact that she and David Hoberman were the two people of authority who persisted in nurturing the infant concept when others had forgotten about Adrian Monk. "The two firm posts that the show's success rests on are Andy and Tony," Jeff Wachtel agrees, not mentioning that he was the one who insisted on holding out until the best actor in America could be found to play the title role.

Wachtel is quick to add, "*Monk* is a collaboration of dozens if not hundreds of people." And Tony Shalhoub is equally quick to share kudos with the ensemble of actors who have shared the load. "*Monk* is a character-driven show," the actor says. "We've had the time to slowly develop the relationships, which makes the series more and more interesting for the audience."

It's tempting to suggest that *Monk* will join that short list of all-time greatest hits revered by fans after generations of other shows are forgotten. Only time will tell, but as the public call for this and other books, along with numerous viewer-driven Web sites dedicated to the series attests, the elements are positioned for a permanent place in the sun.

What makes *Monk* stand out? As Andy Breckman says in his introduction, "*Monk* is a labor of love." And as the Beatles once reminded us, "The love you *take* is equal to the love you *make*." And so, in that sentiment, we as viewers want to say to the people above, and to the people named in the acknowledgements that follow—

Take That.

Afterword

BY TONY SHALHOUB

I like Monk because he is so tender and complicated and funny, and just a joy to portray on-screen. There are little bits of me in him, and bits of other people in him—some from people I know and some from people I haven't even met yet.

I have been so happy with the way fans have reacted to the show and embraced the show. Every episode has its own quirks (certainly *Monk* tries to keep them to a minimum!) and makes for some amusing, as well as some endearing storytelling, that I am proud to be a part.

The cast and crew and the writers especially have done everything in their power and more to make sure that we put out the highest quality program possible. And I think we've done that.

I think Monk will be around for years and years to come, and that the show will go down in television history as one of the all-time detective series greats.

Maybe even one day we will see Monk's OCD cured, and the mystery behind Trudy's murder solved . . . but who knows?

So watch and find out.

Acknowledgments

A highlight of virtually every *Monk* episode is "the summation," a narrated reenactment of the crime. As a dramatic device, the summation has been with us since the earliest mysteries flickered across movie screens many decades ago, which may be why *Monk*'s reenactments usually come in gloriously traditional black and white.

In a sense, this book serves as another kind of summation. Not of a crime, but of the development and execution of a beloved TV show. It covers four seasons of crimes, capers, killers, cops, characters, clues, phobias, eccentricities, and quirks. Of course, we couldn't have highlighted any of this without the help of a whole bunch of experts on those very subjects. They graciously allowed us to watch over their shoulders while they worked, and to probe into the past with our endless questions. To every one of you, we wish to say, "You're the guy."

This book would not have been possible without the encouragement and cooperation of Andy Breckman, New Jersey's Patron Saint of Comedy. Thank you, Andy.

Our very special thanks to David Breckman, Hy Conrad, Jackie de Crinis, Paolo de Oliveira, Dan Dratch, David Hoberman, Jerry Levine, Tony Palmieri, Tom Scharpling, Joe Toplyn, Jeff Wachtel, and Randy Zisk, as well as Stefanie Preston and Shana Stein.

For caring enough to give the very best, our thanks to Tony Shalhoub, Bitty Schram, Traylor Howard, Ted Levine, Jason Gray-Stanford, Stanley Kamel, Emmy Clarke, Melora Hardin, Glenne Headly, Lance Krall, Malcolm McDowell, Max Morrow, Jarrad Paul, and Kane Ritchotte,

For taking care of us on the soundstages, the locations, and the telephone, thank you to Dan Alvarez, Dan Ayers, Ela Barczewksa, Phil Bartko, Jeff Beal, Bonnie Blake, Josh Breckman, Risa Breckman, Charlie Brewer, Deborah Chung, Kate Clarke, Scott Collins, Anya Colloff, Anton Cropper, Jon deGooyer, Olivier Doering, Dan Engelberg, Steve Faust, Fern Field, Toby Forlenza-Willis, Ken Friedman, Daniel Gaeta, Michael Gaspar, Lee Goldberg, Hayley Helmreich, Rich Hobaica, Brigit Jones, Ann Kaiser, Beth Landau, Annie Livingstone, Sheridan MacMillan-Thayer, Kim Meade, Ileane Meltzer, Suzi Mercer, Cameron Meyer, Courtney Morrison, Mike Mullins, Doug Nabors, Melissa Olson, Chuck Parker, Korey Pollard, Jaime Pona, Kim Reed, Rick Rodono, Anthony Santa Croce, Salvatore Savo, Michael Sluchan, Jim Thompson, George Ward, Ric White, Pete Wolk, and everyone else on the *Monk* staff, from accounting to transportation, that we didn't have the pleasure of interrupting . . . er . . . um . . . interviewing.

We want to thank our wonderful editor, Michael Homler, along with Mark Steven Long and Matthew Shear at St. Martin's Press, and Cindy Chang, Veronika Beltran, Julie Chebbi, Dawn Rosenquist, and Jennifer Sandberg at Universal Studios CPG.

Finally, thank you to Jim, Maria and Matthew Block, Mari Castro, Margaret Clark, Florence Erdmann, Gordon Erdmann and Joann Jasinski, Jeff Erdmann and Joyce Kogut, Joe Marconi, Jeff Mooridian, Dave McDonnell, Pam Newton, Ellen Pasternack, and Steve and Terry Wroe for your introductions, interventions, and moral support.

Terry J. Erdmann and Paula M. Block
Hollywood, 2006